Nine
Potteries
in
Kirkcaldy

A History by Jim Bell

Nine Potteries in Kirkcaldy

Published by the Fife Pottery Society
Copyright retained by the publisher and author 2006

ISBN 0-9552268-0-5

Fife Pottery Society grateful acknowledges the financial

assistance given towards the printing cost by

The Strathmartine Trust
Awards For All (Heritage Lottery Fund)
Fife Council Community Grants Scheme
Scottish Co-op

Abbreviations

Throughout this work there are references which indicate the source of the information. For ease the under noted abbreviations have been adopted

*****	Not certain/unreadable	KPR	Kirkcaldy Parish Records
APR	Abbotshall Parish Records	KW	Kirkcaldy Wrights
CR	Census Returns	Numbers	SRO reference
CS	SRO reference	PR	SRO reference
EC	Edinburgh Courant	RHP	SRO plan reference
EG	Edinburgh Gazette	RV	Rateable Value
FA	Fifeshire Advertiser	Sin B	Sinclairtown Burials
FH	Fife Herald	SPHR	Scottish Pottery Historical Review
GR	SRO reference	SRO	Scottish Records Office
Khorn PR	Kinghorn Parish Records	VR	Valuation Roll
KL	Kirkcaldy Cental Library	VS	Vitruvius Scoticus
KM	Kirkcaldy Museum		

CONTENTS

INTRODUCTION

When I started the research for this book some thirty years ago I had the grandiose idea of producing the definitive work on the subject in two years at the most. How wrong I was as such work is only for someone who does not have a "day job"!

In writing this one of my main aims was to avoid introducing my personal opinions especially when dealing with the social aspects unless I was reasonably certain of the facts. To achieve this I have set out the facts as I found them and give sources where possible. The interpretations obviously are my own but I have deliberately used an abundance of qualifying statements such as possible, probable, likely, etc. and leave it to the reader to agree or disagree with my reasoning. In doing this I fully appreciate that it does not enhance the "readability" [such as it is] of the text.

One of the many difficulties I have had is with the term "pottery" which must be unique in being the name of both the place of production and the product. To overcome this I have adopted the convention of using the capital letter [i.e. Pottery] for the works. I have also used the old/alternative spellings for some terms that were in common usage at the time being discussed [eg tile/tyle and sagger/segger] and the use of redware and brownware which are local names for the same product.

I have also chosen to print any quotation from written material in a different type set from spoken and hope that these will help to make the text clearer.

Similarly as the Potteries were geographically close to one another and obviously subjected to same external conditions, such as the national and local economies, unless stated to the contrary any details given regarding one Pottery can be accepted as being the same at the others. It will be noted that the Potteries were not originally within the Burgh of Kirkcaldy.

I also fully accept that no matter how hard I have tried I cannot possibly have gathered all of the facts and more details must exist which I am unaware of. No doubt also as soon as my work is in the public domain new evidence will emerge that is not available as I write. I can only hope that this will add to my efforts.

As would be expected there have been many problems with the attribution of many unmarked pieces and I have in general rejected pieces unless I was very convinced by the evidence. For example this applies to the many pieces of hard paste porcelain, which I was assured "were made at the pottery". Equally I was much happier to accept the source of various "pots" in the possession of the late Miss Isa Wishart who lived literally next door to the Links Pottery which she obviously frequented regularly especially as she was able to show me [and later give me] examples of transfer prints and the copper plate [made about 1860] showing the layout of the Pottery. Certain designs of wares and decoration were common to several Potteries and in many cases they were not given a maker's mark. I illustrate a number of these to show the types of wares manufactured.

The details of the two larger Potteries have been broken down into reasonably sized chapters based on suitable dates usually being a change of ownership although especially when due to a death these may not mean an actual change in the working situation.

In undertaking the research I am greatly indebted to very many friends throughout the Scottish Pottery field for their information, encouragement and patience. In addition it would not have been possible without the help of the various sections of the Scottish Records Office, National Library of Scotland, University of St Andrews, Scottish Pottery Society Archives, Fife Pottery Society and especially Kirkcaldy Library and Museum.

Needless to say my family have been remarkably tolerant and Myra not only trailed around after me on numerous occasions but also did not object very loudly as I filled the house with pots, shards, books and a mountain of paper.

Jim Bell

Chapter 1 <u>**THE EARLY POTTERIES & BRICK AND TYLE WORKS IN LINKTOWN   PRE 1776**</u>

When the interest in the history of Scottish Pottery production restarted in the 1960s it was the commonly held belief that there was almost no potting until well into the Eighteenth Century and that Scotland had been, by and large, a desert until the Nineteenth Century with the introduction of "English" methods. Just why it was considered thus considering that Scotland was rich in suitable clay and fuel is strange. Could it have been because it was thought that the Scots be they post Medieval or Renaissance did not have the wit to become potters or more simply the ignorance of the researcher?

As further investigations have been made it now appears that many of the major burghs in Central Scotland and up the East Coast to Aberdeenshire had Potteries of some type during the Eighteenth Century and very probably much earlier. It appears also that the earliest Potteries were frequently associated with the larger religious establishments if clay was available. Potteries of this type would only continue after the closure of the establishment if the surrounding temporal area could support them.

Kirkcaldy did have such an establishment nearby and later the Burgh was sufficiently large to continue supporting a Pottery although a starting date for one has not yet been established. In common with most others the Potteries were situated outside the Burgh to be close to the clay and fuel and equally importantly to keep the obnoxious smoke and fumes away from the houses.

The area of Abbotshall [now known as Raith] was formerly part of the "Town and Shire of Kirkcaldy" which from the time of Malcolm (III) was under the control of the Abbots of Dunfermline. One of these Abbots established a religious centre or "Hall" within the area thus giving rise to the place name. It is probable that a Pottery was associated with the Hall especially when it is seen that there was a Pottery beside a sister but smaller Establishment at Balchrystie in East Fife.

The site of the Pottery for the later Kirkcaldy Burgh was in Linktown of Abbotshall [now referred to as Linktown or more simply The Links] which was a reasonable distance from the main housing area and had abundant clay and fuel as well as sufficient water for the processing of the clay although, perhaps, not enough to be a source of power. It appears likely that if there were two separate Potteries they were on or about the same site.

The earliest probable date established for a Pottery so far is the 4th of June 1610 when Sir James Scott of Abbotshall granted a Charter to "John Mathie, potter in Linktoun of Abbotshall," for two plots of land both being three roods in area. These two plots were separate one being in Miltown of Abbotshall and the other in Linktown. Neither is accurately described so that the exact locations cannot be established. The Milton land had been occupied by John's grandfather, Alexander, since 16th October 1557 but it is not recorded if Alexander or his son Adam, John's father, were also potters [KM files J.T. Davidson].

From this it can be seen that there was a potter in the area strongly suggesting that there would have also been a Pottery. In making this assumption it must be noted that the term "potter" could be a metal worker although in this case it appears to very unlikely. In an attempt to establish further details the other evidence must be examined.

The legal papers associated with the Mathies are lodged partly in Kirkcaldy Museum and the remainder in Register House although details of the latter section were listed by J. T. Davidson, Solicitor, Kirkcaldy [the list is now lodged in Museum]. These papers were originally from the Methven family and mainly involved their land transactions with the Adam family [details of these two families will be given later] from whom they purchased the Lions House and the Brick and Tile Works and all came from the Kirkcaldy/Links Pottery archives. This strongly suggests that there was a connection between the Mathie Pottery and land owned by Adam and then Methven.

Secondly in his Will of 1815 David Methven [I] referred to a piece of land he had purchased earlier from Adam, as "on which there was a pottery". Surely there could not have been two Potteries in Linktown and this reference must have been to the Mathie Pottery.

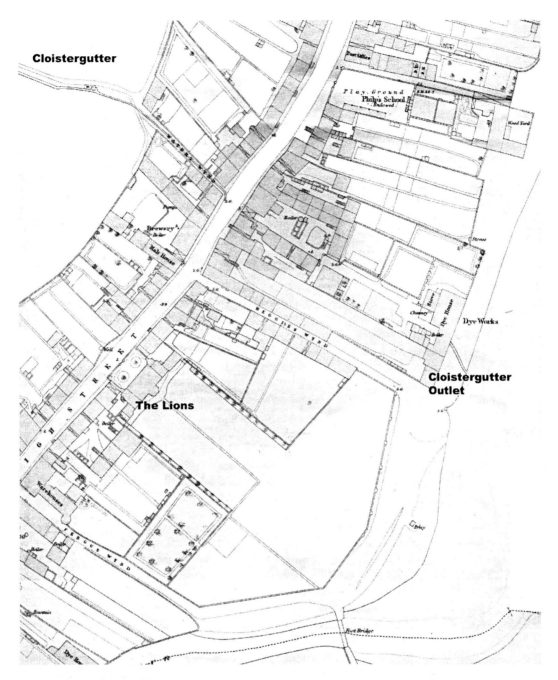

Cloistergutter

Cloistergutter Outlet

The Lions

O.S. 1856

Showing the route of the Cloistergutter & "The Lions"

This land was near to the street now known as Heggies Wynd and was close to a small coal mine that operated at least until the late 1600s and on the south side of the "Cloister Gutter" which was a small stream or drainage ditch that flowed beside a track, which became the route of Ramsay Road and then down Watery Wynd to the sea [OS 1856]. The choice of site was convenient being so close to the required materials for potting, clay, water and fuel. The name of the stream also suggests some religious association, which would fall into line with a possible connection between the Pottery and the Abbots. This stream drained land near to the present Balwearie High School, which in turn is adjacent to one of the possible sites for buildings associated with the Hall. This is somewhat conjectural but if correct could date the Pottery very much earlier than 1610.

It will be noted that by 1610 the area had for obvious reasons been renamed "Abbotshall" after the Abbots although they had lost their power. It was to be a number of years [1650] before the area was subdivided into two Parishes, Abbotshall and Kirkcaldy Burgh. This subdivision gave rise to many tensions and the Burgesses of Kirkcaldy, who held the wealth, were forbidden to purchase goods from the nearby Linktown and Pathhead villages. Just how much this effected trade at the Pottery is unknown but it is hard to imagine that the Burgesses could resist buying the wares at the weekly Linktown markets.

If all these assumptions regarding potting are correct then this would have been a Redware Pottery producing only "coarse redware" from the local clay and perhaps fired by local coal although there was also a plentiful supply of wood locally. There is no mention of any clay lease but it can be assumed that one must have existed and that the clay pit would have been near to the Pottery. Similarly there is no indication of the type of wares produced but they can also be assumed to be similar to those of other Scottish Potteries at that time being mainly drinking and cooking vessels and bowls and although "coarse" by later standards would have been made for a fairly sophisticated market at a time when most people used wooden dishes. Lead, copper and other mineral glazes were probably used and were available from Scottish sources from the Ochil Hills, Kemback, Inverkeithing and on East Lomond Hill in Fife.

To date no archaeological evidence has been found of the Pottery or its products. There is however a reasonable number of pottery shards of the appropriate date from various investigations in the general area but not close enough or in sufficient quantity to be definitely attributable to the Pottery. It would not seem unreasonable to assume that at least some of these did originate in the Pottery. These shards are all made from red clay, which has been made from clay as "dug" having a small proportion of grit and sand. The wares were fairly thick walled [about 10cm] and had been fired sufficiently to turn the outer layers to red leaving the central core grey indicating a lack of oxygen due to the method of firing. The shards show patches of green glaze on both faces indicating the possible use of copper.

The Pottery appears to have been sold to a Peter Harrower in 1630 without unfortunately, his occupation being specified in the legal papers. It seems probable he was a potter as the Pottery appears to have continued for many years and probably into the eighteenth century. For ease of description this Pottery is referred to as the "Mathie Pottery" on all occasions.

The scale of this Pottery would have been very small serving only a fairly local market using the various markets and fairs and with the possibility of limited exports to other areas that traded through Kirkcaldy Harbour. No doubt trade was very dependant on the local and national economic conditions and major events such as the Civil War period when nearly one thousand men were killed in action and the local fleet lost about 60 ships devastated trade [Old Kirkcaldy]. Whatever the scale of potting in Linktown it was only in 1714 that the foundations for the future large scale industrial Pottery were established. This establishment was a Brick and Tyle Works started by the partnership of Robertson and Adam and must be considered first although it is probable that the Mathie Pottery continued to operate when the Works were opened.

LINKS BRICK & TYLE WORKS 1715-1776

For many years William Robertson [b 1656] was "Baillie" to the Countess of Wemyss. This was a managerial position of considerable importance, which enabled him to acquire the small Estate of Gladney near to Cupar where he lived until his employer's death and he became the 'Tacksman of Coal" in Abbotshall. This new position was to take over the tenancy of the coalfield and enable him to operate, on his own behalf, coalmines in the Linktown area especially along the shoreline. The coal in this area is very shallow rarely being more than twenty feet deep. The coal workings stretched along the line of the "High Street of Linkstown" now know as Links Street from the access shaft near to the Mathie Pottery to the future site of the Links Pottery and further although there would have been other access shafts as required. As part of his operations Robertson must have been well aware of the alluvial red clay in the area and the fireclay associated with the coal seams. Although he may not have been fully aware of their full potential he would have been aware of the potting quality of the red clay for the production of coarse brown ware and would have seen "Dutch Pan Tyles" which had been imported from Holland for many years. These imported roof tyles were very much luxury items and were only used on the most expensive houses the others being roofed in thatch or stone as shown in 1641 when Provost James Oswald imported "Slabs and Tiles" from Holland for his house

[KL Harbour History p8].

At the same time there lived in nearby Kirkcaldy a successful builder and architect, John Adam, who was married to Helen Gladstone the daughter of a High Court Judge. Their only surviving child, William [b 30/10/1689 KPR], was educated at the local Grammar School until 1704 when he was sent to the "Low Countries" to continue his education [Linktown of Abbotshall p80].

William as the son of a builder who was being trained to follow his father in business must also have been aware of the use of pan tyles and presumably the Pottery. While abroad as well as studying he is credited with learning the process of making tyles and a method of treating barley to make extra strong beer [VS]. These skills were to prove extremely useful to him when his father died in 1710 and he had to return to take over the business.

The next year Robertson purchased a parcel of land in "Linktoun" as the site for his new home, Gladney House, near to Bute Wynd. He engaged Adam to design and build the house, which illustrated the major influences and training on the young man being an unusual, but attractive, mixture of Dutch and Greek Ionic styles. It was fitted out with a roof of pantyles, which must have been imported from Holland at considerable expense. It also shows the high standard that Adam had reached by the early age of twenty-two years.

Having incurred this expense it must have been a very fortunate association of a coal master with sufficient capital to invest and an enterprising young builder with probably the unique [in Scotland] knowledge of making Dutch pan tyles and the foresight to see the possibilities of using them in his own building works as well as selling them to others gave rise to the Links Brick and Tyle Works.

The basis of this Works was the construction of a Contract between the local landowner, Ramsay of Abbotshall, and the partnership of Robertson and Adam on the 8th. May 1714. The original document, which is still held in Kirkcaldy Museum was modernised in language but not content for a High Court Action in 1857. This version is quoted here for ease of reading [Session Papers 1857 20 May - 12 June {Signet Library V 508}].

> CONTRACT of LEASE between ANDREW RAMSAY of Abbotshall on the one part, and WILLIAM ROBERTSON of Gladney, and WILLIAM ADAM, Mason in Linktown of Abbotshall, on the other part.
> ### At Kirkcaldy, the 8th May 1714
> It is Contracted and finally Agreed between the parties following; that is to say, Mr Andrew Ramsay of Abbotshall, on the one part, and William Robertson of Gladney, and William Adam, of Linktown on the other part, in manner subsequent; that is to say, the said Mr Andrew Ramsay has let and granted, and by these presents, lets, for the duty under written, grants, during the standing of the manufactory after mentioned, to the said William Robertson and William Adam, and their co-partners in the said manufactory, and their heirs and assignes, the liberty and privilege of digging, winning, and away-taking clay in any place within the Barony of Abbotshall they shall think fit, for a tile and brick manufactory, to be erected by them in Linktown, excepting always from the said privilege, the houses, yards, parks, belonging to the said Mr Andrew Ramsay, with feuers properties in Linktown, and also any part or portion of the said Barony that may any ways damage prejudice the said Mr Andrew Ramsay, his mills or coalworks and likewise the said Andrew Ramsay obliges him not to feu or dispone any part of the said Barony in prejudice of the said privilege; and further, the said Andrew Ramsay hereby gives and grants to the said William Robertson and William Adam, and their foresaids, during the said space, the privilege of roads and highways for carrying and transporting the said clay where it is digged to the said manufactory; and also the said Mr Andrew Ramsay obliges him not to set any of the said clay within the said Barony to any other person or persons during the standing of the said manufactory, nor erect any such works himself until such time as the said William Robertson and William Adam, and their foresaids, desist and quit give over the said manufactory; which grant and privilege above mentioned the said Andrew Ramsay obliges him to warrant during the space above mentioned, at

all hands, and against all deadly, as his will. For the which causes the said William Robertson and William Adam bind and oblige them and their foresaids, ***** and severally, to content, pay and deliver to the said Andrew Ramsay, his heirs and assignees, yearly, during the standing of the said manufactory, at the term of Whitsunday, the sum of fifty merks Scots, with five hundred good and sufficient pan-tiles, beginning the first years payment at the term of Whitsunday 1715 years, and that for the year immediately proceeding the said term; and likewise shall content and pay to the said Mr Andrew Robertson what damage he or his tenants may sustain by *** the ground where the clay is digged, and the said highways made, in an arable condition; which two last conditions above mentioned are to be performed at the sight of four neutral honest men, to be chosen mutually for that effect. And finally, both parties bind and oblige them to observe, keep, and fulfil these presents, hic inde, under the penalty of one hundred pounds Scots, by and attour performance; and they consent registration, etc. - Written by James Dumbreck, writer in Edinburgh, and subscribed day, place, month, and year of God above written, before these witnesses,

David Malcolm, writer in Kirkcaldy, and John Manson, vinter there.

[Signed]   And. Ramsay
         W. Robertson
         W. Adam
         D A. Malcolm, witness.
         John Manson, witness.

In this document there is a reference to "Co-partners" who may have existed but their identity has not been established and there is no mention of them in any of the subsequent documents, which suggests they were included as a contingency in case they were required later.

Thus Robertson and Adam were granted the exclusive Right to all of the clay within the Barony of Abbotshall for manufacturing Bricks and Tiles in which not even the owner was allowed to compete with the partners for as long as they chose to use it. For this Right they paid an annual sum of fifty merks Scots [£2.71] and "five hundred good and sufficient pantyles". In addition the Partners had to pay the ground rent of any land they used and to restore the land after the clay was removed.

Since at this date tyles were only available from Holland, these "five hundred pantyles" would have had a reasonably high value but within a few years when the Works were in production the value fell substantially. It is perhaps unreasonable to criticise Ramsay for under estimating the value of the clay and not realising that the cost of tiles would fall so dramatically when ever they became available locally. However if this transaction is an example of Ramsay's business acumen it is not surprising that his creditors sequestered him in 1725 [Linktown of Abbotshall p82].

It should be noted that there is no mention in the Agreement of using the clay for pottery and since the Mathie Pottery was probably still in existence it must have been included in the reference to "Feuers" in the Agreement. Thus the Clay Rights granted to the Partners was apparently for brick and tyle making only. This was to prove an important fact later. It will also be noted that it was expected that the Works would be in production by the following Whitsunday.

Having taken over the lease it was a requirement that the leaseholder had to build a Works to manufacture the Brick and Tyles. To facilitate this Robertson purchased the land for the Works by means of a Charter from Ramsay which was also dated the 8th May 1714 for "yards and ruids on the north side of the Heigh Street of Linktoun" bounded on the east by the "Cossine Gutter" which was one of the several minor drainage ditches in the area [original document in KM]. This "gutter" would have been a source of water for processing the clay but probably not for power. Adam witnessed the legal documents.

Having acquired the land the Works were quickly built presumably by Adam. The construction of this new enterprise would have been assisted by the increase in prosperity brought about by the Union of 1707 although later the sacking of Kirkcaldy Burgh by the Jacobites in 1715 could not have helped it. However as Adam was particularly anti Jacobite any delay would be soon overcome.

No details of the partnership exist or their individual contributions but they were probably equal partners in the business although Robertson wholly owned the site of the original Works. It must be assumed that only Adam had the expertise to design and build the Works and the knowledge to operate it. No doubt also they would have engaged and trained a manager as Adam was so busy in his many enterprises that he would not have had much time to devote to this enterprise.

This Charter introduces a difficulty that recurred through out this period and much later. The confusion is one of orientation. As Kirkcaldy is on the north side of the Forth it was assumed that the shoreline in general lay east-west while in fact it is north-south. This error remains in place names such as the boundaries at the East and West Burns, which are actually at the north and south ends. The error at the Works can be readily seen by examining the plans.

The Works and partnership were successful and the relationship between the partners was further cemented on 30th May 1716 when Adam married Robertson's daughter, Mary, who was only seventeen. She was to make him a fine wife.

On the 20th November of the same year Adam bought land from Ramsay which was described as "Bleaching green and 8 roods of land betwixt ane cast or coall waste on the east and the highway on the north, the yard belonging to Robert Wilson in the west and burn called West Burn and the sea flood" [original documents in KM]. On this land he built the family home "The Lions" presumably to his own design and by his own workmen. At or about the same time he also acquired the land associated with the "Mathie Pottery" which was probably still in operation.

There are no detailed plans existing from that date. The Ordnance Survey plan of 1856 [page3] shows the location of the Lions and the probable site of the Mathie Pottery somewhere between the House and Heggies Wynd. The Cloistergutter is seen in the northeast of the plan and flowed down Watery Wynd. At the lower end it was subsequently taken into a pipe under the buildings to the sea.

THE "LION'S HOUSE," LINKS STREET.

"Lion"

The new house as shown was as would be expected roofed in pan tyles which of course were "very modern" at the time of construction. The name for this house seems to be slightly strange but was presumably associated with the two carved "lions" that decorated the frontage. As will be seen in the photograph they are not particularly lion like. They were retained when the house was eventually demolished and are still in existence.

The gable end of a church showing over the rooftop was built much later on the "Garden" of the house on the other side of the road. This land was acquired by Adam from John Wilson on 29/12/1738 [KM original docs.] described as "My 6 roods of land with houses, biggins, malt barn, kiln, cobble, wells, stables. yard and pertinants .... including the right to win stone and clay". The kiln referred to was, presumably associated with the malt barns and not any Pottery although it will be noted that the landowner had the right to clay on the land, which was a common building material for "clay biggins" as lime mortar when available was very expensive.

William and Mary set up the family home in this house with their four sons, John [b1721] who became heir to the Works, Robert [b1728] and James [b1731], the famous architects and William who was also an architect [VS]. Some of the boys were born in Gladney House the home of Mary's parents.

The Works were soon in production and the products were so popular that as early as 1719 they were supplied to the builders of the new Donibristle House for the Earl of Moray and later were used on Adam's own contract for Hopetown House in 1721 [VS]. Also in 1722 the Heritors of Ballingry resolved to use Links tyles to reroof the school at a cost of £18 Scots per thousand [£1.50] [Linktown of Abbotshall p83].

By this time Robertson [b1656] was an elderly man who probably left the running of most of his affairs to his son, David. Also it is unlikely that either of them took much interest in the day-to-day business in the Tyle Works. Adam was also extremely busy expanding his various businesses in many directions. In *Vitruvius Scoticus* Sir John Clerk is quoted as writing after he visited Linktown in 1728 [when Adam was thirty nine years of age] that

> "I took a little time to consider the Tyle Works as the making required. I could not but admire enough the enterprising temper of the proprietor [Adam] who had at that time near to twenty enterprises, a Barley Mill [at Balbirnie] that produces special barley for strong ale, a brewery. a timber mill, coal works, salt pans, marble works, highways, farms, houses of his own a-building and houses belonging to others not a few. Also at least half a dozen important country houses under construction".

William Adam certainly earned his nickname of "Old Stone and Mortar".

1728 was an eventual year for the partnership when Adam was appointed "a Guild Brother and Burgess" in Edinburgh where he now had a house, near to Robertson's Close and a business. He still retained the family home in Linktown at the "Lions" although he styled himself as "of Kirkcaldy". In that year also Robertson died and left his estate to his son David who was the "Brunton Overseer at the Alloa Coalworks" [Linktown of Abbotshall p83]. As Adam and his new partner and brother-in-law were both heavily committed in other projects it can be assumed that they either employed a manager or that they leased the Works to a tenant. Adam would have been still interested in the Works as a source of materials and, no doubt, income. He still continued to live, at least part time, in Linktown where he added a garden to the Lions in 1738.

Some time prior to 1744 the Works and the associated Tile Works House were leased to James Cranby who occupied them when Adam purchased Robertson's share along with a Wakemill at West Bridge [II/12/1744 original documents in KM. Sassine was not registered until 1747]. These were conveyed to William Adam in Life Rent and his son, John, in Fee. This was a legal device that occurs on several occasions in the Kirkcaldy Potteries, which allows the Life Renter to have complete control of the property during his lifetime but ensured that the property must automatically pass to the Feer. The property cannot be sold by the Life Renter or redirected in his Will without the Feer's permission.

Normally a Wakemill (waukmill) was used for cloth preparation and it seems unusual that this would interest Adam or Robertson. It is tempting to think that since this was on the nearest source of waterpower that it may have been used for preparing the clay for tile making. It should be noted that one hundred years later clay preparation for bricks, was undertaken in a horse mill. This suggestion must be at the best considered doubtful. In addition it should be noted that Adam also had a brewery and this mill was to become a brewery at a later date when it was owned by John Stocks who was one of the witnesses to the sale documents. Another witness was David Hutchison who was described as an "indwelling servant to Mr Adam" supporting the claim that Adam still maintained a home in the area.

On William's death on 24th June 1748 John inherited his father's property in Linktown, Edinburgh, Blairadam and elsewhere, including the Tyle Works, along with many other enterprises. He also succeeded his father as Master Mason for North Britain. Two years later he married Jean Ramsay who, by coincidence, was related to Ramsay of Abbotshall.

It is safe to assume that John also took very little active interest in the Works and that he continued to lease it as the succeeding years brought repeated problems when he was involved in two bank failures which cost him in excess of £18,000 and then he had to assist his brothers with a payment of £30,000 [VS]. Throughout all of his financial problems he retained the ownership of the Works and the "Lions". It is unlikely that he occupied the house and he probably rented it out after his father's death.

Whilst it is obvious that bricks and tiles were made at the Works in reasonably large numbers it is also reasonably certain that pottery was also made during these periods under the ownership of William and John Adam. The evidence is fairly strong and is based on a Court Action in 1855 [Ferguson v Methven X1X. d. 794] at which David Methven[III] gave evidence that his ancestors had produced pottery at the Tile Works from some time prior to 1775. This would have been the limit of his knowledge, which he could claim with certainty although he also averred that pottery had been made "from the earliest period". It can be reasonably assumed therefore that pottery production could and probably was undertaken well before 1775. It will be remembered that William Adam had acquired the "Mathie Pottery" site about 1716 and it could well be that he continued to operate it until production could be transferred to the Tyle Works. A move of this type would have made economic sense as well as having the additional advantage of removing the Pottery with its attendant smoke and fumes away from his new house. While this claim is conjectural it seems to be only reasonable as Adam rarely missed an opportunity to make a profit and especially as he was a friend of John Roebuck, a potter in East Lothian, with whom he was in partnership at the Carron Iron Works. It should also be noted that the Kirkcaldy area was predominantly involved in linen production and that the output increased by about six fold between 1728 and 1776. Surely an opportunity that would not have been missed.

Any pottery produced would have been coarse brownware typical of the vernacular wares made throughout the Central Belt of Scotland. Assuming that pottery was produced in this manner it would explain why the original Partners were happy to accept a limitation on their use of the clay to bricks and tiles. It should be noted that this suggestion was not referred to in any of the subsequent Court Actions which is not surprising as it could have weaken their case

There are also records of Adam dealing in glass tiles [KM]. No source was given for these but it is reasonable to assume they would have come from his Glass Works in East Lothian [The Scottish Glass Industry by J Turnbull].

The extent of Cranby's tenancy is not known. However as stated earlier an ancestor of David Methven[III] was producing pottery at the Tyle Works prior to 1775 and this ancestor was his grandfather, David Methven [I]. The market for the products of the Works must have been helped greatly in 1772 when the law preventing the Burgesses of Kirkcaldy from purchasing goods made in Linktown was revoked.

Little is known regarding David Methven [I] before 1770. It is suggested in a Memo Book in Kirkcaldy Museum, which is associated with the Methven family that he came to the Works in 1769. It also states that David[I] was from the Cupar area and was born about 1740. Although these claims are not substantiated it has to be assumed that the writer had some good reason for making them if only family tradition [KM N Methven papers]. In 1770 David[I] married Elizabeth Stocks, the daughter of John Stocks, Brewer of Links [Khorn PR]. [Note this is the same John Stocks or his son who witnessed the 1744 documents]. This marriage took place in Kinghorn Parish as did the birth of their first son, John, on 10th September 1772 [Khorn PR]. This does not imply that they lived in Kinghorn Burgh as the Parish was large having the West Burn [Tiel] at the south end of the High Street of Linktown [now Links Street] as its boundary with Abbotshall Parish. John Stocks whose brewery was on the Burn had his house on the Kinghorn side. These dates do suggest that David[I] was living in the area by 1770 and make the suggestion that Methven had leased the Works in 1769 reasonable. David set up his home in part of the "Lions" which he rented from Adam [KL M14-1847]. The other part was occupied by James Ogilvie, Collector of Taxes.

It was under the ownership of David Methven[I] and his family that the Links Brick and Tile Works and associated small Pottery were to develop and expand into a major enterprise employing a large workforce producing wares for export throughout the world.

LINKS BRICK AND TILE WORKS AND POTTERY 1776-1827

This period covers the time from when David Methven[I] bought the Links Brick and Tile Works until death. Although his direct input into potting may have been fairly small this period is convenient as it covers the establishment of the separate Links Pottery. Also it covers the start of Custom Records, which give the first true insight into the Potteries in the Kirkcaldy area

Although David[I] in all of his legal documents described himself as a "merchant" even when he owned the Works it is has to be assumed that he had some knowledge of brick and tile making prior to taking over the lease of the Works in 1769 [say] and if so then he may have acquired this knowledge at the Cupar Brick Works. What ever is the truth David certainly was successful and he was able to purchase the Works and the Lions along with a Barley Mill at Balbirnie [near Markinch] and a seat in the Parish Church from John Adam of Maryburn for £400 on 25th June 1776. He made this purchase with a payment of £300 and taking out a bond with Adam for the remaining £100.

It must have been an interesting ceremony when the sale was finalised in 1777 when the two parties met and visited each location accompanied by the necessary witnesses. Firstly Methven handed over the £100 due to Adam who in turn gave him "earth and stone of the ground of the subjects and other symbols requisite as usual after the form and terms of the said Disposition in all Points". If this was typical of the period it must have been very time consuming as the sites were many miles apart [28/2/1795 PR 45.64 N.B. this was the date when the papers were lodged with the Sheriff].

Having finalised these purchases David[I] and discharged the Bond he quickly disposed of the Barley Mill. Whatever his background David[I] certainly was a man of substance as the sums involved were considerable. He established his family home in the Lions including his sons John and David[II] [b1775] and later Alexander [b1779] and George [b1783].

The layout of the Works is shown on Plan RHP 215 [to large to reproduce] originally drawn in 1786 and amended after May 1788 where it is shown that the North East Tile Shade and Tile Works House and Garden were separated from the Tile Works by the access road to the fields. David acquired the access road in May 1788 and the road was subsequently re-routed to the north bringing House and Works into one area. [This new road became known as Pottery Wynd until much later the name was changed to Methven Road]. As David[I] was living in the Lions presumably the house was occupied by a senior employee perhaps a manager. It is significant that this reorganisation of the Works anticipated the opening of the new Turnpike Road from Pettycur to Cupar in 1790, which was immediately followed by a branch Turnpike Road from Gallatown to Crail. The former road literally passed the gate to the Works and naturally made transportation of goods and passengers very much easier by allowing the use of wheeled vehicles

While it is reasonably certain that pottery was being made at the Works prior to David acquiring it there is no doubt that he made it from the start and likely that the firing was undertaken in the tile kilns. David[I] was apparently not satisfied by this and decided to build a separate Pottery. To finance this he borrowed £230 from his father-in-law, John Stocks, on 20th January 1796 using the Works a security [PR 46.248]. The Pottery was built shortly thereafter on the land adjoining tile shade which had been acquire in 1788. Following the usual configuration it was described later as being "on the East wing of the Tile Works". Again the precise date of the Pottery is not known although in a later Court Action James Methven stated that this Pottery had been in operation at least by the very early 1800's.

Although David[I] borrowed this capital to fund his expansion he must have had a successful business as the following year he was in partnership with Stocks to lend £300 to A Sharp and Sons, Manufacturers in Pathhead [now part of Kirkcaldy] [27/8/1797 PR 48.241]. Why he would chose to do this instead of clearing his debt to Stocks must remain a matter for conjecture.

The reason for building the new Pottery was perhaps economic since by that time David[I] must have been at least in his late fifties and although the Brick and Tile Works were successful he had four sons who all worked with him. The business was probably not large enough for the four sons to make a "good living" and therefore some form of expansion was highly desirable. This expansion by building a separate Pottery probably was driven by his eldest son, John.

Although little is known of John's training he must have been fully aware of the production of coarse redware at the Tile Works. However he would have required to gain further experience in the production of superior quality wares. He would also have required to engage extra labour with the required skills. The nearest possible source was at the nearby Gallatown Pottery but it is unlikely that this skill would have been passed onto a potential rival. Of course labour could have been tempted to come to Links simply by offering higher wages. John might therefore have had to travel away from the Kirkcaldy area to gain such experience. One obvious source would have been in East Lothian and no doubt he made many journeys across the Forth since he eventually married in Edinburgh. In the "Memo Book" [KM] he is recorded as being in Leith on the 23rd June 1794 but no reason is given for this specific visit. More importantly he is recorded as being at the "Yarmouth Pig Worke" on 12th April 1801 [NB "Pig" is Scots slang for pottery]. To record this specific visit surely must mean that it was significant and directly connected with the Pottery perhaps to gain the working knowledge of "modern" pottery production or to engage labour or both. It is easy to imagine that if John were a working potter he would have wished to expand the business when the opportunity was available especially as he was contemplating marriage.

John married Mary Moodie in Edinburgh the following year and they set up their home in Links where their son David [IV] was born in 1804 and their daughter, Mary, in 1806 [APR]. It appears that they lived in the Lions perhaps with the two middle brothers. David [I] was living in the Tyle Works House at the time of his wife, Elizabeth's, death on the 1st April 1803 as shown in the funeral notice [KM]. It appears that George was living with his father

David[1] continued to operate the Works in some form of partnership with his four sons while John in addition controlled the new Pottery. Little is known regarding the two middle brothers, David[II] and Alexander except that David[II] married possibly in Cupar and had a son David[III] [b 1798 CR1851]. These brothers both died fairly young and in many ways can be discounted when considering the Works and the Pottery.

A good insight into the Methven family is given in the various Wills written by David[I] which are all held by the Kirkcaldy Museum. In the first written in 1809 when David[1] wishing to settle his affairs prepared a new Will and also cleared his debt to Stocks for £230 [PR 69.19 22/9/1809]. In this Will John was to be given "all and whole that part of my property in Linktown of Abbotshall being the east wing of the Tyle Works ...presently possessed and occupied by the said John Methven as a Pottery with the privilege of digging winning and carrying clay for use of the said Pottery". The remainder of his estate including the Tyle Works and the Lions was to be divided among the four sons "equally betwixt them share and share alike". Although described as a Will this document was much more as David[I] was not simply dividing his Estate on his death but was passing it on to his sons during his life time provided they paid him the peppercorn token of one penny Scots yearly and accepted full responsibility for his debts on death. The details of the properties were given in such a way that the sons could make the necessary changes to the Titles and gain ownership. Assuming that they were aware of this Will the sons did not accept the offer and they took no action.

Although this Will clearly shows that John was operating the Pottery in 18II, when he and others sequestered Alexander Reid, he described himself as "Manufacturer Kirkcaldy" [EC II/4/18II].

One other interesting facet of this Will is David[I]'s opinion of his middle sons, David [II] and Alexander, as although he was prepared to divide his estate between the four sons he expressly forbade David[II] and Alexander from using any part of the estate as security for credit or to sell any part except with the permission of John and George, the eldest and youngest brothers.

It was unfortunate for David[II]'s family that these Title changes were not made at the time as he died on 2nd October 1815 and his heirs lost their right to a major part of the estate. By a strange quirk of fate David[II]'s son, David[III], was to recover from this blow later.

Shortly after this death a new Will was drawn up by David[I], which gives further interesting details of the Links Pottery and the family. David[I] disponed to John and Alexander the Lions and associated land, which for the first time included a reference to a Pottery on the land. They were also given the right to take "clay for any pottery that may be carried on upon the premises" on the payment of £1.05 annually to George who was given the full Clay Right. George's veto on his brother's Alexander actions was withdrawn. Instead any dispute between John and Alexander had to be referred to two neutral men. It would be interesting to know why Alexander was included in this inheritance with John or why their father could foresee disputes between them. David[I] seems to have had a poor opinion of Alexander, which was apparently shared by their aunt, Agnes Stocks, who left John and George 1.5 acres of land at Bridgeton [near the Tiel Burn] and nothing to Alexander[Original Will in KM].

George was to be given The Tyle Works and House as well as the associated Pottery, which were described as "presently possessed by myself and sons with Dwelling House, Kilns, Shades, China Warehouse, Potkilns, Workhouse, Stables and Pedicles". In addition he was to receive all of the remaining Estate being "the whole other lands and heritage and debts heritable and moveable, stocking, furniture, bank notes and money and in general my whole other means". The three sons had to share David[I]'s debts and funeral expenses equally

This Will although slightly confusing, for the first time gives some indication of the business. The confusion is caused by the description of the property left to John and Alexander. On page one of the Will the legal description of the Lions with its adjoining grounds for the first time includes the statement "on which there was a Pottery" suggesting the Pottery no longer existed. While on page 10 it is described as "with the Pottery sometime carried on" which suggests the Pottery was still on the site but not in use. The later suggestion appears to be the most likely and that the buildings still existed but were not in use as a Pottery. However no matter which interpretation is correct there can be no doubt that a Pottery did operate near to the Lions.

Extract 1 from D Methven's Will of 1815

Extract 2 from D Methven's Will of 1815

This Will is of the same type as the earlier one in 1809 as again David[I] offered his Estate to his sons in his lifetime. The various properties are all described in much greater detail as seen in the description of the Tile Works and Pottery. It would also seem appropriate to specify the Pottery if consideration was being given to reopening it. Thus it can not be assumed that the reference to a Pottery at the Lions in the second Will and not in the first implies that the description could not have been equally used in 1809 if David[I] and his lawyer had so chosen. Certainly it would be very strange to imagine that a Pottery had been built and abandoned between 1809 and 1815. As explained earlier this surely must have been the site of the "Mathie" Pottery.

As was seen from the 1809 Will John was operating his father's Pottery and perhaps a wholesale and retail pottery agency. He continued to do so afterwards as shown in 1813 when he sequestered A Reid for a debt for pottery and in the subsequent Action described himself as a "Potter" [9728 PR81-23 12/2/1813].

Although the Pottery at the Tile Works had at least two kilns it must have been reasonably small and restricted in size being an adjunct to the Works and John wished to expand to a greater extent than the site would allow and to gain some independence.

At this time John seems to have been a reasonably successful businessman and surprisingly he was to be left only the minor part of his father's Estate which he had to share with his younger brother while George, the youngest, was to inherit the major share and was appointed executor. Why should this have been? Perhaps John had already been given capital to start his own business or some other assets or alternatively George may have been the favourite. Any interpretation could be correct. Yet again the brothers did not exercise their right to acquire their father's Estate.

John did not build a new Pottery at the Lions, which is hardly surprising as there was a severe trade depression in the country following the end of the Napoleonic War in 1815. However he did open a new Pottery some time before 1827.

Although the starting date is unknown there is no doubt that John did open a new Pottery on land he leased from Fergus of Strathore very close to the Tile Works. This site was across the access road to the North of the Tyle Works [Pottery Wynd/Methven Road]. With this he was independent from his father except for the source of the most important raw material, clay, which he obtained from his father's adjoining clay fields. This is shown in the third Will of David[I] dated 7th December 1826 prepared after the death of Alexander in which John was given the right to take clay for use in his "own Pottery now carried on by him on the east side of the Tyle Works" John was also to inherit the Lions and associated land while George was to be given all the remaining Estate including the Tyle Works, Pottery and Showroom. In this third Will the reference to the previous Pottery at the Lions was dropped as presumably John now had no intention of reopening a Pottery on that land.

While there is a doubt regarding the starting date of John's independent Pottery there are some clues that are worth considering. Firstly in the sequestration of William Inch in 1819 John was described as "Potter in Linktown of Kirkcaldy" which certainly suggests that he was potting at that time [CS 239/M45/76]. However in Piggot's Directory of Trade in 1825 he was listed as a "China and Glass Merchant" which in turn suggests that he was simply a dealer and not a manufacturer. Judging by other evidence from this publication little credence can be given to omissions such as this. To add to the confusion in the 1826 Will the Works and associated Pottery are described as "presently possessed by myself [David[I]] and sons", John and George, which suggests that John still had an interest in the business that might still have included potting. To complicate matters even further in Piggot's Directory 1825 the business is listed as David Methven and Son [i.e. George].

A positive connection of John with pottery dealing, if not manufacturing, is found in the Custom Records for the Kirkcaldy Area [Page 19] which list John as exporting 1560 pieces of earthenware on 20th September 1820 and the further loads between 1822 and 1825. These loads are all fairly small and hardly exceed 3000 pieces in the best year. There is nothing in the records that suggests the origin of the wares and since John was also a "China Dealer" they could have been made elsewhere than at the Links Pottery. It should be noted that the unit cost of the Methven pieces was usually higher than those from the Fife Pottery, which was producing and exporting whiteware. This could have been because those from Methven were re-exports and of a much higher quality or more likely that they were made in Links and the higher price was due simply to the large size e.g. milk basins or butter jars. Lastly John's nephew, David[III], in a later Court Action claimed that he had started working as a potter before 1818 with his uncle John although this could have been at his grandfathers Pottery.

Thus the doubts remain as while it would appear that John might have considered giving up all interest in his father's Pottery in 1815 and he was potting somewhere in 1818 he certainly had his own Pottery by 1826. He also had exported wares in the intervening years. The most likely scenario is that he continued at his father's Pottery for a time until the end of the depression [say 1820] when he opened his own Pottery. Until further evidence is available there has to be doubts although it is hard to imagine that John an ambitious if not always successful businessman who had a keen interest in potting would have remained at his father's small Pottery until the mid 1820's. He would have had to consider the severe trade depressions of 1810, 1816 and 1819. These doubts must remain.

In building up his business John was assisted by his son, David[IV], who by 1825 was acting as an agent for his father in the exports. John also employed and trained his nephew, David[III] and later employed him in another potting enterprise in Cupar, which is the subject of a separate chapter. Thus yet another David Methven contributed to potting in the Links.

It is interesting and confusing to note that when Alexander's burial was recorded [14/6/1818] in Kirkcaldy he was described as "son of David Methven, pottery, Linktown". It is not known who recorded this death but is strange that David[I] should be described as a "potter" when he owned a major Brick & Tile Works with an associated small pottery

While these limited historical facts are available there are, to date, no known examples of the wares produced. It is reasonably certain that only brown ware was made and unlikely that any flint was used in the body except perhaps towards the end of this period. This does not imply that only poor quality was produced as the local clay fires to a hard non-porous body which can last for hundreds of years when exposed to the weather as roof tiles. Thus although the pieces may have been fairly heavy with the use of suitable glazes a good standard of functional product could have been made.

During this period George Methven continued to work with his father in the Brick and Tile Work and was probably in control from about 1815. In the 1815 and 1826 Wills he was to be given the Works including the associated Pottery along with the Clay Right and most of his father's personal property. It should be noted that George was being associated with the Pottery and China warehouse and could have both produced pottery and operated a pottery wholesale and retail business. This is unlikely, as George seems to have had very little interest in potting even at a later time when he owned an active Pottery. From the terms of the Wills and other evidence it appears that John was the potter and George was content to be a brick and tile maker. This would have been no hardship to George as the Works were obviously very successful and as will be seen later much more profitable than the Pottery.

Little is known of the Works except the brief details shown on the 1786 plan [RHP215] prior to the construction of the Pottery and in the various Wills. The business was successful remaining in operation through the various trade depressions. As well as making bricks and roof [pan] tiles with the local red clay he also made floor tiles [pavings] as well as a small number of drainage tiles to supply the small local market. The term pavings is difficult to define but were probably the redware unglazed tiles [approximately 30cm square and 7cms thick] found in an archaeological excavation of the Tile Works House in October 2000. In addition he would have used fireclay at least to make firebricks as this material, which is associated with the coal measures, was readily available. It would not be unreasonable to assume that the kilns at the two new Potteries built by the Methvens were constructed of firebricks of their own manufacture.

Fireclay products must be fired at a much higher temperature than brown clay and required a separate kiln[s]. At that time the type of kiln used for fireclay products was very similar to a pottery kiln and it is quite possible that the Potkilns adjoining the Tyle Works were adapted for that use when pottery production was moved to the new site.

.Roof tiles at that time were valued at £4 per thousand as shown in the Court Action Methven v Lord Minto to recover £33 being the cost of 8250 tiles [CS 239 Box 337 W/2/D]. Similarly in 1813 the "Raith Papers" give roof tiles the same value and show that David[1] paid an annual feu-duty of £2.78 on the land at the clay field, which adjoined the Works [KM files].

By the end of the eighteenth century in excess of 75,000 bricks and tiles were being manufactured annually in the Kirkcaldy area and taxed at £300 [Statistical Account for Fife 1791]. The precise source of these bricks is not given and there may well have been other Brick and Tile Works in the area. Indeed considering the abundant red and fireclay it would be surprising if no one had considered opening a rival business outwith the Abbotshall area. However if any such work existed it must have been small and short-lived and it can be reasonably assumed that the bulk of the taxed production, if not all, came from the Links Works. Strangely the same Statistical Account states that bricks and tiles were regularly imported into Dysart from Aberdeen. These would have been exclusively made from red clay. It seems odd at first that a heavy and relatively low valued cargo such as this should have been brought from Aberdeen when an equally good product was available locally. This is probably a case of ships coming in ballast for coal and carrying bricks and tiles instead of stones that had no commercial value. Also there is a local tradition of importation of roof tiles from Holland for the same reason. It should also be remembered that although Adam is credited with introducing tile making to Scotland he did not have a patent on this product and he would have been copied by many others as was the case in Cupar where a new Brick and Tyle Works was opened in 1764.

In the Custom Records for the Kirkcaldy area there are many entries for the exportation of bricks and occasionally tiles in sailing ships. No prime source is given for the bricks as with the exception of one all of the loads were registered by persons who as far as are known were not local producers. When it is remembered that in this case "Kirkcaldy" covers the coast from Aberdour to Leven and that the bricks could have been made anywhere in the area or indeed be re-exports from other areas sources other than Links must be considered. However unless further evidence becomes available it can be assumed that the bulk of these loads were made at the Links Works. It should be noted that only overseas loads were subject to this tax. There was also considerable coastwise trade both in sailing ships and steam powered such as the daily steam ships to Leith, which were not taxed and therefore not recorded. This is clearly shown by lists published in the Clyde Commercial Advertiser published between 1806 and 1810 that lists several loads of bricks being delivered in 1807 to Port Glasgow from Kirkcaldy, which are not recorded for taxation purposes. This reference to Kirkcaldy was the dispatching harbour not the Customs Area and it can be accepted that these Bricks were produced at the Links Works.

6/6/1807   8,000 bricks,   9/6/1807   9.000 bricks,   28/7/1807   II,000 bricks,
21/9/1807   11,000 bricks   &   21/10/1807   4,000 bricks.

Exports of Bricks from Kirkcaldy Tax Area

DATE	VESSEL & DESTINATION	LOAD	EXPORTER	VALUE
23/3/1772	Betty for Granada	4,000 Bricks	Dalgleish	
		1,000 Tyles		
30/5/1772	Adventure for Antigua	20,000 Bricks	Parker	
16/6/1775	John & Elizabeth	40,000 Tyles		
	for Copenhagen	6,000 Paving	David	
		6,000 Bricks	Methven	
29/4/1786	Balborn for Gibralter	1,400 Bricks	Shaw	
14/4/1789	Margaret for Gottenburgh	2,000 Bricks	Oliphant	
6/8/1796	Ann for Hamburgh	2,000 Bricks	Gordon	
16/4/1801	Emanuel for Mandale	12,000 Bricks	D Alison	£17
16/6/1806	Emanuel for Mandale	12,000 Bricks	D Alison	£10
13/9/1806	Hope For Peterburgh	30,000 Bricks	D Alison	£105
		10 tons Clay	D Alison	£7.50
20/3/1811	Minerva for Quebec	12,000 Bricks	Bennet	
1/7/1815	Ruby for St Petersburgh	20.000 Firebricks	H Bisset	£80
		10tons Clay		£10
3/8/1818	Flemming for St Petersburgh	15,000 Firebricks	H Bisset	£45
10/8/1819	Harmony for St Petersburgh	15,000 Firebricks	H Bisset	£90
		10 tons Fireclay		
16/7/1821	Robert for St Petersburgh	20,000 Firebricks	H Bisset	£75
		15 tons Fireclay		£11

The type of bricks delivered is not specified nor is their value. However as bricks were regularly exported from the Clyde to other destinations it must be assumed the bricks from Kirkcaldy had some special quality and from the other evidence given later it seems probable that they would have been fireclay bricks. If correct this would suggest that the Links Brick Works and others in the Forth area were leading the field in fireclay production.

The details of the overseas exports are shown in the previous table from the Custom Records for "Kirkcaldy" and it is worthwhile considering them in detail. It should be remembered that there was at least one other Brick & Tile Works at Leven in the Kirkcaldy Taxation area at this time. It is not known if this Works made fireclay products at this time.

The first two loads were sent to the West Indies in 1772 and were probably red clay tiles and judging by the rest of the ship's cargo were destined for the Sugar Plantations as "Slave" clothing was also included in the load. The second of these loads, 20,000 bricks, was a substantial quantity. The next in 1775 was the only load sent by directly D. Methven and was dispatched prior to him purchasing the Works confirming that he had control prior to acquiring them. It was also the only load sent to Copenhagen. This may be attributable to the Master of the vessel, John Methven, who might have been David[I]'s brother as he had one of that name who died in the West Indies in 1780. It is also strange that although David[I] registered the load with the Customs Authorities he had a substantial change of mind and only sent 25,600 pantiles and no bricks or paving slabs. From this entry it is now confirmed that, at least by that time he had diversified from simply making bricks and pantiles into also making paving [floor tiles].

The small loads listed seem uneconomic until the full manifest of the vessels are studied when it is seen that small loads of bricks are frequently accompanied by iron fireplaces presumably for timber built houses. Small loads continued and where values were given the cost of the bricks were in the £1.00 to £1.50 per thousand until 1806 when the first load was sent to St Petersburg [Russia]. The value of the bricks increased to about £3.50 per thousand. The type of brick was not specified but as this higher value was later only given to firebricks it can be assumed that these bricks were of that type and this is, probably, the earliest reference to fireclay products at the Links Works.

As stated earlier fireclay, which is a product of the coal seams, was abundantly available in the Links area either as a waste product from the coal workings or by quarrying. It was a more expensive material than the alluvial clay to obtain and much more expensive to process into bricks etc. Although nothing is known of the working methods at the Works in the early 1800's it is known that in 1848 and probably much later red clay was processed for bricks in a horse mill whilst the much harder fireclay required a steam driven mill. Further as the only real advantage that firebricks had over common clay bricks was their ability to withstand much higher temperatures it was only with the expansion of industry, especially iron smelting, during the Industrial Revolution that this additional cost could be justified. Thus expansion into fireclay processing at the Works possibly required the installation of steam power to drive the mill machinery. It certainly was very convenient that the demand for fireclay products caused by the Industrial Revolution was aided by the availability of the new machinery due to that Revolution. There is no doubt that the demand for firebricks in Russia at that time can be credited to the expansion of industry there after the failed Napoleonic invasion and that the demand increased after the end of the War.

Nearly all of the exports were made by H Bisset who was probably the East Lothian brick and tile maker of the same name who regularly sent firebricks to Russia from East Lothian [Custom Records]. If this assumption is correct then it says much for the quality of these bricks, which were considered to be of sufficient value in Russia to secure repeat orders and were considered suitable by a rival maker. There is one clue that helps to strengthen the claim that the bricks were made at the Links Works as one load in 1822 was exported by "Mr Swan for Mr Bisset". This "Mr Swan" was probably the linen agent of that name who dealt extensively with the Baltic area. Strangely his family was later to own a Brick and Tile Works in the Links area.

Thus in 1826 the Tyle Works bought by David[I] had grown into a substantial business operated by George while his elder brother, John, had his own Pottery on leased land at which he used clay from his father's clay fields. As before the father was prepared to hand over his Estate to his sons who yet again did not accept his offer. On this occasion it did not matter as David[I] died the following year[1827] "of old age and debility" and was buried in a "sief" in Abbotshall Church Yard near to his wife and two sons [APR]. The gravesite is well marked and continued in use by the family.

These two notices come from the Methven family records. The later one contains a footnote added at a much later date.

SIR,

My Wife, ELEZEBATH STOCKS, Died 1ſt. April, and is to be Interred in Abbotſhall Church Yard, on Tueſday the 5th. Current, at 12 o'Clock noon.

The Favour of your Preſence to acompany the Fueneral from my houſe here to the placé of Interemet will very much Oblege

SIR

Links Tyle—work

April 4ᵗʰ 1803

Your Humble Servt.

David Methven

Chapter 2   GALLATOWN POTTERY

While David[I] and especially John Methven were developing pottery production in the Links as an extra to brick and tyle making rivals were in operation in nearby Gallatown village [N.B. there are several spellings of the name even in the one document], which is now part of Kirkcaldy as is Linktown. Little is known about the early days or the products of this Pottery but it was to give rise to one of the larger and more important Potteries in the area.

Although various dates are suggested for the start of Gallatown Pottery: - P McVeigh 1786, R, Insh 1780, G Quail 1790 and Fleming 1817 none of these dates is substantiated although any of the first four could be correct. Fleming is definitely wrong although 1817 is not without significance.

The earliest reference found so far is in the Edinburgh Courant of 19th May 1810.

DISSOLUTION OF COPARTNERY

The Pottery Business carried on at Gallowtown under the firm of GALLATOWN POTTERY COMPANY was DISSOLVED on the first day of January last.
[signed] Will. Mackie
          William Grant, for the children of the deceased William Grant, Wright,
in Kirkcaldy

Gallowtown, 1st May 1810

N.B. The business is now carried on by Robert Paterson and Andrew Gray, potters at Gallatown, under the firm of Paterson and Gray. The new company beg leave to return thanks to their friends and the public for the liberal encouragement they have met since their commencement in business and having procured a large supply of first materials, and employed the best workmen they trust their wares will be inferior to none in the Kingdom. They therefore solict a continuance of public favour. Dealers will be served on the most liberal terms, and pointed attention given to orders addressed to Paterson and Gray, Gallatown Pottery by Dysart.

Thus while it is certain that this Pottery was in operation prior to 1810 there is only an indication of the type of ware being produced or the status of the Pottery. It can be stated with reasonable authority that in 1810 the Pottery was of sufficient size and reputation to make it worthwhile and necessary to publish this Notice in a national newspaper. Similarly the expression "large supply of first materials" cannot reasonably be considered to refer to the local red clay, which was abundant throughout the Central Belt of Scotland and used extensively for the manufacture of brownware [e.g. Links and Cupar]. From the tone of this notice and considering the market it was obviously aimed at it can be assumed that the Gallatown Pottery was and had been, even for a short time earlier, manufacturing whiteware. This assumption implies that at least white clay and flint must have been imported to Dysart. There is no indication of the starting date nor has any been found to date. It is necessary therefore to consider the evidence.

Firstly there was in Gallatown in the first half of the nineteenth century a building known as the Old [Auld] Pottery at a time when the newer Fife Pottery was in operation. It would not be unreasonable therefore to assume that this "Old" Pottery predated the Fife Pottery. Thus when it is recorded that this property had been purchased by William Grant [wright], one of the partners listed, on January 31st 1800 [PR.53-473] it seems reasonable to assume that this was the site of the Gallatown Pottery. In the legal papers the land is described as being "33 falls with dwelling house and stables" which suggests there was no Pottery on the land in 1800 and that the Pottery was constructed after that date. This need not be true as for reasons of legal continuity of Titles the description of land and its contents often remains the same although the buildings on it had changed. This is clearly illustrated in the future transactions of this land and at the Links Brick and Tyle Works. It could well be that the land had been rented from the owner, James Laing Currie, prior to 1800 and the building converted into a Pottery. However with only this evidence it would only be safe to assume that the Pottery dated from 1800[circa].

Secondly the partners must be considered. The late William Grant referred to in the 1810 notice was registered as a "Wright of Kirkcaldy" and was a house builder carrying out speculative development up to at least 1806 [PR57-103 & PR61-176]. William Mackie [born 1748] was also a Wright but interestingly his son James [born 1784] was a potter [Sin B]. Could this indicate that if not also a potter that William certainly had an interest in potting?

Thirdly the location of the Pottery - is it important? Gallatown although within the Parish of Dysart at that time is some one-mile from the Burgh and harbour. Dysart was one of the most important burghs in Scotland and up to 1690 was larger on a taxation basis than Kirkcaldy. Thus as explained in Chapter 1 regarding the Links area it was a possible location for a Pottery as there was clay and coal in abundance. If a Pottery had been built it would have been outside the Burgh. However there is no positive proof of such a Pottery and the available evidence has to be examined.

Gallatown is about 250 feet above sea level and up a very steep hill which caused problems for horse drawn carts which were usually sent "half loaded" and extra trace horses were required to pull them up the hill. In the Gallatown area there is a reasonable ground water supply but no running water capable of driving machinery. From these it appears reasonable to assume that if anyone was considering starting a Whiteware Pottery from scratch then it would have been situated as near to the harbour and to sea level as possible to facilitate the importation of the necessary materials, at least clay and flint. There was also the possibility of a better water supply especially for power. From these alone Gallatown is an unlikely location for a new Whiteware Pottery and it is more likely that when potting started in Gallatown it was with a Redware Pottery using local clay and coal or wood and that this developed into the Gallatown Pottery probably but not necessarily on the "Grant" site. In addition there was an ecclesiastical establishment at St. Serfs in Dysart Burgh, which could have supported a Pottery. Any starting date would be guess work; however if the assumptions made are correct there is no reason why the starting date could not match that of the Mathie Pottery in Linktown.

Exports from Kirkcaldy Tax Area pre 1817

Date	Vessel/Destination	Load/Value	Exporter	Unit Cost
10/10/1776	Friendship for St Martinique	4 Crates of Earthenware	D Robertson	
17/7/1780	Thomas & Mary for Greenock	2 Crates of Earthenware £10	D Alison	
19/7/1790	Morningside for Gottenburgh	11 Casks, 1 Tierce 13 Casks British Stoneware £64	John Grant	
17/10/1792	Neptune for Charlestown South Carolina	15 Crates Brown Earthenware £19		
24/9/1796	Margaret for Gottenburgh	3 Crates British Earthenware £17	Alexander Hill	
8/10/1812	Juniper for Christainsand	16 Crates Earthenware £64	Master for Alex. Hill	
16/12/1812	Betsy for Oporto	1 Cask Ew £14	W Adam	
24/8/1814	Tvends for Kiertimunde	7 Crates [233kg] Earthenware £50	I. F. & T. C. Dennwaid	
26/9/1814	Charlotte Louisa for Stratsmond	12 Crates [254 kg] Earthenware £50	Alexander McFarlane	
11/2/1815	Lively for Bremen	17 Crates [12,012 pieces] Ew £95 17 Crates [11,076 pieces] Ew £110	Alex Elder & Co. E & T Millie	0.8p 1p
12/9/1815	Heelwe for Amsterdam	20 Crates [14,000 pieces] Ew. £110	Alex Elder & Co.	0.8p
20/11/1815	Endevor of Dysart for Bremen	18,000 pieces Earthenware £150	Gray & Co	0.83p
20/9/1816	Forth for Bremen	34,875 pieces Earthenware £241	A Elder & Co.	0.7p

Fourthly the shipping records as shown in the List of Custom Records of Exports pre 1817 there were exports of pottery, mainly earthenware, from the Kirkcaldy tax area. In these cases it is probable that they were sent out through Kirkcaldy or Dysart harbours. Whilst this evidence cannot be taken as proof of pottery production it surely must give a strong indication, as it is unlikely they were all simply re-exports. One load is of particular interest when on 19/7/1790 a load of approximately 10,000 pieces was sent to Gottenburgh. Surely this was made locally and can it be pure coincidence that the exporter was John Grant who could have been William Grant's father [K.W.]? It will be noted that this load was declared as "stoneware" but it is difficult to know how accurate this description was as there was no difference for tax purposes between white earthenware and stoneware and in the Staffordshire Potteries until at least 1837 [FH 16/11/1837] the two names were synonymous. There are no records of any imports of clay or flint during this period but this in no way means that they were not imported as clay and ground flint were not recorded by the Tax Collector at other ports on the Forth where it is known for certain they were landed. It appears they were taxed, if required, at the port of dispatch. In addition it appears highly unlikely that a load of this size would have been all redware.

The loads in 1776 and 1780 are also interesting but again only indicative. D Robertson who did not pay any tax exported the first a load of "4 crates of earthenware". This can imply that either the tax had been paid elsewhere or that there was no tax on "earthenware" at that time. Alternatively St Martinique may have been a tax-free area. Although H.M. Customs are unable to clarify these points it is likely and that the pieces were made locally. Judging by the ship's cargo the bulk of the 1776 load was being sent to Slave owners and this load could well have be cheap redware for that purpose. The 1780 load again although small adds to the theory of local production at a Pottery other than the Links which probably would not be capable of the manufacture of the good quality earthenware and certainly not the "stoneware" at the dates when the exports were made. In addition since this load was sent to Greenock and tax was paid in Kirkcaldy the earthenware must have bee destined to go overseas after Greenock. As there were many redware Potteries in the Clyde area such a load had a specific importance and would have been whiteware

From this evidence it appears highly likely but far from conclusively proven that there was indeed a Pottery in Gallatown in the later part of the eighteenth century and that at least from 1780 whiteware was produced although earlier dates cannot be ruled out. Such a date would follow the spread of creamware from Staffordshire after its development by Wedgwood in 1764.

Whatever the story prior to 1810 after that date the picture is much clearer as at last it is certain that there was a potter in the company, Andrew Gray. Andrew was born on 30/11/1782 but unfortunately his father's trade is not given [DyPR]. He married Mary Irvine on 7/7/1804 and in the burial records of their children he is described as "potter" [SinB].

The new partnership of Paterson and Gray was expanded within a few months when they were joined by Andrew's brother, Archibald, and the firm reformed as Paterson and Grays. Paterson must have played only a small part in the Company as he left it on 5th April 18II after only sixteen months. This change in the Company was advertised in the Edinburgh Courant of IIth April 18II

COPARTNERY DISSOLVED

The Pottery Business formerly carried on at Gallatown, under the firm of Mess. Paterson and Grays, was this 5th. April 1811 DISSOLVED by mutual consent.

[Signed] Robt. Paterson
        Archibald Gray   James Smite witness
        Andw. Gray   Wm. Mackie witness

The POTTERY BUSINESS, formerly carried on under the firm of Mess. Paterson and Grays is in future to be carried on under the firm of Mess. Smith, Grays and Co.

[Signed] James Smith
        Archibald Gray

Andrew Gray

Gallatown April 5 1811.

[Note the name Smite is probably a printing error and should have been Smith the new partner]

From this it is seen that Wm. Mackie had remained interested in the Pottery and perhaps he is the "and Co". Certainly from the Parish Records the families of Gray, Grant and Mackie were intermarried and several of the male Grays were potters although not necessarily directly related to Andrew and Archibald.

Like Paterson before him Smith is an anonymous character although the fact that his name is given first in the company title would suggest some form of superiority he left the firm very quickly as when the vessel "Industry of Port Soy" delivered 40tons of flint stones to the "Kirkcaldy" Customs area on 4th December 1812 it was consigned to "Gray and Company". No official notice was published regarding this change in the partnership so the composition of the firm is uncertain. The use of the term "and Company" suggests that there were other partners but again if they did exist they were probably only financial.

Imports of Flint to Kirkcaldy Tax area pre 1817

Date	Vessel	From	Load
4/12/1812	Industry of Port Soy	Banff	40 tons of white flint stone
1/6/1813	Triton of Exmouth	Plymouth	7 tons of china stone
30/4/1815	Red Rose	Newcastle	5 tons of white flint stone
3/7/1815	Jane of Kirkcaldy	Leith	5 tons of china stone
19/8/1815	Rose of Leven	Newcastle	5 tons of flint stone
27/4/1816	Lismouth	London	60 tons of flint stone

After 1812 the picture is much clearer and a reasonable history can be obtained. The importation of 40 tons of flint stones late that year shows much about the Grays. Firstly they were ambitious and wished to have more control over their operations. Secondly their demand for flint must have been large enough to justify the expense of a Flint Mill. Thirdly they were making or intended to make a good quality product with flint in the body. It also implies that they had or expected to have access to a flint mill. The location of this mill is not certain. This first load appears to be very much an experiment as was the 7-ton load of China Stone the following year [1813], which was delivered to a James Gray. It can be reasonably assumed that James was associated with the Pottery although no details of him are known. Perhaps he was the unspecified "and Company". This was the only load received of this material in its unprocessed state for several years and presumably the experiment of processing was a failure. In 1815 at total of fifteen tons of flint was imported followed by fifty tons in 1816 which might indicate a substantial increase in out put. This flint was processed at the Burn Mill on the River Leven very near to Leven Harbour. This mill was leased from the Durrie Estate [Christie] some time after 1/3/1813 until 1829. In his book "Loch Leven & River Leven"[p175] D Munro shows that on 1/3/1813 the mill was occupied by Alex. Ballingal as a grain mill. Also on p51 that in 1828 during the Gray tenancy "the rent or yearly value of the water fall was £13". The "fall" was the head of water available to drive the mill.

This mill although some ten miles from Dysart was still very convenient as it was very close to Leven Harbour and shipping between the two harbours was easy. It should also be remembered that the Customs Authorities did not record the movement of ground flint.

No pottery was exported in the first eleven year of the Nineteenth Century, which was probably due as much to the Napoleonic War as the lack of production. The first load in 1812 was again substantial being about 15,000 pieces and was taken by the Master of the ship to Christainsand [Norway]. Since this Master traded regularly with Forth Ports he must have been aware of the availability of whiteware at the Lothian ports and as he chose "Kirkcaldy" as his source for a commercial venture this load must have been a local product and of reasonably high quality. It is simply described as "earthenware" which would cover the products of the Gallatown and Links Potteries. However judging by the limited knowledge of these Potteries available Gallatown is, by far, the most likely source.

On 20/11/1815 the picture changed when Gray & Co. were sufficiently confident to export 18,000 pieces of earthenware to Bremen. Certainly by April 1817 the Grays were producing whiteware both painted and printed at Gallatown Pottery as shown in the cover letter [SRO 41/20 112] for a consignment of pottery sent to Mr Duncan Thomson a potter and pottery dealer in East Lothian which contained: -

Gallotown Pottery   8th April 1817

Mr Duncan Thomson   Bot. of Gray & Co.

8 doz. BE Dinners	£0-17- 4
BE Tureens	£2-10- 6
10 doz Bakers	£1-13- 0
8 doz. Chambers	£1- 0- 0
12 doz Basons & Bowls	£1-10- 0
4 doz. Basons & bowls, Dipt	£0-13 -0
4 Doz. Mugs Dipt.	£0-14- 0
4 doz. Bowls Enamd.	£0-18- 0
1 doz. Poringers Enamd.	£0- 4- 6
1 doz. Cans Enamd.	£0- 4- 3
20 Teapots Painted	£0-15- 0
2 doz. Teas Printed	£0- 7- 0
Crates cordage and straw	£0-15- 0
	£12- 1- 7

Sir   We have shipped the above for you and one other for delivery to Geo. Shaw this day in the Jean Fraser Master who sails this afternoon if the weather permits. Have annexed George's Invoice which will make only one postage between you and him. Trust you have got safe and sound home and will not neglect to send us a good supply of B. Wares as soon as possible.

Your most obedient servant

Gray & Co.

Many of the items quoted are further subdivided to give different sizes e.g. the "Chambers 8 doz." are broken down into 4/4 and 4/6 which can be taken as 4 "dozen" at 4 or 6 pieces to the "dozen". This practise of referring to a quantity of pottery as being a "dozen" but not necessarily meaning twelve continues to this day. The teapots were supplied as "1 & 8/12 dozen" [i.e. 20] but in this case one dozen did mean twelve.

The total value of the load was £12.08 including packing and from the prices quoted it is seen that the cost of each item was in the region of 1p to 2p with the exception of the teapots, which cost 4p. These prices compare with those charged later in the early 1820's. Also there can be little doubt that the "printed" wares were whiteware and probably the same applied to "painted" wares. "Enamelled" wares could be whiteware or brownware. However as the Grays were so keen to have a supply of brownware from Thomson surely must indicate that they were not making that type of ware. It also suggests that the Grays considered the Links Pottery brownwares products as being unsuitable for their trade.

There can also be little doubt that many other loads were sent "coastwise" i.e. by ship to other British ports but these would not be recorded by the Customs. In considering the Customs Records it must be remembered that there was at least one other Pottery in the area at Links although it is more likely that the bulk of the exported earthenware did come from Gallatown Pottery.

It is interesting to note that in 1812 the foreign export trade restarted after a lapse since 1796 and whilst this can be attributed in part to the change in the political climate as Napoleon's grip on the Baltic area lessened it cannot be pure coincidence that 1812 also marked an expansion in production at Gallatown Pottery as suggested by the importation of flint. Certainly a supplier able to produce loads totalling some 26,000 pieces must have had a highly productive Pottery and not a primitive affair as suggested by Fleming. It must be noted that dealers or agents and apparently not the original producer sent most of these loads

The Grays continued their operation at the Gallatown Pottery and no doubt contributed to the substantial loads, which were exported until 1817 [circa.] when they gave up the lease of the Pottery.

In trying to establish the history of the Pottery the Old Parish Records are of very limited use as they in general do not give the occupation of the entrants. The various graveyard records are slightly more helpful as they do give this detail. They do not give the age or place of birth. In the St. Dennis Graveyard, which was in the Burgh of Dysart, a few potters are recorded up to 1817:- John Guillen [died 1806], Francis Henderson [working potter in 1808], Peter Turnbull [died 1814] who is described as "that belongs to the Pottery" and in the Dysart burial records a James Beatton "that belongs to Dysart Pottery". These last two descriptions are presumably expressions akin to "associated" or "employed" and not some form of bondage! Also "Dysart Pottery" is presumably a description of Gallatown Pottery, which was within Dysart Parish; however it could be an entirely different and unknown Pottery.

When Gray & Co. quit the Gallatown Pottery James Grant who had inherited the property [PR II1.224] from his father leased the Pottery to new tenants, the firm of Messers Reid & Adie, who continued to operate it for whiteware production. By 1821 James had immigrated to Frankfort, Kentucky, USA after passing the Pottery to David Grant of Port Glasgow on 21/8/1820 [PR 1290.16]. The relationship if any between James and David has not been established. Later on 4/4/1822 the Pottery was offered for sale or rent [FH] as Reid and Aidie's lease was nearing termination. Judging from this date and following the usual leasing methods it appears that Reid and Aidie had taken a five-year lease possibly from Whitsunday 1817. If this were correct then the Grays would have left the Gallatown Pottery on or by that date.

POTTERY TO BE LET OR SOLD

To be sold by public roup within the house of George Downie vinter Kirkcaldy 2nd. May 1822.

The premises situated in Wester Gallatown presently occupied by Messers Reid and Adie with the whole utensils necessary for carrying on the works. Also 40 or 50 Tons of White & Blue Clay. Title Deeds in the hands of Mr Galloway Town Clerk Dysart.

If not sold the Pottery will be let at Whitsunday first. 2nd April 1822

In the "For Sale" notice it is advertised as a going concern with all the "utensils necessary for carrying on the works". They also advertised 40 of 50 tons of white and blue clay for sale showing that whiteware was still being produced and that such clays were imported without being recorded for taxation purposes.

This sale was unsuccessful and it has not been established if David was ever able to lease the property as a Pottery again. It is hard to imagine that in this period of severe trade depression taking over a Pottery would have been an attractive proposition although John Methven may have given it serious consideration.

Certainly by 1841 it was occupied by weavers [CR]. David eventually sold the Pottery to James Robertson [carter] in 1852 [20/9/1852 PR 294.189] when for the first time it was described as "now fitted out as a Pottery" which suggests that the kiln[s] and workshops still existed. Thus Gallatown Pottery came to an end with a much mystery as it started.

Wares

So far no wares from the Gallatown Pottery have been positively identified and there is only the vague descriptions given in the letter and sale notice. Equally no shard evidence is available.

In his book "Scottish East Coast Potteries" Patrick McVeigh illustrates a "marriage" jug for Wm Beveridge and Helen Shoulbread, which he dates as c1805 and as being made at the Gallatown Pottery. No evidence is given for this attribution except the proximity of Beveridge's home and the Pottery. There is no reason to assume this jug does not commemorate the marriage, which is recorded in the Dysart Parish Records as being on the 8th. November 1777. The wife is recorded as Shoulbraid in this and when William Beveridge reported to the Dysart Kirk Session in 1797 that his eldest son John had been born on the 5th June 1786. Whilst it would be a lovely idea to accept this as proof of whiteware production in Gallatown Pottery at this early date further evidence is required as the mug, which is now held in Kirkcaldy Museum, could well have been made in the East Lothian Potteries or elsewhere.

Further evidence is required before any positive attributions can be made.

Chapter 3

FIFE POTTERY 1817 to 1829

By 1816 [circa] the Grays who were obviously very successful found their rented Gallatown Pottery very restricted in size and lacked room to expand. This was easily overcome as they were sufficiently well funded to develop their own Pottery. To achieve this they leased an area of land from the Rosslyn Estate not far from the Gallatown Pottery. This land amounted to almost one acre and was situated in Pottery Street as shown on the plan of Gallatown, which was surveyed about 1826. The Pottery is the building in the shape of an open square just above the **y** of "Pottery". The lease must have contained an option to buy as they built a substantial pottery on the land at a cost of about £1500 surely a substantial investment [E.C. 10/6/1826]. The buildings were completed in 1817 and described later as "erected...upon an extensive and approved plan" [EC 30/II/1827]. It would have been to a modern design and contained three kilns that required 60,000 firebricks in their construction [F.H. 14/8/1828]. A quantity of bricks of this size would have been made fairly locally and very probably at the Links Brick and Tyle Works. Even if they did not make the bricks the Methvens, especially John, must have looked with envy at this rival with a much superior Pottery. Indeed the design was so good that over a century later an ex-manager, McKenzie, remarked on the high quality of the layout. The Grays obviously had to find a new Trade Name having left the Gallatown Pottery and they decided to use "Gray & Co." for trading purposes although there are references to the "Fife Pottery Company". The property was named the "Fife Pottery". Within the Pottery grounds they appear to have also constructed a dwelling house. This is not mentioned in any of the sale documents. This house was, probably occupied by Archibald Gray.

If as suggested in the previous chapter Gray & Company gave up their lease to Gallatown on 15th May 1817 is seems reasonable to assume that from that date they were fully committed to the new Fife Pottery. Such a major development must have required an influx of new highly skilled labour which could only be found away from the immediate area [It should be noted that the Gallatown Pottery was still in operation]. At that time they apparently also engage new apprentices one of whom, Andrew Nicolson, was indentured for five years to be trained as a platemaker and printer. Fortunately his indenture papers still exist and the legible contents shown are a copy of part of the original. This remarkable document is slightly peculiar as it was written in 1820 and is retrospective to 1817. Andrew was about 11 years of age when he started his apprenticeship and was given board and lodgings, probably living in the Pottery. The limitations on his life style were strict and somewhat strange for a boy of his age. He appears to have been expected to work at nights if required although his working hours are not specified. It is interesting to note that although he was classified as being trained as a potter he was to be specifically limited to platemaking and printing showing that even as early as that date this new Pottery had been set out on a production line basis with tradesmen concentrating on restricted parts of the potter's trade. This also shows conclusively that Gray & Co. where making transferred printed wares.

> It is Contracted and Agreed upon between Gray and Company, Potters in Gallatown on the one part and Andrew Nicolson son of Alexander Nicolson Sailor in Parkhead with the special advice and consent of his said Father on the other Part in manner following. That is to say the said Andrew Nicolson hereby becomes bound as Apprentice and Servant to the said Gray and Company in the Art and Occupation of a Potter as a Platemaker and Printer, and that for the period of Five years complete from and after the Fifteenth day of May eighteen hundred and seventeen, which notwithstanding the date hereof is hereby declared to have been the said Andrew Nicolson entry to his apprenticeship during which space the said Andrew Nicolson with consent foresaid hereby Binds and Obliges himself faithfully, diligently and honestly to serve the said Gray and Company their

heirs and survivors in the above mentioned art and occupation by night and by day, and not to absent or withdraw himself from his said master's service without liberty asked and obtained, and if he do on the contrary he shall serve two days for each days absence and that after the expiry of this Indenture, and he shall consent and pay to the said Masters two pennies for each penny loss they shall suffer of sustain through his default. That he shall abstain and refrain from all vicious company and gaming, excess in drinking, night walking and debauchery, and fro all every idle exercise that may in any way divert him from his said Master's service. Neither shall he be accessory to mobs or *****: That he shall no sooner *** his Master's prejudice their goods or good name but shall immediately and make the same known to them and prevent the same to the utmost of his power and shall in all respects so behave himself to his said Masters as becomes a dutiful and obedient Apprentice and for faithful performance of the whole Premisses. James Robertson Potter in Wester Gallatown hereby becomes *** as his Cautioner and Security for which causes and on the other Part the said Gray and Company hereby Bind and Oblige themselves and their heirs and Successors to teach and instruct the said Andrew Nicolson in the art and trade of Potter, at least in each of the branches of the said business called Platemaker and Printer and shall *** nor conceal from him any part ****** do their utmost endeavour to cause the said Andrew Nicolson ***** as they daily practice there themselves or their said apprentice has capacity to learn and understand. And further to pay to the said Andrew Nicolson their apprentice **** Board **** during the period of this Indenture the following sums and in proportions after specified viz. Three Shillings per week for the first year, Three Shillings and sixpence per week for the second year, Four Shillings per week for the third year, Four Shillings and sixpence for the fourth year and Five Shillings per week for the last year thereof. And lastly both parties Bind and Oblige themselves to perform the respective parts of the promises to each other under the penalty of Five Pounds Sterling to be paid by the party failing to the party observing or willing to observe the same over and above performance and Consent to the Registration thereof in the Books of Council and Session or others competent that****

Their Procurators - In Witness thereof those present written on Stamped Paper by William Mclean Apprentice to Andrew Galloway Writer in Kirkcaldy are *** by the said Parties at Hawklymuir the fourth day of July Eighteen hundred and twenty years before these witnesses the said Andrew Galloway and William Mitchell his Apprentice.

Signed
Andrew Galloway   witness
William Mitchell   witness

"Gray & Co."
Andrew Nicolson
James Robertson

Extract from the Indenture from Gray & Company

The Grays continued with their Flint Mill at Burn Mill in Leven, which was operated on their behalf by Colon [Colin?] Keir, flint miller, who was Andrew Gray's brother-in-law [SinB]. They imported flint stones in reasonably large loads between 1817 & 1822 from several different sources but the location of the exporting ports suggests that they mainly were through agents and not the prime source. As there were no imports between 1817 and 1821 it has to be assumed that their stock covered that period or they were importing ground flint.

This map was published at a later date. It shows the Burn Mill in the top left hand corner. The harbour was at the mouth of the River Leven in the bottom right hand corner. The mill was served by a mill lade off the river and the place name is still in use today.

Imports of Flint to Kirkcaldy Tax Area from 1817

Date	Vessel	From	Load
7/3/1817	Hind of Aberdeen	Landwich	60 tons of Flint Stones
16/6/1817	Mary	Banff	23 tons of Flint Stones
7/9/1817	Two Sisters	London	30 tons White Flint Stones
1/10/1817	Provedence of Aberdeen		70 tons of Flint Stones
11/10/1820	Open Boat	Portobello	2 Tons of China Stone
19/10/1820	Isabella of Banff		2 tons China Stone
7/3/1821	Trainer Young	London	80 tons of Flint Stones
1/5/1822	Agnes Lawson	London	90 tons of Flint stones

Although "earthenware" was exported from "Kirkcaldy" on a fairly regular basis and in reasonably large loads during 1816 &17 they were all by anonymous dealers or ships' masters until 4/8/1817 [P 28] when the first load direct from the Pottery was sent by Gray & Co. to Christainsand in the vessel "Emanuel". This load amounted to 17 crates of 4800 pieces of "common earthenware" which was valued at £75 plus packing valued at £5. Although the tax was only eight shillings [40p] this still represents a very substantial investment. The "Emanuel" traded regularly with "Kirkcaldy" from its homeport of Christainsand usually delivering wood or flax. This load although one among several could well mark the full opening of the new Fife Pottery and does show the confidence the Grays must have had in their operations and the products. It must be remembered that until 1822 the

Exports from Kirkcaldy Tax Area after 1817

Date	Vessel	Load/Value	Exporter	Unit Cost
12/6/1817	Christain for ?	7 Crates/6,000 pieces Earthenware £35	T. R. Robertson	0.6p
1/7/1817	Christain for ?	4,000 pieces Ew Earthenware £35	A Young	0.9p
22/7/1817	Peggy for Bremen	14 Crates/4,000 pieces Ew 1,5000 pieces E w £150 3,000 pieces Ew £30	A Young I & H Wallace A. Young	
4/8/1817	Emanuel Christainsand	4,800 pieces Ew Earthenware £75	Gray & Co	1.6p
2/8/1818	Five Sisters for ?	13 Crates/2,500 pieces Earthenware £52	Reymart	2p
3/9/1818	Caroline for Steton	800 pieces Earthenware £10	Elliot Briggs & Roberts	1.25p
5/4/1819	Pilot for Christainsand	2 Crates/1,440 pieces Earthenware	G Malcolm	
1/7/1819	Five Sisters for Christainsand	6 Crates/3,600 pieces Ew 6,350 pieces Ew £15.25	Reymart	0.24p
2/8/1820	Emanuel for Christainsand	14 Crates/4,000 pieces Ew 1560 pieces Ew £4.5 4,000 pieces Ew £45	Master John Methven Gray & Co	0.3p 1.13p
15/6/1821	Emanuel for Christainsand	3,800 pieces Earthenware £35	Gray & Co	0.9p
13/8/1821	Ria Scogwell for?	14 Crares/4,500 pieces Earthenware £18		0.4p
1/5/1822	Emanuel for Christainsand	1.560 pieces Ew £10 2,000 pieces Ew £15.25	John Methven Gray & Co	0.64p 0.5p
20/10/1822	Emanuel for Christainsand	2160 pieces Ew £10 2,000 pieces Ew £10	John Methven Gray & Co	0.46p 0.5p
29/4/1823	Familien for Dran	2,000 pieces Ew Earthenware £13.75	Gray & Co	0.69p
13/5/1823	Emanuel for Christainsand	500 pieces Ew £3.75 1,000 pieces Ew £5.5 4,000 pieces Ew £15	John Methven Gray & Co Gray & Co	0.75p 0.55p 0.38p
26/6/1823	Familien for Dran	20.000 pieces Earthenware £160	Gray & Co	0.8p
1/8/1823	Emanuel for Christainsand	1,000 pieces Ew £8 730 pieces Ew £0	Gray & Co Master	0.8p
2/4/1824	Emanuel for Christainsand	3,000 pieces Ew £19 500 pieces Ew £0	Gray & Co Master	0.6p
19/5/1824	Margaret for Quebec	4,000 pieces Earthenware £25	R Bisset for Alex Balfour	0.6p
24/5/1824	Emanuel for Christainsand	12,000 pieces Ew £73 650 pieces Ew £5.75 500 pieces Ew £0	Gray & Co John Methven Master	0.61p 0.88p
31/5/1824	Fruchenden for Stottenburgh	12,000 pieces Earthenware £42	Gray & Co	0.35p
17/8/1824	Emanuel for Christainsand	800 pieces Earthenware £0	Master	
3/9/1824	Emanuel for Christainsand	525 pieces Ew £4.5 2,500 pieces Ew £0	David Methven Master	0.86p
24/3/1825	Emanuel for Christainsand	6.000 pieces Ew 650 pieces Ew £4.75	Gray & Co John Methven	0,73p
20/5/1825	? For Stollenburgh	6.500 pieces Ew £45	Gray & Co	0.69p
3/7/1825	Emanuel for Christainsand	5,000 pieces Ew £33.5	Gray & Co	0.67p
7/10/1825	Facheile for Soon	5.470 pieces Ew £22 1,255 Ew £10	Gray & Co D for J Methven	0.4p 0.8p
15/12/1825	Isabelia for Lisbon	900 pieces Ew £7	Barclay F. Gray	0.78p

Gallatown Pottery was in operation and that any export not listed as being by Gray & Co. could have come from that source.

They traded successfully and Andrew and his wife, Margaret Irvine, were able to purchase a new family home on 24/10/1819 [PR II1.224] very shortly after the death of their son, William, on 3/9/1819 [SinB]. This house and yard, amounting to 40 ells of land, was in West Gallatown near the Pottery. Following this A &A Gray purchased the ground on which the Pottery was built from the Earl of Rosslyn in 1820 although the Feu Charter was not registered until the following year [2/1/1821 PR II7.237]. The Title was held in the names of "Archibald and Andrew Gray, potters in West Gallatown" and not by the Company. The land was described as "That Piece of land ... where on the said A & A Gray have erected a Pottery".

It is a tribute to the Grays that in a period of some nine years, which included the trade depression after the Napoleonic War they had developed their business, purchased a house and land and built a new Pottery without apparently having to borrow any substantial sums of money although the possibility of the "& Co." should not be forgotten.

It is easy to imagine the happiness and confidence they must have felt at the start of 1821. This happy state of affairs did not last long and the brothers' financial position was soon so poor that they were forced to borrow £600 from the Glasgow Banking Company on 14th February 1822 [P.P. 124.76]. Whilst no reason is given for this loan, which was secured against the property, it is unlikely that they had any desire to expand further. The Customs Records do give a strong indication regarding the trading conditions at this time as in 1820 the Grays only exported 5800 pieces and during the next year they had no exports. It can be assumed therefore that the funds were required for trading purposes. This loan was to mark the start of a period of severe trade depression throughout Britain, which was to last for some six years. The conditions were such that over this period workers wages were reduced by fifty per cent and very many of the self employed weavers were unable to find any work. This depression was not fully international as the rate of exporting did improve after the loan was taken out as shown by the totals, 1823 - 4,000 pieces, 1824 - 18,000 pieces and 1825 - 42,000 pieces. There were also small quantities sent by other agents where the source is not given. The majority of the exports went to North Europe and the Baltic areas. Two notable exceptions were on 19/5/1824 when a small load, 4,000 pieces, was sent to Quebec and the last recorded load of 900 pieces on 15/12/1825 destined for Lisbon. This load was sent by Barclay F Gray who was an Edinburgh timber merchant as well as a "China" dealer who in turn was to be sequestered within a few years. No relationship has so far been established between Barclay and A&A Gray.

Although the Grays continued trading and exporting up to the end of 1825 the business was not viable and they had been forced to raise other bank loans: - National Bank of Scotland £3II, Commercial Bank of Scotland £125 and the Fife Banking Company £302 [CS46 May 1830]. These loans were all unsecured against any property. They also had a considerable number of trading and personal debts.

To add to their problems Andrew Gray, potter and feuer, died 21/3/1825 [SinB] and was buried in the same grave as his two sons, Peter and William. He was succeeded by his son, Andrew[II], who inherited his father's share in the Pottery. Although Andrew[II] did take Title to his share in the Pottery on 18th. January 1826 [PR 146.244] he did not become a partner in the business [CS46/1830/ 40]. Andrew [II] was also a potter but could only have been in his late teens and therefore can in effect be ignored when considering the Pottery.

Before considering the demise of the Pottery it is worthwhile examining the details contained in the Custom Records. Firstly it will be noted that John Methven only exported from 1820 and usually in the same ships as Gray & Co. Also his loads were always fairly low, 1560 pieces being the largest and very much smaller than those from the Grays. It is likely also that the bulk of the larger loads sent by other than the potters originated at Fife Pottery.

Considering 1817 it will be noticed that the unit cost increased from 0.88p to 1.0p in July to 1.56p in August. This was followed by an increase to 2.08p in August 1818. An increase of this magnitude cannot be attributed to inflation and must be due to either to an increase in size of the individual pieces or an improvement in the quality or both. Since it is mainly whiteware being considered and that this would have been mainly tableware "better quality" is the only acceptable reason. It cannot be pure coincidence that this occurred shortly after the opening of the new Pottery. This high value was not maintained and there was a gradual decline over the next few years until by 1820 it fell to well under 1.0p. This reduction in value would have been associated with the general decline in trade, which contributed to the trading difficulties suffered by the Grays. This is well illustrated in two articles in the Edinburgh Courant [28/6/1827] which reported on "Distressed Workers" and that mason's wages which had been 26/- [£1.30] in 1825 fell to 17/- [£0.85] in 1826 and to 13/- [£0.65] in 1827 and later on 2/7/1827 in a "Report to Parliament for the year 1826" that "In earthenware, glass and indeed in every field there has been a sensible decline"

Archibald continued trading as sole partner for a very short time until he was sequestered on 21st March 1826. The creditors of the Fife Pottery Company met on 14th April 1826 and appointed Henry Normand and John Barclay as Trustees to settle the affairs [it will be noted that the creditors used the formal name of the Company which generally had not been used by the partners in their day to day trading]. Henry Normand was an accountant with offices both locally and in Edinburgh. The Trustees had collectively made a loan of £150 to the Grays through their Company, The Dysart Coal & Salt Company, which was also due £85 for supplying coal to the Pottery.

No doubt the creditors, many of whom operated at a considerable distance, were content to leave the problems to local experts although they also appointed William Swan, agent for the Glasgow Bank in Kirkcaldy, Robert Kirk, agent for the Commercial Bank Co. and John Meldrum Merchant in Edinburgh as Commissioners to oversee the dealings.

When the Trustees examined the Company they found that the assets, even on paper, were substantially below the debts. The main assets were listed as "Earthenware stock in hand £610, pottery materials £219, bricks and tiles £587 and rags and old iron £138" [Wemyss Ware" by Davis and Rankine, no primary reference given]. Added to these was the value of the Pottery less the £600 due to the Glasgow Bank that was treated as a preferential creditor. There were also a good number of business debts due to the Company by customers, which were not detailed.

The large value of brick and tiles is somewhat surprising as the stock of these items is almost equal to that of the stock of pottery. This does seem strange and especially as the Grays had concentrated on the production of whiteware and the existence of brick and tile making facilities were never mentioned in any of the "For Sale" notices for the Pottery. Assuming however that the bricks and tiles had been made at the Pottery then the tiles would have been made of the local red clay whilst the bricks could have been made from either red or fire clays or both as these clays were available locally. However in a later "For Sale" notice [FH 29/II/1827] it states "...a fire brick works might be carried on " which suggests that only red clay could have been used. However perhaps the bricks and tiles were those used to build the kilns and workshops [FH 14th August 1828]. The fairly large amount of scrap is not unusual as at that time and for a long time thereafter scrap [glass, rags and iron] was exchanged for pottery [usually substandard] by itinerant dealers who used it to trade both with the Pottery and their customers.

The Trustees proceeded to recover the debts to the Company and prepared to sell the assets, if possible. To achieve this they took over the Title for the Pottery from the Glasgow Bank who then became only creditors for the £600 plus the interest accrued up to that date of sequestration [9/4/1827 PR 124.76]. The Pottery was also put up for sale along with the remaining stock.

The Pottery proved difficult to sell and fortunately the "For Sale" notices give a very good insight into the Pottery. It must be remembered that such notices would have set out the good points and any problems would have been minimized. None the less it is unlikely that any claim made had to be reasonably accurate if future court action was to be avoided.

Edinburgh Courant   19 March, 2nd. and 30th. April 1827.

FOR SALE
FIFE POTTERY NEAR KIRKCALDY
There will be exposed for sale by public roup, within McGlaslan's Inn Kirkcaldy upon the 22nd. day of May next at II o'clock forenoon in virtue of powers contained in a bond and disposition in security. All and WHOLE of that PIECE of GROUND in the form of a square, part of the lands of HAWKELYMUIR consisting of about one acre and lying on the south of the road leading from Parkhead to Wester Gallatown and on which buildings for a Pottery are erected. The buildings were erected only a few years ago for a Pottery on an extensive scale and the plan of the works it is believed to be inferior to none in Scotland, and being in the vicinity of coal and fire clay and within a mile of the ports of Kirkcaldy and Dysart and upon the Road to Cupar, Dundee etc. few situations will be found preferable. The works will be continued in operation till the day of the sale and being the only white and coloured ware pottery on the north of the Forth it commands a very extensive inland sale. The feu duty is moderate. The

title deeds are in the hands of Henry Normand, merchant in Dysart, to whom or to William Hunt W.S. or Andrew Galloway, writer in Kirkcaldy, application may be made for further particulars.
POTTERY UTENSILS ETC.
TO be sold by public roup at the Kirkcaldy Pottery on Tuesday the 22nd. of May next. The following ARTICLES belonging to the sequestrated Estate of Gray and Co. consisting of the whole stock of Manufactured Ware of all description, Materials, Utensils, Rags, and Machinery of a Flint Mill connected with the Pottery. Also about 8 tons of Mill Stones and one Share in the Kirkcaldy and Leith Shipping Company.

The Roup to commence within the Pottery Square at 1 o'clock and to continue until the whole is sold off. For particulars application may be made to Henry Normand the Trustee or at the work.

Dysart 17th. March 1827

This sale was unsuccessful and the property was readvertised in the Edinburgh Courant on 29th. November and 6th December 1827.

FOR SALE
FIFE POTTERY, NEAR KIRKCALDY
Upset Price Reduced
There will be exposed for sale by public roup, at the Fife Pottery, upon Wednesday the 26th of December next, at II o'clock forenoon, the following parts of the Sequestered Estates of Gray and Co:-
That RANGE of BUILDINGS at WESTER GALLATOWN, erected a few years ago for the purpose of a pottery, upon an extensive and approved plan, and being in the immediate vicinity of coal, an extensive field of fireclay, lying within a mile of the shipping ports of Kirkcaldy and Dysart, and upon the line of the Great North road to Cupar, Dundee etc. few situations will be found so well adapted for a pottery. A firebrick work might also be carried on here with great advantage. The work is still in operation; and being the only white and coloured ware pottery on the north of the Forth, it commands a very extensive inland sale. The feu duty is moderate. Should the pottery be sold, the purchaser may have the utensils and machinery of the flint mill at Leven at valuation; in the event of it not selling, these will not be disposed of. The materials on hand are for sale, and offers therefore may be given in to the trustee. The manufactured ware will be sold as formerly by the trustee, for ready money only; and as the whole estate must be readily realised a liberal discount will be given to dealers purchasing in quantities. The title deeds are in the hands of Henry Normand, Merchant, Dysart, to whom or to William Hunt, W.S., or Andrew Galloway, Writer, Kirkcaldy, application may be made for further particulars.
Edinburgh, 20th. Nov. 1827

This second sale must also have been a failure and the Trustees must have been increasingly concerned that they might never recover any part of the creditor's money. The Pottery was quickly readvertised, again in the Edinburgh Courant, on the 10th. January 1828 in the hope that a reduced price might tempt a purchaser.

POTTERY FOR SALE
Upset Price Reduced to £600
The FIFE POTTERY, at Gallatown, as formerly advertised will again be again exposed to SALE, by public Roup, within the premises, upon Thursday the 24th, current at eleven o'clock forenoon at the reduced price of £600. Arrangements are in progress, by which the whole or greater part of the price may be allowed to remain over the property for a term of years, at reasonable

conditions. And as the erection of the work, only ten years ago, cost nearly three times the amount of the upset price, so advantageous a purchase is rarely to be met with. The whole stock of manufactured ware is now selling off for ready money, 20 percent. discount being allowed to dealers buying in quantities. Apply Henry Normand, Dysart, the trustee; to Andrew Galloway, writer, there or to William Hunt, W.S. 19 Leopold Place Edinburgh.
Dysart 5th. Jan. 1828

The rapidity of the timing of this sale would suggest that the Trustees considered that a purchaser was available "at the right price". If so they were misguided as like the earlier ones this sale failed. The Trustees were more cautious at their meeting on 26th. February 1828 [E.C. 6/2/1828] as they did not readvertise until 30th. June 1828 again in the Edinburgh Courant when they were more tentative.

POTTERY FOR SALE

THE FIFE POTTERY as formerly advertised. Apply Hendry Normand, accountant, the trustee, No. 13 Annandale Street Edinburgh
28th, June 1828.

Yet again this sale of the Pottery was unsuccessful and the Trustees tried once more this time in a different market by advertising in "The Fife Herald", which circulated in the Perth, Cupar and Dundee areas, on the 14th. August 1828. This notice, which gave the very short time of five days, was for a public roup on 19th August and was similar to the earlier ones but also contained: -

.... The extensive premises belonging to the sequestered estate of Gray and Co. and presently used as a pottery. The property at trifling expense could be converted to a warehouse or weaver shop. It covers an acre of ground and was erected within these 12 years at £1500.
The upset price now reduced to £550.
N.B. In the three kilns in the premises it is estimated to be 60,000 firebricks which would be well adapted for partitions and could be taken down without injury to the property .....

When the creditors met on 26th. November [E.C. 8/II/1828] it was, perhaps, to learn that a bid had been made as the Pottery was sold in February of the next year to John Methven of Links Pottery.

The various legal documents were witnessed by James Beaton [potter] who remained with the Pottery and eventually became the manager and William Dalziel [Clerk at the Pottery]. The fact that these two employees were still available at the Pottery implies that the creditors had kept it open, perhaps only as a very small operation, while trying to sell it although this is not mentioned in the later notices. This would not have been surprising as there had been a large upturn in trading shortly after the sequestration. To do this the creditors would have required expertise which they did not have. This may have been found in James Beaton or by retaining Archibald Gray both of whom had the required skill. Another possibility that has been suggested is John Methven who was a Master Potter but had little or no experience of whiteware production.

The precise details of the sale are not given. Although the upset price was only £550 John took a Bond for that sum [30/1/1890 408.161] and also borrowed a further £600 from the Trustees again secured by the Pottery [GR 2161:282 13/12/1842]. It can be assumed that he paid in the region of £II50 for the Pottery and the equipment and stock. If this price is correct then John certainly made a very good bargain as the trade in all types of pottery had continued to increase to such an extent that should have enabled the business to progress from strength to strength.

WARES

Unfortunately there is very little known of the details of the products of Fife Pottery during this period The only clearly marked pieces are two plaques in Strathkelvin Museum which are clearly incised "Fife Pottery 1827". This is outwith the period of the Grays but can be assumed to be typical. They are regretfully not a great deal of help as they are a simple rectangular shape and feature in relief a bust of King George[1V] being typical of the wares commemorating the 1822 Royal Visit to Edinburgh. The body is plain white earthenware with a slightly blueish glaze. Just why this type of piece was produced so long after the visit and marked in such a clear but unusual way is conjectural. One possible reason is that they might have been samples perhaps illustrating the type body produced. Any guess is possible.

In SPHR No 5 [1980] at page 54 there is a description of a small shard found in Fife but not near to the Pottery. This is from an undecorated plate with an impressed mark of a "whelk" shell surrounded by a circle and the inscription "FIFE POTTERY" and "? & Co". the ? being a missing section. It is possible that the missing portion could be "Gray" and if so some of the examples of plates bearing the impressed whelk mark could be from this period. However the mystery remains and this subject will be discussed later.

Chapter 4   **LINKS AND FIFE POTTERIES**
                                                     JOHN METHVEN 1827 - 1837

For much of this short period the two Potteries were under the same ownership and therefore can be considered together.

At the time of his father's death in 1827 John was successfully operating his own Links Pottery on land leased from Fergus of Strathore where he used "Abbotshall" clay and was also a "china and glass dealer" in both Links and Cupar. He inherited the "Lions" which was his family home and more importantly the right to continue taking clay for the Pottery from his brother's clayfield on the payment of £1 per annum to George [KM Files]. Although he was forbidden to use the clay to compete with his brother's Brick and Tyle Works this restriction would not have troubled him as he was first and foremost a potter.

John assisted by his son, David[IV], in the Links and his nephew, David [II1], in Cupar survived the trade depression that finished Gray & Co. and he appears to have been much more financially sound. This depression gave him an ideal opportunity to expand significantly when he acquired the Fife Pottery in 1829 by taking over the bond against the property [289-178 21/5/1885] and borrowing the balance. He may also have continued using the name of Fife Pottery Company.

Earlier on the 24th. June 1826 John's only daughter, Mary, had married Robert Heron in Abbotshall [APR]. Robert is described as "a Merchant and son of a Baker". His father had a substantial baker's business, which along with many others went into sequestration shortly after the marriage. When John acquired the Fife Pottery Robert moved to Gallatown to assist in the operations at Fife Pottery whilst David [1V] remained at the Links Pottery probably as his father's second-in-command. It will be remembered that David[1V] had trained as a potter with his father and acted as his agent but it is not known if Robert had any training in potting. Robert and Mary set up their home in the Fife Pottery House and no doubt gradually took over more responsibility for the day to day running of the Pottery. There can be no doubt that John was still very much in charge of both Potteries as shown when Robert only acted as his assistant in the sequestration of William McCrea, China and Stoneware Dealer, in Kirkcaldy in 1830 [CS96-4268].

John acquired the land on which his Links Pottery was built on the 9th. February 1828 [31/8/1829 PR 171.213] and the Fife Pottery in February 1829 [PR 289-178 21/5/1885]. The land at the Links Pottery was described as "houses and ground behind the same on where a pottery has been lately built" which does not help to establish the starting date of the Pottery as the term "lately" is somewhat vague. This section of land and a front elevation of the row of houses is shown on plan number RHP 580/4. His financial resources must have been stretched as at the same time he had to raise a loan of £1000 from his uncle, John Stocks, on 29th. August 1829 [PR171.217] using his Links Pottery as security. This loan would have been used to make the purchase and to revitalise and improve the Links Pottery.

Thus in a period of about one year John, although heavily in debt, gained control of the two major Potteries in the Kirkcaldy area. Following on from the recent period of advantageous trading conditions this should have been a very fortuitous time for businessmen, as the age of heavy engineering started about 1830 with the attendant increase in the domestic market and the potential availability of new machinery, which along with the abundance of labour due to the "Highland Clearances" allowed manufacturers to cut production costs. It was not to prove so as the following year, 1831, there was mass unemployment and a new Labour Acts which attempted to restrict the working hours of workers under the age of eighteen years to "no night work and no more than 69 hours". These factors must have severely restricted the market and increased the cost of production. An indication of the economic conditions during the early 1830's is seen when in 1836 bread had increased in price by 1p per loaf [about 30 per cent] and the potato crop failed. To add to these problems the price of coal went up by 100 per cent an increase that must also have had a profound effect on the production costs.

For this period there are two significant sources of information, the Customs Records up to 1830 and the Kirkcaldy Harbour Records for 1832-1834. In this case, unlike Custom Records, the latter are for that harbour only.

IMPORTS BY JOHN METHVEN TO KIRKCALDY HARBOUR

DATE	FROM	LOAD
6/12/1832	London	38 tons of flint stone (value £41.2)
12/12/1832	Newcastle	2 casks of glass, 2 tierce plaster
25/1/1833	Newcastle	7 casks of lead, 1 tierce of glass
26/1/1833	London	6 parcels
19/3/1833	London	3 chests
19/3/1833	Newcastle	3 casks of lead (24)
10/4/1833	Newcastle	2 casks of lead
13/4/1833	Overside	Flint stone
		Overside =landed on beach
20/5/1833	Newcastle	1 hogshead of glass
7/6/1833	London	2 casks
28/6/1833	Newcastle	1 tierce of glass
20/7/1833	Newcastle	ground flint (160), 6 casks lead (51)
12/9/1833	Newcastle	1 hogs head glass, 2 casks lead
28/9/1833	Newcastle	2 casks lead red (120)
19/10/1833	Glasgow	1 tierce of glass
14/11/1833	Newcastle	1cask ofglass
13/12/1833	Newcastle	3 casks of lead
23/12/1833	Glasgow	1 crate, 24 jars
6/1/1834	Newcastle	2 casks of lead
5/2/1834	Newcastle	2 casks of glass, 4 casks of lead
1/3/1834	Newcastle	1 cask of Paris White
28/4/1834	Dundee	2 casks of lead
17/5/1834	Glasgow	1 hogshead of glass
5/6/1834	Newcastle	4 casks of lead red & white, 1 hgh. & 1 teir. of glass

EXPORTS BY JOHN METHVEN FROM KIRKCALDY HARBOUR

DATE	DESTINATION	LOAD
8/12/1832	London	34 Bags of rags
18/12/1832	Newcastle	4 casks of old iron (4cwts)
2/2/1833	Newcastle	22 bags of rags & 3 casks of old iron
2/2/1833	Dundee	3 chests
23/3/1833	Newcastle	2 casks of old iron(30) & 15 mats of rags
27/5/1833	Newcastle	3 casks of old iron (30) & 25 bags of rags
27/5/1833	Dundee	1 Crate of Earthenware
20/6/1833	Dundee	1 Crate of Earthenware
5/7/1833	Newcastle	7 casks of old iron, 42 mats of rags
24/7/1833	Dundee	1 Crate
24/7/1833	Newcastle	4 casks of old iron,17 bags of rags
24/8/1833	Newcastle	2 casks of old iron, mats of rags (42)
26/8/1833	Dundee	4 crates
10/10/1833	Dundee	1 Crate of Earthenware
28/10/1833	Newcastle	7 casks of old iron, 46 mats of rags
17/12/1833	Newcastle	5 casks of old iron, ?rags
14/1/1834	Newcastle	3 casks of old iron,1 cask of cullet, 26 bags of rags
7/3/1834	Newcastle	2 crates of old iron
19/3/1834	Newcastle	40 mats of rags
24/3/1834	Glasgow	1 cask of cullet sent by D Methven
15/4/1834	Newcastle	20 mats of rags, 2 casks of iron, 1 cask of cullet
22/4/1834	Dundee	1 crate
12/5/1834	Dundee	1 Box of Earthenware
12/5/1834	Newcastle	17 mats of rags, 1 hogshead of old iron
19/5/1834	Newcastle	16 mats of rags, 2 hogshead of old iron
20/6/1834	Newcastle	4 casks of old iron, 1 cask of cullet, 2 crates & 2 mats of rags

The Custom records are equally as important in as much that they show that during this period John Methven did not export any pottery overseas although he did send some coastwise to other British harbours which would not have been recorded by the Customs. Similarly he is not listed as importing any unprocessed flint stones during this period. However In the Harbour Records it is seen that he took delivery of 38 tons of flintstone on the 6th December 1832 and as this is not in the Custom Records it maybe that the Customs no longer required to record this or it was processed or ground flint. Earlier on 13/4/1832 one load is recorded as flint being "Overside" from a boat on its way to Fisherrow No details are given of the quantity or the importer but it safe to assume it was John Methven and presumably the load had landed directly onto the beach near to the Pottery as such deliveries were not uncommon at that time and presumably attractive as they were "free". The possibility of other loads of this nature being made and going unrecorded cannot be ignored. On 20th July 1833 John imported 160 tons of "ground flint" from Newcastle suggesting that the earlier imports were also "ground" and that he did not have a Flint Mill. It is not known if John had taken up the offer of the machinery and grinding stones from the Burn Mill [Leven]. He did lease the Balwearie Mill some time prior to 1836 when the section on Abbotshall Parish was written for the "New Statistical Account of 1845" [P.157]. The same section also reports that there was a Pottery in the Parish making brown earthenware. The precise starting date of the flint mill remains a doubt although some date in the period 1833 — 1836 is the most likely.

As well as the very occasional imports of flint John regularly took delivery of plaster of Paris [Paris White] and white and red lead which he would have used in both Potteries. The plaster of Paris was used for making moulds for "pressing" hollow ware and for the jollies and jiggers. The two leads would have been made into glazes. Unfortunately the quantities of all of these materials are frequently given as "casks" which although indicative does not give a precise weight. It appears that a cask could be up to eight hundredweight [approximately 400 KG].

As well a Pottery materials John regularly imported glass from Newcastle and other unspecified loads, mainly from London. The glass would have been sold in his wholesale and retail outlets and the other loads were probably china or earthenware for the same purpose.

Naturally on occasions he also exported earthenware to other ports and in return received scrap iron, glass and rags, which he in turn exported to Newcastle. There were also occasional loads registered to David Methven and Robert Heron that were unspecified. There can be no doubt that John was very much in control.

There are no records of John receiving any clay during this period. This only to be expected as the white clay required was all for the Fife Pottery and would have been shipped through the Dysart Harbour.

Imports & Exports by Others

DATE	IM/EXPORTER	LOAD
12/12/1832	Ian Black - import	1,600 tiles
12/12/1832	J Bums - import	8 tons coal, 1ton flint, 1 cask stucco, 10cwts. clay
18/12/1832	J Bums - export	2 casks of old iron 4 cwts
2/1/1833	J Bums - import	10 tons whitening, 10 tons of coal
8/1/1833	J Bums - export	3 barrels of old iron "ballast"
25/1/1833	J Bums - import	8 tons of coal
10/4/1833	A Bird - import	2 casks of lead
10/4/1833	J Bums - import	21 tons of coal, 4 tons of whitening
18/4/1833	M Rigney - export	1 cask old iron
18/4/1833	J Bums - export	4 casks & ? of old iron (2tons), 15 mats of rags
1/5/1833	M Laysell - import	3,500 tiles
4/5/1833	J Bums - export	old iron
20/5/1833	J Bums - import	Whitening and Coals
27/5/1833	J Bums - export	25 casks of old iron
5/7/1833	J Bums - export	old iron "ballast"
20/8/1833	J Bums - import	20 tons of coal, 9 tons of whitening
24/8/1833	J Bums - export	5 casks of old iron
24/8/1833	M Rigney - export	2 casks od old iron
12/9/1833	M Rigney - import	earthenware
12/9/1833	J Bums - import	4 tons of whitening, 10 tons of coal, 1,000 tiles
28/9/1833	J Bums - import	1/2 "keel" of coal
14/11/1833	J Bums - import	10 tons of coal, 7 tons of whitening
17/12/1833	J Bums - export	5 casks of old iron, 2 trunks
5/2/1834	J Bums - import	12 tons whitening, 1 mill, 2 grindstones

During this period and frequently on the same vessel as John Methven other merchants had similar loads, especially James Burns who imported stucco, whitening, coal and very occasionally clay and flint from Newcastle. In return he also sent loads of scrap. Judging from the low proportion of clay and flint it suggests that Burns was not a potter but simply a "stucco ornament" maker but the possibility of him having a connection with potting cannot be ruled out. The importation of coal by him to Kirkcaldy is surprising and suggests that it must have had a special property [e.g. high heat]. Also recorded was Martin Rigney a local very successful China & Glass dealer who, judging by the exports of iron, also dealt with the scrap trade. The other few similar loads listed are very minor and not connected with pottery production.

This picture of John and his extended family running two Potteries in the Kirkcaldy area along with the "china and glass" salerooms in Links and Cupar would appear to be one of success but all was not well. Although he had firmly established the Links Pottery on which his successors were to build a very prosperous future and continued the operations at the Fife Pottery, which was also to make its mark on the Scottish Pottery field, he was considerably in debt and not trading at a profit. This period came to a tragic end when David[IV] died on 28/3/1837 unmarried. To add to this sorrow John's financial affairs were in such a poor state that the Commercial Bank of Scotland took over the titles for the Links Pottery, the Lions and the Fife Pottery as well as some other minor properties. This was done despite the fact that the major properties had already been used as security for loans. John's affairs were indeed in a sorry state when he died very shortly thereafter on 9/8/1837 leaving his whole estate and debts to his daughter and son-in-law, Mary and Robert Heron. With hind sight it would be easy to criticise John for his financial state and to compare him to his brother, George, however this would perhaps be unfair without considering the general financial conditions in the country at that time.

In settling John's estate as Trustee Robert Heron took two significant steps which although slightly outwith the dates for this chapter are added here as they give an insight into John Methven's operations. Firstly as Executor and heir Robert wrote to all of the creditors explaining the situation and requesting time and suggesting a scheme to clear the debts. One of these creditors was the Minton Pottery in Stoke who replied accepting Robert's proposals [SPS 606/93]

> Stoke Septem. 5 - 1837
> Mr R Heron
> Fife Pottery
> Scotland
> Sir
> We are duly in receipt of your letter of the 1st inst.
>
> We have little doubt but will find all the other creditors thankful that we duly considered your communication and shall be happy to conform to the arrangement you propose. Methven's affairs have fallen into such honourable hands. The crate we last sent we trust you will take to account if you can be of little moment but to us it would be inconvenient to have it returned on our hands - we very little doubt on this head [?] Our traveller has we expect called on you and you will probably have communicated any thing more on this subject which you deem necessary.
> We would suggest that you get the trust deed drawn up as soon as possible and that it may be sent round the creditors for signature.
> We shall be happy to hear again from you if necessary.
> We are your obedient serv.
> Minton and Boyle

This letter shows just how bad John Methven's affairs were prior to his death. Indeed it would appear that his creditors had been close to taking action. It also shows that Minton at least had very little respect for John as a businessman. It appears that John's China Saleroom [Wareroom] in Linktown had been included in the sale of Links Pottery. Who ever owned the Saleroom it was decided to sell the stock, which contained a considerable amount of imported wares. This sale was advertised in the Fife Herald on 16th November 1837 some three months after John's death.

Sale of
China and Stone-ware cut and plain Crystal
At the late
Mr John Methven's Warerooms
Linktown Kirkcaldy
To be sold, without reserve at a great reduction in price for ready money only

The friends and customers of the late Mr John Methven are most respectfully informed that the sale of the whole STOCK consisting of Rich China Tea and Breakfast sets, Dinner & Dessert services in Stoneware and a great variety of Cut Crystal in Decanters, Dessert Dishes, Jellies, Salts, Wine Glasses etc. has now commenced and will continue until the whole is Sold off, that all the affairs connected with the Estate may be brought to a close as soon as possible. There is a great variety of Rich China Tea Sets which owing to having been in stock for some time will be sold at half their real value.

The Stock on hand being well known it is only necessary to state that it consists of almost every Article in the Trade. Country Dealers supplied, as usual, on the most liberal terms.

Linktown Kdy. 9th Nov. 1837

It should be noted that even at this date the term "stoneware" is used for wares that would now be referred to as earthenware, a confusion that was covered in Chapter 1.

This sale notice is in itself not abnormal and is typical of others of the period although, perhaps, the mention of goods being "in stock for some time" does give an indication of the state of the business. The details do however give a good indication of the type of goods normally stocked. These were all bought in to be resold with the possible exception of some of the earthenware, which might have been made at the Fife Pottery. There is no indication that any of the products from the Links Pottery were for sale. The glass and crystal must have been made outwith the area and probably in Newcastle or Glasgow judging by the Harbour Records.

John's death was recorded in Kirkcaldy Parish were he was listed as "of Pottery Warehouse, Linktown". This is surprising as he also owned two Potteries and also described himself as "a potter". Does this mean he lived at the warehouse and if so why was his death recorded in Kirkcaldy Parish? As expected with the Methven family confusion and doubt are never far away.

The impression given of John is that although obviously ambitious he was not a good businessman. He had however kept the two Potteries in production. The wares from the Fife Pottery will be considered later.

Chapter 5   JOHN AND DAVID METHVEN[III]
THE CUPAR CONNECTION 1825 - 1837

As explained in Chapter 1 there is a tradition that David[I] had lived in the Cupar area prior to going to Links and that he learnt the art of brick and tile making there although no firm connection has been established regarding him in Cupar or any Works in that area.

Certainly there had been a tradition of potting in Cupar from at least the eighteenth century and of brick and tile making since 1764 [circa]. This subject has been well documented in the entry in the "Tayside and Fife Archaeological Journal", Vol. 2 [1996] 27-41 by C J M and P FdeC Martin.

What ever his father's connection with Cupar John Methven expanded his Links Pottery business there when he opened a new china and glass shop in St Catherine Street in 1825 and advertised for trade in the Fife Herald of 23rd June of that year

New Crystal & China Warehouse Cupar
John   Methven
Manufacturer of Earthenware Kirkcaldy

Begs to inform the Nobility and Gentry of Cupar and neighbourhood that he has opened that commodious and extensive warehouse in St Catherine's Street opposite the Commercial Bank.

With complete assortment of Glass, China and Stoneware from Wedgewood, Spode and other principal manufacturers in England

Cupar 23 June 1825

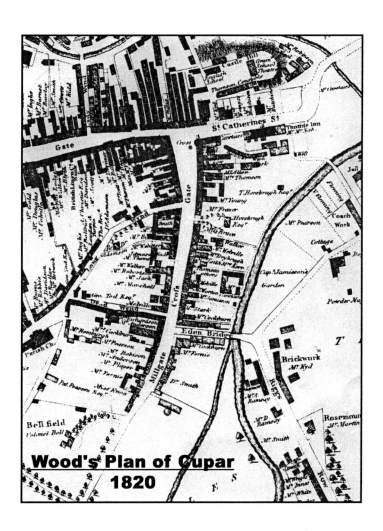

Even if there was no family connection Cupar was not an unusual choice as it was connected to Kirkcaldy by a good road, for those days, and judging by the newspapers he had no serious rival except itinerant but not necessarily poor quality dealers.

This property must have been rented and was presumably the same one he bought from R Hutchison, builder, on 7/10/1826 [GR 1624.125]. This property was described as "the west most shop in the east most of the two houses on the south side of Hope Street [now called St. Catherine Street] Cupar with two cellars". John did not register this purchase until 1830 when he used the property as security to borrow £400 from the Right Reverend D Low of Pittenweem [GR 1624.125]. It is more likely that this need for funding was due to his expansion in the Kirkcaldy area than for the Cupar section of his enterprises.

Although this new shop/warehouse was reasonably close to his main business and home in Links John still required a manager. This was easily found within the family as he had been employing his nephew David[III] since the death of his brother David[II] in 1815 and had trained him as a potter. It should be remembered that David[III] was left £150 on his grandfather's [David [I]] death in 1827 and in the Will dated 7th December 1826 he was described as "in Cupar" showing that indeed he was living there at that time

In later Court Case in 1848 Cupar Sheriff Court David claimed that he had worked as a potter for his uncles, John and George, from about 1818 until the date of the trial except for a short time of two and a half years when he was "a Potter in his own right". This would seem to suggest that John also had a Pottery near Cupar as well as the shop or perhaps that David[III] only worked part time in Cupar and still was potting at Links. So far there is no evidence to suggest that John had a Pottery in Cupar and it is not unreasonable to suggest that if he had a Pottery he would have advertised this fact. Never the less David[III] did make this claim, under oath, in the Cupar Sheriff Court at a time well within living memory such that if it was false it could have been easily challenged with the subsequent legal implications.

David[III] continued to manage his uncle's business until 1833 when they entered into some form of lease and David took it over. This was advertised, again, in the Fife Herald on 20th June 1833.

China Crystal and Stoneware
St Catherine Street Cupar
John Methven thanks his patrons and informs that the business has passed to David Methven and requests early payment of debts.
                                                          Cupar 19 June 1833

After a short period David[III] had organised his new business to his own satisfaction and having acquired new stock he in turn advertised in the Fife Herald on 5th December 1833

China Glass and Stoneware
St Catherine Street Cupar
D Methven begs to acquaint the inhabitants of Cupar that the above establishment [which he has conducted since it opened] is now carried on his own account.

This notice was published again on 29th May 1834 with the extra offer to "to supply dealers and hawkers with all sorts of articles at Pottery prices".

David [III] following on the family tradition of potting also opened his own Pottery in Cupar. This was achieved by leasing the local Cupar Pottery. The starting date for this lease is not known. It was however advertised in the Fife Herald on 19th February 1835 and bearing in mind the caveat in later Court Case it has to be assumed that David [III] had taken over the lease a short time before the advertisement.

David Methven China, Crystal and Stoneware Merchant Cupar
begs to inform the public that in addition to his establishment in St Catherine Street he carrys on a pottery at the Bridgehill in all its branches and has on hand at all times a large supply of well finished garden pots, sea kail covers, chimney cans and vases of all shapes, water and steam pipes and every kind of brownware.

This Pottery must have been situated near to the Brick Works although its precise location is not shown on the Wood Plan of 1820. It was perhaps the buildings situated slightly to the north east of the Brick Works. The list of products is very comprehensive and presumably typical of Brownware Potteries at that period. The wares would have been made from the local clay probably without the addition of flint or any other "improver". No doubt the interior of certain pots would have been lined with white clay slip that must have been imported as were the necessary glazes and kiln furniture.

David[III] placed another advertisement for his shop goods on 18th February 1836 but did not advertise the Pottery again until 1837 after the death of his uncle and landlord of the shop, John Methven. This death could have caused David [III1] problems as the ownership of the shop passed to his cousin, Mary, and her husband Robert Heron but fortunately this was not the case. It was instead to prove to be a fantastic opportunity when he was invited to return to Links to work with his uncle George. This he readily accepted.

Before he could leave Cupar he had to dispose of his pottery dealers business and the lease of the Pottery. To achieve this he placed a notice in the Fife Advertiser on 12th October 1837.

China Crystal and Stoneware Trade for Sale and Pottery to Let
In consequence of MR DAVID METHVEN leaving Cupar to carry on the business of his late Uncle, MR JOHN METHVEN, at Kirkcaldy, the extensive Establishment carried on by himself at Cupar, is to be disposed of. The business has been established for thirteen years and stock in trade is large and well selected.
The Pottery, at which Chimney Cans, Flower Pots and Brownware of all descriptions manufactured, is the most northern in Scotland and has supplied a great part of Fife, Forfar and Perthshire for several years, and the trade may be extended to great advantage.
Further particulars will be learned, and the Stock and Premises seen on application to Mr. Methven. Offers for the whole will be received until the 1st day of November next.   Cupar II th. Oct. 1837

The shop proved easily to dispose of and the lease and business were transferred to James Cousins the following December as shown by the notice in the Fife Herald [14/12/1837].

Crystal, China and Stoneware Establishment
St Catherine Street
David Methven left Cupar to carry out business thanks everyone for support. Business now with Mr. James Cousins

Cupar Dec. 9 1837

James Cousins will carry on the business as conducted by Mr. Methven. Has purchased the whole stock and will dispose of at reduced prices to give way for new stock

The Pottery was not so easily disposed of and David[III] probably kept it open while he searched for a tenant who he eventually found in May 1838 and the lease was taken over by James Armstrong as seen in the Fife Herald 3/5/1838.

CUPAR POTTERY

James Armstrong Having taken over the lease of the above Pottery recently wrought by D Methven begs to inform china dealers and others that it is now in full operation and orders will meet prompt attention.

A large supply of brownware, chimney cans and flower pots etc. always in stock.

Cupar Pottery 1 May 1838

With this the direct connection of the Methven family with potting in the Cupar area ended although the shop remained in the ownership of the Herons who had inherited it from the late John Methven.

Cousins continued to operate the shop there until the Whitsunday Term of 1844 when the lease was due for termination and Robert Heron advertised it for let [FH 4/1/1844] at a rent of £25 and was said to be "gas lit". The lease was transferred to a James Armstrong who was presumably the one who had leased the Pottery. He in turn traded in the shop for a short time until May 1846 when he announced he was retiring and advertised a "sale" of his extensive stock including "English Milk Basins and Butter Cans" [FH 21/5/1847]. Having quit the shop he held a "Roup" [auction] of his remaining stock in November [FH 15/10/1846]. There was no mention of the Pottery at that time and it would be safe to assume that his connection with the Cupar Pottery had terminated when the land including the Brick and Tile Works [D Smith] was sold to the Railway Company. It should be noted that Smith had started making redware at his Works in September 1832 [FH 13/9/1832].

The shop was yet again advertised on 1st April 1847 as "occupied by Armstrong" [FH 1/4/1847]. It is not known if this attempt was successful. However as Robert Heron cleared John Methven's debt on the shop on 16th November 1849 [PR 315.109] and sold the property to G Hutton, China Merchant, Cupar two years later [21/1/1851 PR315.109] perhaps Hutton had taken over the lease. With this all connections with Cupar were finally severed.

Chapter 6   GEORGE METHVEN 1827 — 1847

On the death of his father, David [I] George inherited much of the estate under the conditions of David [I]'s Disposition and Settlement [Will] dated 7th December 1826 and he took Title to the property on the 20th December 1828 [PR 165.283]. The main property was listed as "Tyle and Brick Works on the north side of the High Street of Linktown with dwelling house, kilns, sheds, china warehouse, potkiln, workhouse and stables. He also inherited a tenement in Heggies Wynd called Barnyard consisting of "four houses and ground behind". He was also heir to most of the Movable Estate and must have been a wealthy man.

Although all of these details are well recorded it must be remembered that as David[I] was a very old man at his death [there are various estimates between 80 and 100 years of age] George would have been running the Works for many years and therefore the change of ownership is unlikely to have made any significant difference at the Works

Although he had the potential to be a potter as well as tyle and brick maker it appears he had no interest in the former and it is likely that the "pot kiln" was not used for its original purpose after John Methven opened his new Links Pottery. This is not to say that the pot kiln was unused as it could simply have been transferred to firing products from the Works perhaps fireclay. [NB the descriptions given in various documents vary as "potkiln" is given in both singular and plural]. Whilst as explained earlier it is reasonably certain that the scope of the works had expanded to include the use of fireclay well before this date it is only known that bricks and tiles were made although these could have been of different styles and for different uses. It does not seem unreasonable to assume that this major enterprise had expanded into the production of other domestic and commercial wares such as pipes and troughs that may have been salt glazed as required. Certainly these and many other different products were made later.

Similarly George now owned the China Warehouse but, again, it is not known if he operated a sales business there at that time as he did not appear to have advertised this type of enterprise and did not appear to have shown any interest in it. It should be remembered that John already had such a business associated with his Pottery, which was literally next door.

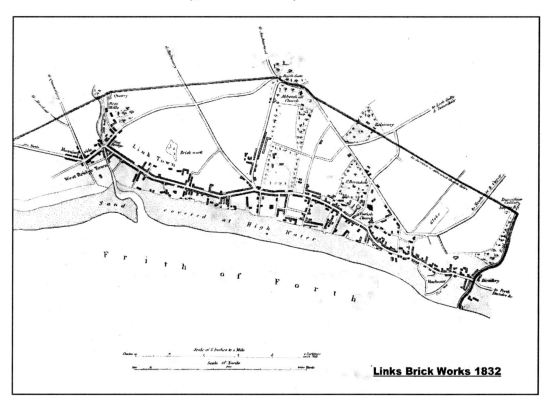

Links Brick Works 1832

George must have ran a successful business as he soon started to expand by acquiring land adjacent to the Works starting with the "Gardeners House" and "the west most of the line of cottages fronting the High Street" as shown on Plan RHP 215 [9/2/1830 PR 180.79]. Further purchases were made in 1830 when an adjacent section of land was bought [10/9/1830 PR 180.83] and later in 1832 when the "Garden Ground" was acquired from John Fergus [1/6/1832 GR 1677.164]. By these purchases George and his brother, John, now owned a large section of land that were separated by the access road to the adjoining fields including the clayfield.

It will be noted in the plan of 1832 that the clay field and Works are shown but there is no indication of John Methven's Pottery.

Throughout all of these transactions George did not apparently require to raise any extra capital and it can be assumed he was sufficiently wealthy to fund them out of savings and profits.

George who was unmarried had no direct heir and by that time was in his late "forties" without anyone to assist and succeed him. There were two obvious possibilities, his two nephews, David[IV] and David[III] who was living and operating in Cupar [see Chapter 6]. Any choice George may have had was removed in 1837 when David[IV] died. Shortly after this death George made a Will naming David[III] as his main benefactor on 12th May 1837. Whether he did this to tempt David[III] to join him or simply to regularise his affairs is not known and is unimportant as the situation was brought to a head by the sudden death of his brother, John, later that year.

As seems to be the usual state of affairs with the Methven family George's Disposition and Settlement [Will] of 12th May 1837 had a peculiarity as he bequeathed the Brick and Tile Works to David[III] and whom failing to David[III]'s second son James. One can only guess as to why the first son, David[V], was excluded especially as the boys were only six and eleven years old at the time. The only suitable reason was that David[V] was not considered to be very healthy. It should be noted that although this bequest was for the complete Works there was no mention of any Pottery at the Works and that George referred to himself simply as a "Brick and Tyle Maker" adding to the belief that he did not operate his "Pottery" or the "Warehouse" which he had inherited at least on paper.

As explained elsewhere John's heirs Robert and Mary Heron were obliged to sell off the Links Pottery to settle the most pressing debts and George acquired it on the 15th December 1837 for the price of £1,500. The sale included "the large Warehouse and other houses and the Pottery situated behind with the whole machinery, work looms and utensils fixed and movable" There was also a requirement that the Pottery must not obstruct the "air" to the tile shades. This restriction had been placed on John when he built the Pottery but had no effect once the Works and Pottery were under the same ownership. Thus George now had as far as the Titles were concerned two Potteries and two warehouses and had not shown much if any interest in operating either type of business. There can be only one answer to this, David[III], who as early as 12th October 1837 had advertised in the Fife Herald that he was taking over his late uncle's [John Methven] business. From this it appears that David[III] returned to The Links Tile Works on the understanding that the Pottery would be acquired shortly. This apparent delay was due to a problem with the Title of the Pottery that took a short time to overcome and it appears that there was some family arrangement by which George took over the Pottery whilst the matters were cleared. It was indeed a strange turn of events that brought David[III] back to the Links Works and the Pottery which he must have thought he had lost any interest in on the death his father, David[II].

There can be no doubt that David[III] was the driving force behind the Pottery and he was soon taken into partnership with his uncle in the new firm of "George Methven and Co., Potters and China Merchants," [GR 1921.251] but not apparently in the Brick and Tile Works which he was heir to. This again was not surprising as David[III] was very experienced in Pottery production and selling and probably had little or no experience in brick and tile making.

Links Pottery continued making brown ware with perhaps cane ware no doubt to a reasonably high standard and although it was to be a few years before any details were available it is likely that significant improvements were soon made to the Pottery and the products. Perhaps also the output increased due to generally improving financial situation in the Pottery and Works as well as in the general economy since an extra clay field was required. This was rented from the Raith Estate in 1839 at an annual rent of £28 [Raith Papers]. [NB Raith Estate is almost the same land as Abbotshall

Estate]. This land was the Links Acres that was a short distance to the west of the Pottery and was an extension to the original clay field. Any land not required immediately for clay extraction would have been used for grazing the horses and general crops including straw, which was used for packing pottery.

The suggestion that the running of the Pottery was left to David[III] is further borne out in the Census of 1841 when George is listed as a "Tyle Maker" while David[III] was an "Earthenware Manufacturer". David[III]'s elder son, David[V], was by then working as an "apprentice clerk" presumably with his great uncle George. Perhaps the fact that he was in the office instead of being on the production side supports the suggestion regarding his poor health. The other son, James, was still at school as were the three daughters, Elizabeth, Robina and Janet.

This Census Returns also list the workers in the area with their occupation and age and whether they were born in Scotland or not. If Scottish it also indicates if they were born within or outside Fifeshire. On occasions by examining the details of the birthplaces of each member of the family it illustrates that workers moved around the country to obtain work. From the 1841 lists there were 30 Pottery workers in Abbotshall and only two listed for the Works. This later figure is obviously incorrect as seen from the labour details given in the Court Action. This "error" must be due to the fact that the majority of the workers in the Works were unskilled and could have been simply listed as "labourer".

Of the Pottery workers there were 6 potter journeymen, 19 potters, 3 apprentice potters and 2 pottery labourers. Although not stated, presumably the journeymen were more highly skilled than plain potters. Of those listed the majority were born in Fifeshire and probably fairly local, whilst seven were born outwith Fifeshire including one from England and another from Ireland. They were all fairly young men being in the range of twenty to thirty years of age which would mean that they started their working life during John Methven's ownership. The use of the very general term "potter" would suggest that they were skilled in the general work of a potter and although perhaps carrying out only one task were capable of undertaking many aspects of the work.

In 1841 there was another major enterprise being undertaken which was to prove very troublesome to the Methvens although the outcome was very favourable to them and the Pottery researcher. In that year a railway was being constructed through Kirkcaldy and passed a short distance to the west of the working clay field. The lawyer, Mr Lees, acting for the Edinburgh and Northern Railway Company wrote to George.

> -   Mr Lees to Mr G. Methven.
>   Edinburgh 15th June 1841
> Dear Sir,
>   I beg to inform you that it will be necessary to keep the
> works of your clay 5 yards clear of the Embankment of the
> Railway.

While this demand would not have an immediate effect on the business it meant that George was denied the use of the clay under the railway and access to the clay fields to the west of the railway. He responded in two ways. First by writing through his lawyers, Messers Pearson and Jackson, that he was "the sole putative tenant" under the Clay Lease and secondly by dissolving, by mutual consent, the Company of George Methven and Co. on the 6th October 1841 [EG 1841 p348]. This was done presumably to make any legal argument about ownership easier as David[III] continued to manage the Pottery and was appointed manager of the whole concern two years later.

George evaluated his claim for "losses" at £7,236.87 but was only offered only £500 by the Railway Company and after a long and acrimonious correspondence the parties became deadlocked on the question of who should appoint the "oversman" to adjudicate in the proposed arbitration. Finally to overcome the problem the matter was taken to the High Court where the Railway Company demanded evidence of the claimants' right to the clay. Fortunately George was able to produce the original Clay Lease along with his father's Will and his Sasine of 1828 for the Works. After a long legal action Lord Fullerton ruled that George had a Right to the clay by "servitude or otherwise" and the matter was referred for evaluation of the compensation at the Sheriff Court, if necessary.

Needless to say Court action was required and in the submission great details of the Works between

1838 and 1846 and the Pottery from 1841 to 1846 were submitted which give a considerable insight into the operations of both enterprises. The choice of two different periods would seem to suggest that there had been a substantial alteration in the Pottery between 1838 and 1841 which had led to an expansion in output and profitability probably associated with new and improved methods and an increased range of products. It has to be assumed that the profits from the Pottery, if any, prior to 1841 were so small that they were not worth considering or would have adversely effected the Court submission. This would not be surprising as David[III] was an ambitious young man and probably his uncle John Methven had not felt the need to improve the quality of the products as he also owned the much more sophisticated Fife Pottery at which he was producing much higher quality whiteware. He was also heavily in debt and would not have had sufficient capital to undertake significant improvements.

Thus the details given in the Court Case for the Pottery are unlikely to be typical of the period prior to the 1841. The full details were submitted on 27th August 1847 and can be assumed to be reasonably accurate as the accounts and other business and financial papers had to be submitted to the Railway for investigation. There can be no doubt that they would have been presented in such a way that gave as favourable situation as possible. The valuations have been converted to pounds sterling

Valuation of Property   TABLE C1

Large Tyle Shed in Park	311
3 Tyle Sheds at Works	758
Engine House and Shed	100
2 Brick Stoves	266
2 Tyle Kilns	300
1 Brick Kiln	60
Old Warehouse	322
Stable, Loft, Firebrick Shed & Gig House	467
Dwelling House	230
Ground at Works	253
Garden & Wash House	180
Ground at Store	70
Total	3317
Pottery in Whole	800
Utensils at Same	477
Total	**£5594**

Output of Pottery   OCT 1842-OCT 184   TABLE C2

Black Teapots 49 Doz.	12.25
Flowerpots & Flats 359 Doz.	24.67
Chimney Cans 216	12.85
Chimney Cans Moulded 35	7.80
Extras	13.52
2nd Ware 239 Doz.	16.27
Total	605.46
Expenses in 36 Kilns	468.00
Profit	137.46
Business Profit over 8.5 years	**£4999.47**

From Table C1 it is seen that even when the non-industrial buildings [house, washhouse etc] are discounted the Works were of more value than the Pottery and this is reflected in the respective outputs and profits [Table C2]. Indeed when it is seen [Table C 10] that the Works made some two to three times the profit compared to the Pottery it is easy to understand George's apparent lack of interest in potting especially as his original Pottery was presumably a much smaller and primitive affair than the current Links Pottery. It is also interesting to note that the Improved Pottery with equipment was now only valued at £1277 when it had been purchased for £1500 some ten years earlier. Whilst it must be borne in mind that these valuations were made for different purposes it appears that George had either made a very disadvantageous purchase of the Pottery or more likely there were other items such as the wareroom in the transaction.

To substantiate the claim details of the cost of each process was given.

Items of Expenses   TABLE C3
On Dishes or Brown Ware Each Kiln

Clay Digging & Milling	0.43
Coals for Kiln 7.5 carts @ 0.48	3.59
Coals for Pan 4 carts @ 0.30	1.22
Coals for Stove 1 cart @ 0.30	0.30
Red Lead 2.45, Flint 0.09, Shavings 0.50	3.10
Rent of Pottery	0.70
Wear & Tear	0.20
Wages	5.30
Total	**£14.77**

N.B. The average expense of 34 Kilns of Chimney Cans and Brown Ware takes as they follow one another in the Kiln Book is assumed as the expense of each Kiln in the prefixed state.

Items of Expenses   TABLE C4
On Chimney Cans and Flower Pots Each Kiln

Digging and Milling Clay	0.42
Coals for Kiln 6 carts @ 0.49	2.87
Coals for Stove 1 cart @ 0.31	0,31
Rent of Pottery	0.70
Wear and Tear	0.20
Total	**£10.50**

In the sale description in 1837 the Pottery is described as having "machinery" which might suggest that there was some form of power and perhaps that steam power was used at least for the clay preparation. However by the time of this Court Case it is certain that the preparation, at least, was steam powered since there was a requirement for "coals for the pan[mill]". It is probable that "wheel drivers" would have manually powered the wheels, lathes etc.

For the year quoted, 1842/43 [Table C2] there was only 36 firings that could have been accommodated in one kiln. However as there were "kilns" there must have been at least two, which could have been used if required. Certainly by 1846 when profits had gone up by about fifty percent with the associated increase in output more than one kiln would have been required [Table C10].

As would be expected the whole submission concentrated on the local brown clay with only very minor references to white clay and fireclay. The products quoted throughout the papers were described as brownware, black teapots, flowerpots and flats, chimney cans [plain and ornamental], jugs, tumblers, gold lustre teapots and dishes. All of these were made from the local red clay although any caneware dishes and gold lustre teapots might have required a proportion of white clay to "lighten" the colour of the body. It was also claimed that the clay was of superior quality and could be made into caneware without "boiling" the clay. This process was required in poorer clays to remove impurities such as iron. The wares were lead glazed where necessary and the body contained flint, which presumably was obtained from Robert Heron's Balwearie Flint Mill [Table C3]. Flint in the mixture would also help to lighten the colour of the body.

From Table C3 it is seen that there was an additional expense for the "pan". This reference was to a pan mill that would have been used to produce finer clay that was smooth and free from lumps. This superior clay would have been required for the production of pottery that must have been relatively thin walled when compared to such products as chimney cans. This suggestion is borne out, in part, by the submitted statement made by William Street, the Pottery Foreman, that "pottery clay is always the best quality and mixed with power". It is also interesting to note how cheap clay was if the supply was local and privately owned. From the details in Table C3 & C5 it appears that there was approximately 3 cubic yards of clay in each kiln load and 1 cubic yard of clay had a "Pottery" value of about 3/-[15p]. As would be expected this was below the retail values quoted for pottery clay since it would have been for lower quality. The comparative cost of glaze [£2.45] was surprisingly high considering the relatively small amounts used while flint at 9p also seems a very low cost. Shavings at 50p are a mystery as it is difficult to establish the quantity this indicates, as is the use unless it was for packing the wares for dispatch.

Of the materials used coal was by far the most costly at £5.1 per kiln firing. Coal of two grades was used. The best, presumably that capable of producing the highest temperature, was used in the kiln while cheaper and poorer coal was suitable for the drying stove and steam raising for the pan mill. The quantities quoted are in "carts" which judging by other details supplied was equivalent to about 10 cwts [500 KG.]. From this it appears that the kilns were fairly small if they only required such a small quantity of coal per firing. Although not stated it can be assumed that the bulk of the brownware was thrown on wheels which were probably manually driven by wheel drivers, usually women or children. There is no one listed in the 1841 Census Returns as specifically undertaking such work and such workers would have been considered as labourers. The wages of skilled workers were not stated but would have been higher than the 2/2 [11p] per day paid to labourers in the clay field.

The types of brownware were not fully specified and it has to be assumed that they were similar to those produced by David[III] at Cupar [Chapter 5] and could have been lined with a layer of white clay slip when required. Some of these pieces, especially those for farming or commercial use, would have been quite large and with a correspondingly high unit cost.

The cost of various products was given which also give an indication of the relative sizes.

RELATIVE COSTS   TABLE C5

Black Teapots

30 doz. Per cu. Yd. clay @ 0.22 per doz.	8.25
Expenses to manufacture	4.65
Profit	**£3.60**

Brownware

60 doz. Per cu. Yd. Clay @ 0.13 per doz,	7.50
Expenses to manufacture	4.59
Profit	**£2.91**

Chimney Cans

100 per cu. yd. Clay @ 0.05 each	5.00
Expenses to manufacture	2.74
Profit	**£2.26**

TABLE C5   Continued
Garden Pots

60 doz. Per cu. yd. Clay @ 0.08 per doz.		4.50
Expenses to manufacture		1.92
	Profit	**£2.58**

Gold Lustre Teapots

30 doz. Per cu. yd. Clay @ 0.90 per doz.		27.00
Expenses to manufacture		13.18
	Profit	**£13.82**

Of the specials only teapots were specified and caneware if produced ignored perhaps as it required a good proportion of white clay and its inclusion in the claim might have added an unnecessary complication. Again it can be assumed that the teapots were thrown or on occasions moulded if more awkward or non-cylindrical shapes were required. Similarly the handles and spouts would, probably, have been moulded. The Black teapots were made of the local clay hidden under a black glaze while gold lustre that might have required an addition of white clay to the body was covered with a clear glaze giving a light brown finish, which in turn was covered with the gold lustre finish. This in part would account for the large difference in the costs between the two types [black 26p per dozen and gold 90p per dozen]. The different final glazes would also contribute to the costs. Gold lustre wares also required a third firing which again would have added to the unit cost. A third firing might have been required also for Black Wares if they were decorated overglaze but judging by the relative costs this is unlikely. Black teapots were listed in the annual output [Table C2] although the quantity was very low. Gold Lustre was not quoted perhaps as the quantities were so low or perhaps because production of this type of ware did not start until after 1843 and before 1848. Again although not stated the wares, especially at the glazing stage, would have been packed in saggers and separated by some form of stilt or spacer. In this and on most occasions quantities are quoted in "dozens" without specifying if this represents twelve pieces or a "potters dozen" roughly the same quantity. Perhaps as these details were part of a Court submission intended for non-potters a dozen was simply twelve.

From Table C2 it is seen that the annual throughput was some 5,600 "dozen" pieces, excluding the fairly small number of chimney cans. Most of these items [with the exception of flowerpots and flats and chimney cans] would have been glazes requiring two firings. Therefore since 34 kiln firings were required it can be estimated that a kiln held about 300 dozen. This number of firings per annum could have been accommodated in one kiln at about ten days per firings but as the Pottery, apparently had more than one it can be assumed that the individual firings took longer than that period. By 1847 the output of the Pottery had reached its maximum and the foreman, W Street, claimed that consideration was being given to building a new kiln.

Items of Expenses   On Roof Tiles per 1,000 tiles   **TABLE C 6**

ITEM	COST
Tirring per cu. Yd. 1p Digging Clay 2p per cu. yd. Therefore 3 cu. yds.	0.11
It requires 9 men & 2 horses to win 60 cu. yds. of clay. Men's wages IIp per day each. The charge for horses and men 30p per day	
Milling & taking to mill house	0.09
Coal for milling engine	0.05
Moulding 9p Washing off 10p placing 7p	0.26
Kiln setting including wheeling	0.05
Kiln firing	0.05
Coals for kiln at the rate of 9 tons per kiln of 15,000 tiles	0.27
Drawing kiln	0.06
Breakages at rate of 400 per kiln of 15,000	0.05
Wear and tear 4p loading carts 1p	0.05
Rent of premises excluding clay	0.18
Discount & bad debts	0.15
Total	**£1.33**

Items of Expenses On Drain Tiles per 1,000 tiles   TABLE C7

ITEM	COST
Tirring 1p Digging clay 2p per cu. yd.	0.11
Milling and taking to table	0.06
Coals for milling engine	0.05
Moulding 6p Washing off 6p Facing 6p	0.18
Kiln setting including wheeling	0.07
Coals for kiln at 9 tons per 18,000 tiles at 9/6 per ton	0.28
Drawing kiln	0.05
Rent of premises excluding clay	0.06
Discount & bad debts	0.06
Total	**£1.93**

Items of Expenses   On Bricks per 1,000 bricks   TABLE C8

N.B. As in the case of roof tiles [10 men are required in this case] the clay digging is not done on piece rate and requires 10 men wheeling being substituted for cartage the manufacturing being carried on near the clay field.

ITEM	COST
Tirring 1p per cu. yd. & Digging clay 2p per cu. yd. Wheeling to bing and watering 2p per cu. yd. Tirring & clay of equal depth 3 cu. yd. per 1,000 bricks	0.10
Milling allowing one horse @18p for two tables	0.02
Making including all expenses to hakes	0.28
Wheeling setting & firing	0.10
Coals for kiln at 45p per ton — 11 tons per 25,000 bricks which each kiln contains at rate of 9 cwts per 1,000 bricks	0.21
Drawing kiln	0.05
Loading carts	0.01
Breakages	0.02
Rent of premises excluding clay	0.09
Cost per 1,000	0.90
Duty per 1,000	0.31
Total	**£1.20**

Output from Brick and Tile Works   TABLE C9

YEAR	ROOF TILES	DRAINAGE TILES	BRICKS
1838	243,100	3,320	314,300
1839	301,200	69,900	376,000
1840	133,000	273,400	180,300
1841	175,400	138,000	216,600
1842	172,500	II0.600	191,600
1843	203.000	251,000	200,900
1844	175,400	138,00	216,620
1845	169,700	996,000	410.600
1846	II6,700	722,300	716,200

It was stated that the manufacturing price and selling price per thousand were :-

ITEM	COST PRICE	SELLING PRICE
Roof Tiles	1.33	3.00
Drainage Tiles	0.93	2.00
Bricks	1.20	1.65

The total profit for this period was £4,999-9-4 based on the quoted wholesale selling price. Extra profits could be made with retail sales. The tax on bricks was 30p per thousand

Profits in Brick and Tile Works and Pottery   TABLE C10

YEAR	B & T WORKS	POTTERY	BUSINESS
1838	557.49		
1839	742.45		
1840	598.88		
1841	524.99		
1842	419.50	131.84	551.34
1843	425.16	132.46	467.62
1844	305.02	162.07	462.09
1845	647.48	167.69	815.17
1846	778.30	212.86	991.16

1846 is based on six months only
All based on wholesale prices. N B The greater proportion of pottery sold as retail

It is surprising that the profits for the first six months of 1846 are greater than for the whole of 1845

The Brick and Tile Works was the more successful side of the business making in most of the years quoted [Table C10] two to three times the profit of the Pottery. The brick output [Table C9] although fluctuating from year to year showed a general increase and doubled between 1838 and 1846 when the output seems to have reached its limit for the one kiln even though the Works were operating all year round. On the other hand the production of Roof Tiles dropped to less than 50% over the same period perhaps due to a recession in new buildings or because of competition from slates and other Tile Works. This was more than compensated for by the fantastic increase in the production of Drainage Tiles that increased from 3,320 in 1838 to 996,000 in 1845. This increase in demand was due to the very powerful "Improvement Movement" in land, which entailed, among other factors, the installation of land drains. This was frequently done on an "Improvement Lease" in which the tenant could offset the cost of the drainage works against the land rent. An agreement that was welcome by both tenant and landlord. Details of this type of arrangement are well illustrated in the Court Action *Hard v Anstruther* [CS 233H 12-16] that contains the Caiplie Tile Works Day Books for 1843-1846 [CS 96 3945/ 3946]. Caiplie is between Crail and Anstruther. It is also seen from these papers that the production costs in the Links Works were roughly similar to those at Caiplie as were the selling prices. By today's standards the "mark up" quoted in Table C9 of 100% for Tiles and 50% for bricks seem to be excessive although they were accepted by the customers perhaps on the "Hobson's Choice" principle.

It will be noted in Table C1 which gives details of the property that there were one large and three small tyle sheds and two tyle kilns which could have been used for either roof or drainage tiles as required. These tyle kilns must have been reasonably large as they had a capacity of 15,000 roof tiles or 18,000 drainage tiles [Table C6 & C7] and must have been in almost continuous use especially in 1845 when in excess of 1,000,000 tiles were made which would have required in the region of 65 firings.

The clay for tiles was prepared in a steam driven mill and the roof tiles were probably machine made. The process is not known for certain but was probably the same as used later where clay was rolled out into flat sheets of a predetermined thickness and then cut into suitable pieces that were then pressed into oiled wooden moulds [bats] to form the appropriate shape. On the other hand drainage tiles as seen in the few marked cylindrical examples known might have been extruded which if correct would suggest a power driven mechanical process. However as no allowance is made for this in the report [Tables C6 & C7] it has to be assumed they were hand made by forming them round a cylindrical mandrel. A more basic type of a horseshoe shape sitting on a separate base was also in use at that time and these would have been hand made by simply "bending" the piece of clay over a cylindrical piece of wood of suitable diameter. After moulding the roof and field tiles were "washed off and faced" to give the final product that were transferred in boggies to the tile sheds were they were placed to the dry prior to firing.

Bricks only required poorer quality clay, which was processed in a horse mill and were all made by hand. In the submission George stated that a horse was capable of supplying two brick tables and valued at 19p per day compared to a workman in the Brick Works who was paid 11p per day. Writing much later in 1909 [FA 13/1/1909] Robert Hunter recalls starting in the Brick Works in 1846 at the age of ten years when he was paid 0.25p per hour. His working day was 10.5 hours and his weekly wage 50p including a bonus. Brick makers worked in teams of six and could produce 4,000 bricks per day for which they were collectively paid 50p bonus.

The manufacture of bricks had one great advantage as it was undertaken near to the clay field thus reducing the transportation costs. The process was similar although simpler than tile making. Predetermined weights of clay were thrown into a wooden mould that had been oiled and covered with sawdust. This clay was pushed into the mould to form the required shape, usually rectangular. Drawing a wire along the top of the mould cut off the surplus clay. George seems to have adopted the usual dimensions of 9 inches by 4.5 inches [22.4 cms. by 11.2 cms.] for his standard brick. Other sizes were easily accommodated, as the moulds were simple wooden boxes. However as it is not possible to date these items no "specials" can be attributed with certainty to this period except "large bricks" [see later]. After moulding was complete the moulds were turned over and given a sharp blow that dropped the brick onto a wooden board. When full the boards were taken to the drying sheds [Hakes] where they were left to dry by wind action. After drying they were stacked and fired in the single kiln that had a capacity of 25,000 bricks. The completed bricks were carted to a nearby store area for uplift by customers.

Bricks, which cost in the region of £0.85 per 1,000 to produce, were subjected to a tax of £0.31 being approximately 30% that naturally increased the cost considerably. This "high" price was not a deterrent to sales and George had difficulty in supplying demand until he changed from seasonal to full time production about 1845 when the output increased substantially to reach a figure of over 1,000,000 in 1846. This quantity would have required about forty firings showing that, allowing for the loss of production due to inclement weather in the winter, it must have been possible to complete a firing in about one week.

Throughout all of the submission there are few references to fireclay. One by D Landale, an "Expert Witness", in which he gave comparative costs for clays. Fireclay as would be expected was much more expensive to purchase and work. The other is in Table C1 which lists a "Fire Brick Shed" There was no indication of the products which can be assumed to have been mainly firebricks and kiln bedding with perhaps the industrial and farming equipment made at a later date such as troughs and pedestals. There is by this time no indication of a separate kiln for this type nor of the old potkilns. Equally there is no mention of the type product or the quantities produced. It has to be assumed that all fireclay products were fired in the tile kilns and would have been separate firings as higher temperatures were required. There is no mention of salt glaze being used but this cannot be ruled out for both fire and brown clay.

From these details a picture of the business can be established and it can be seen that the greatest asset was the clay as not only was it of a very good quality and cheap it was ideally located. The entire clay field was on higher ground than the Works so that once removed from the pit it was conveyed downhill following the long established practice of avoiding moving weights uphill against gravity wherever possible. This height advantage had one other great advantage as by installing a drain culvert down to the sea beach the clay pits could be kept free of water at all times without the use of pumps. As part of the claim against the Railway Company George required that this be continued and that culvert be built under the railway embankment

From the Table of Business Profits [Table C10] there can be no doubt that George had a very successful enterprise based mainly on the Works although the Pottery was steadily improving. It should also be noted that he only quoted wholesale prices in these calculations but as he was able to sell "the greater proportion as retail" through his warehouse the total business profits were even higher. In this Table he only included the Pottery from 1842 despite the fact hat he had gained ownership in 1838. No doubt George and his advisers would have chosen the information to be presented with care so that it would present the best case and it appears likely that the Pottery before 1842 was of a substantially lower standard than after that date. This is not supported by the fact that George only valued the Pottery at £1277 including all equipment and machinery while he bought it for £1,500 in 1837.

Throughout this submission George was careful only to supply figures applying to the Works and Pottery although he left no doubt that the profit in retailing pottery was much higher. Such sales could have been made at the dispatch or packing areas of the Pottery but he may have retained the use of one of his warehouses. As early as 1841 he appeared to have decided to give up the retailing of other manufacturer□s goods and advertised it all for sale. [Fife Herald July 15th 1841]

Extensive Sale of China Stoneware and Crystal in Kirkcaldy

G Methven and Co. of the Links Pottery having resolved to devote more of their attention to the manufacture of fine goods have this day commenced a sale of their valuable stock of English Dinner, Breakfast and Tea Sets, Crystal Etc. in that large shop lately occupied by Mr Syme, Flesher.
Auction every evening at 7 o'clock and private sale during the day.

This sale could not have been entirely successful or there was a change of mind as in 1847 there was still a stock of china valued at £68.35 [SC-20-23-4] and it can be assumed he continued this side of the business.

When the evaluation of the claim eventually was laid before the Cupar Sheriff Court in January 1847 the proceedings were again held up by Colonel Ferguson of Raith who tried to reopen his claim that he and not George Methven was entitled to the compensation. The Sheriff was not sympathetic to this especially as it had already been tried on almost the same grounds in the High Court with the exception that on this occasion Ferguson appeared to have the support of the Railway Company. The Sheriff found in favour of George and commented that case submitted had not been helped by the fact that Ferguson and the Railway Company had retained the same firm of lawyers.

When the compensation claim started the "expert" witnesses who had already provided written statement were called to explain and where necessary expand their opinions thus providing further details into the business.

Michel Wilson, Foreman to Mr Methven. When asked his opinion of the general state of the Works replied "...was at the Works in old Mr Methven's time [David[1]] and knew that the business was a good concern and his trade had been greatly improved. During the last year they had found it impossible to supply demand. Although the Works had been considerably extended the demand would still exceed supply. Mr Methven is at this moment contracted to extend the Works. ....". When asked for details regarding the production of drain tiles he was equally enthusiastic "Parties come from a great distance for their tiles from Falkland - 12 miles - from Kinross - twice the distance and other places equally far off. No other works of this kind exist in the district except Mr Methven's". When cross-examined he stated that over the last 21 years they had used about 5 acres of the clay field and that "he had never heard of clay at Dysart or Grange".

The reports of the examination and cross-examination are very lengthy and the following are the more important details

M Wilson:- "Tiles are best made in summer as they are interfered by frost and rain - but are made all year round".

"Works consist of brick tables. kilns, stoves, shades etc. at the brick works: - there are two houses where the moulders work. These are temporary erections of brick and wood which can be moved at pleasure".
"Working the same way as always ....they removed the brick kilns once in 3 or 4 years ....varies according to the clay thickness".

Allan Livingston, Brick and Tile Merchant Portobello, was called as an external expert witness and although he was listed as a "Merchant" he also gave details of production. He also claimed that he "sends bricks all over the world". This is at first sight a somewhat ambitious claim until it is remembered that bricks were sent to many countries from "Kirkcaldy" during David[1]'s time. He supplied costs the production of roof tiles on the basis that 1,000 roof tiles which required 8 cwts [400kg] of coal for firing and for drainage tiles and bricks which required 10 cwts [500kg] per 1,000. These costs were similar to those at the Links Works

Peter Grant, Excise man in Kirkcaldy:- Was called only to substantiate the output of the Brickworks based on the tax paid. He lodged the following list

YEAR	COMMON BRICKS	LARGE BRICKS
1842	243,300	8,800
1843	260,700	2,200
1844	158,400	13,200
1845	379,500	3,300
1846	1,060,400	3,300

He also explained that Methven made a "kind of square brick which do not pay duty and are not in the calculations". [these may be the pavings referred to earlier] Surprisingly these quantities are, with the exception of 1846, smaller, than the outputs claimed by George [Table C9]. Presumably this does not mean that George was failing to declare his full output to avoid tax payments.

W Bisset, Manager of the Brick and Tile Works near Leven stated ".. at his works clay was 5/- [25p] per ton. .... There were no other works in the neighbourhood except Mr Methven's and theirs in which brick and tiles were sold. ... At our manufactory we made 100,000 bricks and the same number of house tiles and a larger number of drain tiles ". It can be assumed that these claims are reasonably accurate as they were presented to the Court and went unchallenged. From this it is seen that George had a great deal of control over his market and his only nearby competitor was much smaller and was at a sufficient distance not to be in serious competition as road haulage was so difficult

As it would only be expected that the foreman would praise his master's business on this occasion perhaps his statements have to be treated with caution. However from these details it is seen that the business had expanded over many years with acceleration over the last few years under, presumably, the influence of David[III]. Also that drainage tiles were of such value to landowners that they were prepared to transport them many miles over the very poor roads which must have been an awkward journey.

John Lindsay, superintended the digging of clay for Mr Methven: - "They wheeled the tirr behind the face and made up the ground as they worked and prepared it for cropping". This use of "tirr" appeared on several occasions when the clay working was discussed and is a term used to cover both the removal of the over burden to expose the clay and for the material removed. It was and still is the normal practice to remove the tirr a short distance from the working area usually into the hole left by the extraction of clay. The topsoil portion of the tirr would have been laid aside to be returned once the workings were finished to return the ground to a "cropping" condition. This method ensured that no unwanted material was allowed to fall into the workings and contaminate the clay. Although not stated presumably land drainage would have been installed. Also there is no reference to infilling the void left other than by the tirr when the clay was removed and the general ground level was probably lowered. Judging by the amount of pottery wasters found in the area, which in now occupied by housing, the clay field must have also been used as a dumpsite for rejected products. The quantities of these would not have made a significant alteration to the final ground levels.

Having produced all of this expert testimony regarding the technical side of the business it only remained to try and confirm the financial statements made. For this purpose Robert Hunter was called. He was a Potter from Leith who had served as a clerk with Methven and had no doubts regarding the accuracy of the "books kept at the Works" he also explained that "Cash sales were not entered into the books but he thought they would amount to £10-£15 a month". This evidence was corroborated by "Mr Methven, another clerk at the Works, at a subsequent time". This "Mr Methven" would have been the elder great-nephew, David[V] who at least in 1841 was working as a clerk at the Works [CR 1841].

As would be expected George also called his Accountant, Andrew Templeton, to speak to the figures submitted. He claimed that on an average over the last five years they had used 100 cu.yds [90 cu.m] of clay per annum. He also claimed that the Railway Company were large purchasers of bricks from Methven for use on the building of the Dumfermline to Thornton Railway which hardly helped the Railway Company's case regarding the alleged poor quality of the bricks.

In reply the Railway Company tried to devalue the clay and quoted figures from an abortive attempt at Grange [between Kirkcaldy and Kinghorn] to open a Brick and Tile Works a few years earlier. George's lawyer suggested that this was a trick as the Works were only advertised and never opened. Indeed the Railway case was so badly presented that when the expert presented to the Court, Henry Struthers, Brick and Tile Maker at Wardlaw, claimed that having examined the Grange clay on behalf of Colonel Ferguson of Raith he found it to be "suitable for brick and tile making" he also had to admit that he had only seen "about twelve bricks". This evidence did not impress the Sheriff. Several other brickmakers were called including Mr Adam of Glasgow who went as far as claiming that "he would not take Mr Methven's clay as a gift" a most surprising claim for clay that had been used in for brick and tile making for some 120 years. The evidence from the other experts was not much better. Having started badly the lawyer for the Railway then produced an Accountant from Edinburgh, R Spottiswoode, who claimed that "he had examined Mr Methven's books and found them to be in a very confused state". This should have been very strong evidence except when challenged he had to admit that he had not seen all of the books and that he had therefore made errors in his examination.

The lawyer for the Railway also tried to make a case that the current prices for all products were unreasonably high for valuation use as they were dependant on the lack of local competition a situation which would be altered when the railway was completed and the subsequent easing in transportation would expand markets and bring down prices. This was an interesting argument that was to prove wrong as the ease of transportation only served to destroy many of the small Works at the expense of the larger such as at Links.

The Jury retired and having considered the evidence returned to the Court at 9 pm having valued the lost clay under the Railway at £4,318, The Sheriff agreed and made an award of that value to George [FH 21/2/1847]. The Sheriff also ruled that "in respect of the verdict being given a sum larger than that previously offered by the Railway Company that the Railway Company would have to pay all costs, charges and expenses". The Railway Company also had to provide a drainage culvert under the railway embankment approximately one metre square and an access arch 4.2 m wide and 3.6m high. This arch still exists and serves as an access to Balwearie High School. George was also cautioned that within the Term of the lease he should not sell unprocessed clay, a warning that would not have bothered George as his sales of clay were insignificant.

On hearing this good news a large celebration was arranged at the Works as reported in the Fife Herald on the 4th February 1847.

-Entertainment to Mr Methven's Workpeople. On Friday last week Mr Methven, Brick and Tile maker Kirkcaldy on the head of the success of the late trial gave his workmen and their wives and children to the number of 200 a grand fete in one of the workshops or stoves where drain tiles are dried which was seated and cleaned out for the occasion. After all were met pies were served by the stewards: after which Mr D Methven in the absence of Mr George Methven who was indisposed was called to the chair. He made a short speech and ended with proposing "The health of Mr George Methven" which was drunk with all honours. various other toasts were given including the following - Mr A Templeton gave "The Potters" Mr Ellice [a master potter] gave "Prosperity to the Methvens" Mr Steel proposed "The Generals of the Clayfields" [meaning Messers Pearson and Jackson we suppose who were present] Mr Pearson replied stating that they had only done their duty particularly considering the state of Mr Methven's Health which rendered him unable to do anything himself and thanked the meeting . Mr Templeton gave "Prosperity to Potters Wives and Families". There were also numerous songs sung in the course of the evening. In the intervals between the songs and speeches dancing was kept up to the music of four fiddles and ginger beer, cordial and toddy were abundantly supplied. The dances were kept up until one o'clock next morning. On Saturday the festivities were again commenced but now "Willie Young" was beginning to take effect. However the company got on with great spirit having now got Mr George Methven into the chair and dancing singing and drinking were continued until Saturday night when aching heads and weary limbs put an end to all

It seems to have been a remarkable celebration which George could well afford having been awarded such a significant sum of money by the Court. It would be interesting to know if the workers had to attend their work on Saturday. Considering that the working week was over sixty hours and that the report does not mention any time off it is very likely that the workers had to include a day's work in their festivities as Saturday was considered to be a normal working day and even the Sheriff Court had sat until 9 pm on the previous Saturday when considering the Case.

Throughout the legal action there were many references to George's poor health and indeed there was an unsuccessful attempt to delay the final Court appearance as he was unable to make the journey to Cupar to attend. Also during the Trial one of the witnesses for the Railway Company could not identify George except as "The old gentleman who rides in a gig".

George died a few months after the Court Case on the 19th June 1847. In his Will of 1837 which he had expanded on the 24th October 1845 to include the Pottery [SC-20-23-4] he left the Brick and Tile Works along with the Pottery and Warehouse to David[III] in life rent and to James Methven, David[III]'s younger son, in fee. Why he should have carried on this preference for James over his elder brother, David [V] has not been established but as this Will was prepared on 12th May 1837 when the two brothers were still children [David[V] b 1825 and James b 1829] it can only be assumed the family tradition that the major factor was David [V]'s poor health is correct.

George's other property in Heggies Wynd, the Barnyards, was given to Mary Heron, his niece, except for the "West Most House" which was left to David [III] and James on similar conditions as the main property which may imply that this house had some connection with the Pottery. David[V] was also left in Fee the whole of the Personal and movable Estate to be shared equally with his sisters, Elizabeth, Robina and Jessie. Again their father was given the Life Rent of their shares. There were also a number of small legacies to various individuals including the housekeeper, Harriet Campbell. This "Life Rent and Fee" type of Will was strange and very awkward to administrate and gave many problems later on.

George's Will and Inventory of Assets was registered at the Sheriff Court in Cupar on the 29th January 1848 by David[III] and his younger son, James, who were the major inheritors. The Inventory was prepared by James Cooper of Caledonian Pottery, Glasgow and Allan Livingstone [J], Brick and Tyle Maker, Portobello [SC-20-23-4 29/2/1848]. A copy of this document and another submitted after the payment by the Railway Company. Selected sections are given here for ease of description.

POTTERY

Stock of Crystal	82.48
Stock of China	66.35
Stock of Earthenware	422.95
Stock of Rags	138.70
Stock of Iron	41.04
Warehouse Furniture	10.31
Pottery Manufacturer's Utensils	128.84
Stock of Materials in Pottery	219.60
Value of Stock of Pottery in Operation	39.20
Horses	100.00
Harness Etc.	53.75
Crops	75.00
Household Furniture	43.60
Value of Brick & Tile Utensils	95.36
Total	**£1,828.38**

BRICK & TILE WORKS

Court Action	4,318.00
Interest	86.95
Debts Due	238.02
Total	**£4,742.98**

The grand total value of the movable estate was therefore valued at £6,571 of which the Court Award with interest amounted to some £4,400. With this the value of the inheritance to David[V] and his sisters had increased substantially giving them a potential share of £1,100 each compared to James's potential inheritance of the property, which was valued at £3317 [Table C1]. For some reason there were no funds listed either for the business or as George's personal savings although there can be little doubt they existed. Similarly the property was not listed as an asset as its value was much larger than the outstanding debt of £800.

The debts listed due to the Brick and Tile Works were from farmers and builders who were, obviously, the main customers. The list included Sir Charles Adam of Blair Adam who was a descendant of the original owner, William Adam. As would be expected the debtors for the Pottery and presumably the Warehouse were mainly pottery retailers and the list shows that they traded mainly in Fife which could be supplied by road and Perth and Angus by sea. The debtors listed were W Child [Edinburgh], Rt. Hon. Earl of Leven and Melville, D Martin & Co. [Dundee], Cooper & Balbourne [Dundee], White [Alloa], Mrs Richards [Carnoustie], Lawson [Kelty], Thomson [Perth], Wilson [Dundee], Mapin [Dunfermline], McNair [Dunfermline], Smith [Dundee], Arthur [Springfield], Gray & Muir [Edinburgh], Miss Duff [Elie], Henderson [Cupar] and Wright Bros. [Glassworks Newcastle]. The debtors listed in Newcastle and probably Edinburgh were likely to be credits for scrap [EG Wrights Glass Works, Newcastle]

Also from this Inventory there can be no doubt that George was supplying pottery in exchange for scrap iron and glass and rags continuing the practice started by his brother, John. Also George seems to have had a remarkably large stock of earthenware [£443] that presumably would have been mainly of his own manufacture. The quantity that this represents is hard to estimate as it is not stated if the valuation was based on manufacturing costs or selling price. However assuming that 60 dozen [not necessarily 12] pieces of earthenware had a value of £8 this gives a stock of about 3,000 dozen.

The same comments apply to the Works with a stock valued at £290 which at cost price of [say] £1.50 per thousand would give a total stock of 240,000 which hardly suggests that George was unable to meet the demand for his products unless, of course, he was now operating the new kiln referred to in the Court case. This assumed figure would have been reduced significantly if there were a large stock of fireclay goods.

It will also be noted that the Railway Company had not paid the award made by the Court and that interest was accruing. It was left to David[III] to eventually obtain the final settlement that was added later to George's assets. There is no mention of the possibility of the Court also awarding expenses.

At his death George owned property to the value of approximately £5,000, a movable estate of nearly the same amount and only comparatively small debts. David[III] and his family were extremely lucky to have such an inheritance, which they were to make good use of.

Chapter 7   Links/Kirkcaldy Pottery 1847 - 1928

Fortunately George had prepared a new Disposition and Settlement [Will] on the 24th October 1847 shortly before his death in which he made David[II1] and his second son, James, his "Heirs in Provision" for the Pottery and Tile Works. They were able to register the various properties in their ownership [PR 273.171] as well as clearing the debt of £800 against the property to D Morgan [PR 290.98]. David[II1]'s other children were also due to inherit George's moveable estate on the same basis.

David Methven[II1]

Mrs David Methven[II1]

David Methven[V]

James Methven

At last under the control of David[III] a reasonably accurate picture of the business can be established as at that time there was an increase in Official Documentation such as local taxation based on the "Rateable Value" of the property. Also at this time there was the start of the publication of local newspapers and the Ordnance Survey Plans.

Shortly after George's death David[III] moved with his family, wife, two sons and three daughters, to the Tile Works House from a nearby house owned by Robert Heron of Fife Pottery [FA 2/10/1847] which was described as "consisting of 4 apartments, kitchen, washing house and stable and a good garden".

Although George's Will had contained the unusual "Life Rent and Fee" it did not make any immediate difference to David[III] who now had control of the business and all of his uncle George's assets although there would be certain limitations under the "Life Rent" conditions. To overcome any restrictions and reinforce the family business arrangements the firm was renamed "David Methven and Sons" at Links Brick and Tile Works and Pottery thus returning to the business name used at one time by his grandfather David[I].

David[III] had shown all along that he was ambitious and no doubt would have wished to expand especially as he now should have had access to the very substantial Court Award. The most obvious and chosen method of expansion was to go into full-scale whiteware production. There was also the possibility of expanding the output and range of products at the Brick and Tile Works which was not missed but was not as spectacular as the expansion of the Pottery. The Pottery was rebuilt to introduce whiteware production using imported white clays from southwest England thereby preparing to compete with the other local and national manufacturers on equal terms. This expansion was either extremely fortuitous or more probably based on a sound knowledge of the potential market as the demand for this more refined product was expanding rapidly as the lower classes became relatively more affluent and sophisticated by with desires for a little "luxury" in their lives. The timing could well have been influenced by the recent development of jollies and jiggers, which allowed a very high out put per worker of hollow and flat wares without the need to train the workers in all the skills of a potter.

To achieve these changes in production the Pottery and the workforce had to be expanded. Unfortunately there was no requirement to submit the proposal or plans to the authorities and the exact starting date is not known although a reasonable estimate can be made.

In the legal papers at the transfer of the property it was extensively defined as

> "The Tyle and Brick Works with dwelling House, Kilns, Sheds, Warehouse, Pot Kilns, Stables and other buildings. Tenement of ground with the Warehouse thereon fronting the Street [Links Street] and the Pottery there behind the said houses and Warehouse connected therewith. Tenement of land with erections thereon called the Strawyard adjoining the said Pottery and Garden adjoining the said Tyle and Brick works and Pottery. Walls enclosing the same....".

It will be noted that the reference to Potkilns at the Works still continued although from the Valuation of 1846 [Table C1] it is known that if they existed they were now used for a different purpose. There are two warehouses listed and presumably the one in front of the Pottery was used for that section of the business. The other in the Works could have been put to any use. To this inherited land they were to add further acquired land in Bridgeton in 1856 and at Milton Road in 1860 [2/6/1856 PR310.269 & 4/4/1860 695.177]

Throughout the whole of the recent Court Action there was no reference to use of white clay except as an additive to red clay to produce caneware and lustre ware. It was also probably used as a slip to form the inner surface of some of the brownware. More importantly there is no reference to the production of whiteware. This lack of reference cannot be taken as conclusive evidence that it was not produced at that time, as the use of white clay would not have added to their Case that was solely considering the red clay.

It could well be that the production of whiteware had been planned during the last few years of George's life and even that minor amounts had been made as a change of this nature would have required a great deal of planning and experimentation. At a seminar organized by the Scottish Pottery Society one piece was produced that had a backstamp which appeared to be "G M & S". However there was nothing in the printed pattern that could identify the producer or give an indication of such an early date. In addition George was unmarried and had no son associated with his business. This remains a mystery.

What ever the precise date there can be no doubt that it is under David[III] large-scale production was achieved. No firm date for this has been established but it is perhaps significant that a new Pottery Manager, W. Low, was engaged in 1849 [FA 23/7/1859] as although David[III] would have been well versed in redware production to a reasonable standard he could have had only little or no experience in whiteware production. Certainly by 1851 David [III] had opened a large whiteware Pottery as can be seen in the Census Returns for that year in which he is listed as employing 76 men, 29 boys and 19 women in the business being a total of 124. When compared to 1841 when the listed workforce was only about twenty, although probably slightly higher, the magnitude of the expansion can be seen. From the details of the individual employees is seen that the bulk of the expansion was in the Pottery. Most of the workers are simply described by the general terms of "potters" or "pottery labourers" however there a few listed who could have only been employed in the production of whiteware: - Frances Leese [England] pottery painter, Mathew Eath [England] transferer, Robert Holborn [England] pottery painter, James Low [Prestonpans] pottery painter and Mary and Jane Hunter [local] spongers. It will be noted that the highly skilled workers all came from areas well away from Kirkcaldy which is hardly unexpected as it would not have been possible to recruit a sufficient number of new skilled employees locally where the only source would have been at the Fife Pottery. This importation of labour is seen throughout the pottery workers listed. It is also worth noting from the family details given that many of these workers had been in other different pottery areas prior to coming to the Links Pottery.

The other skills listed are presser, flat presser, dipt turner, thrower and "kigger maker". This last term is obscure and was probably an error and should have been "sagger". The other trades listed could apply to both brown and whitewares. The use of the general term "potter" to cover the majority of the skilled worker probably reflects their actual trade in as much as they would have trained to carry out the various tasks associated with potting and although they might have been employed at any one time in carrying out one specific process they were capable of transferring to other types of work within the scope of a potter. The age of high specialization had not yet arrived in Links Pottery

In this 1851 Census Return David[V] and his younger brother, James, are both listed as "Partner with Father" and following on from the 1841 Census Returns when David [V] was listed as a clerk it is likely that he had remained in the office while James was employed on the production side of the business. Both sons were still unmarried and living with their father in the Tile Works House along with one of their sisters, Robina. It is also interesting to note that at the date of the 1851 Census David[III] had a visitor, Robert Clough a potter from Ripon, Yorkshire. Any conclusion from this would only be speculative and Robert might simply have been a friend who had made this long journey to visit the area. However it is tempting to think that he could have been an expert called in to advise on the expansion.

David[III] following on from his uncle still was not free from the Court as the Railway Company had failed to pay the monies awarded claiming that they were bankrupt and could not raise the capital. On this basis they claimed that David[III] was not a preferential creditor and should only be awarded £874 for his claim. David[III] was forced to return to the High Court in March 1853 counter claiming that the Railway Company were lying and the problem was that the shareholders had failed to make the required interim payments. The Judge agreed with David[III] and instructed the Railway Company to pay the sum due along with interest and the legal expenses of £1200 incurred by the Methvens. In making the judgment he described the Company as "most nimous and vexatious" a comment that seems to sum up their whole attitude. Payment was finally made after this ruling.

Considerable costs must have been incurred in the expansion of the Pottery and since David[III] had not borrowed capital secured against the property it is possible that David[III] might have borrowed against the Court Award and if so he would now have been able to clear any debts. This injection of funds came at a very fortuitous time as the outbreak of the Crimea War in 1854 brought a slump in trade that was to last for nearly ten years.

David[III] having taken his two sons into partnership was not happy with the conditions of George's Will with respect to the two sons and he persuaded James that they were unfair. James "in obedience to and on the recommendation of his father" agreed that he and David[V] should exchange with each other one half of their potential inheritance from George which they were due to receive on the death of their father, David[III]. This arrangement was formalized on the 13th February 1854 [SC 20-22-35] the same date as David[V] entered into an Ante Nuptial Contract of Marriage with Ellen Cox of Dundee. As part of these arrangements David[III] agreed to give each son a 5% share of the business which was now known as "David Methven and Sons", while he retained the other 90%. David[III] further promised that he would leave the sons equal shares in his Estate. Perhaps since David[V] as eldest son might have expected to inherit a major share of his father's Estate the financial arrangements were equitable despite the fact that control over the business property seems the greatest asset. To avoid to many future arguments a "Real Burden [value] of £1800" on the Property was agreed. From this and from future problems it can be seen that George's Will, although no doubt well intentioned, was a source of many problems.

The Methven/Cox marital arrangements were somewhat unusual as David[V]'s two sisters, Elizabeth and Janet, married two of Ellen Cox's brothers. These would have been considered as "good marriages" as the Cox family although by that date already well established was to become the largest of the Jute Weavers in Dundee.

As if the Methvens had not had enough of the Courts, David[III] found himself back in the High Court again in 1855 when Ferguson who owned the Raith Estate, that included the Abbotshall Clay, claimed that David[III] was using the clay contrary to the 1714 Agreement which he argued stipulated that only bricks and tiles could be made. He further claimed that the Agreement did not allow the sale of clay. David[III] counter claimed that this situation was not new and that it was "custom of trade". Further that "from the earliest period, at least for eighty years past, the clay had been used for the manufacture of brownware" and that "brownware had been made for upwards of fifty years from Abbotshall clay in buildings or property in Linktown by his ancestors". A second Action was raised by Ferguson who further claimed that David[III] was not even entitled to make "collars and pipes" from the clay. Both of these actions were unsuccessful and costs were awarded against Ferguson. One can only imagine why he would have raised these Actions when he must have been fully aware of the Railway Cases and of the general situation at the Pottery and Works.

After 1856 further information became available when all property was assessed for local taxation. This assessment gave a notional value to the property that was supposed to reflect the rent that could be obtained in the open market. The importance of these values is that they give an indication of the relative value of individual properties. The Valuation Rolls also list the owners and occupiers of the various properties. These details are not always correct

As would be expected David[III], the father and senior partner, was in full control of the business while James was responsible for the Tile Works and no doubt also learning the art of potting. David[V] continued in his administrative roll. In addition they employed managers in each section who would more accurately described as "Works Managers". The Tile Works Manager was Boswell Lindsay until he retired in 1866. He lived in a company house that was given a Rateable Value [R.V.] of £4 showing that it must have been of a reasonable size as a potter typically lived in a rented house with a R.V. of £1.5 - £2. The owner's houses were valued at about £30 showing the considerable difference in their lifestyle to that of their employees.

The Pottery Manager from 1849 [circa] was William Lowe who was held in such high esteem by the workers that when he was due to return to his work after a prolonged illness, dropsy, they made a collection and proposed to hold a soiree on the 21st July at which he was to be presented with a suitable gift. Unfortunately he died on the 13th and never received his gift, "a massive and beautiful snuff box" [FA 23/7/1859] He was succeeded as manager by James McKee who is believed to have trained in Glasgow [FA 7/7/1866].

The first R.V. given for the Links Brick and Tile Works including the Pottery and associated properties was £115 some 50% more than the Fife Pottery. This value surprisingly dropped to £110 the following year then climbed steadily to £215 by 1864. This increase of nearly 100% during a period of restricted trade was a remarkable achievement by any standard and was not matched at the Fife Pottery.

In the same year [1856] the Ordnance Survey published their first edition that had been surveyed in 1853 and shows in considerable detail the layout of the Pottery and Works at the time of the survey. To be included in this plan the buildings must have existed but need not have been in full operation. Indeed judging by the increase in the R.V. perhaps the buildings were not in a fully operational condition when surveyed. The expansion would have been presumably linked to the access to funding which must have been extremely easy after the Railway paid the Court Award in 1853.

From the plans it is seen that the whole premises were laid out in three separate, although interconnected, sections. These were the Clay field and associated Brickworks, the Tile and Fireclay Works and the Pottery.

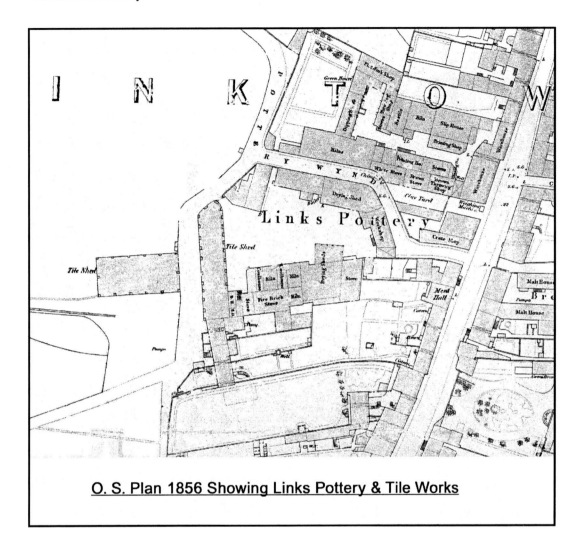

O. S. Plan 1856 Showing Links Pottery & Tile Works

The Tile and Fireclay Works were situated on the south side of Pottery Wynd [now known as Methven Road] this being the site of the original Brick and Tyle Works and the earlier and now defunct Pottery. Within this area there was a large workshop on the east side in which they apparently made the tiles [roof, floor and drainage] and perhaps the firebricks, as there is no obvious alternative building within the premises. After moulding the tiles were dried in one of two sheds. The one on the west side, the "tile shed", appears to have been a simple structure that was open to the wind while the other on the north, the "drying shed" probably used the waste heat from the adjoining boiler which was use to drive a steam engine [FA 4/3/1854]. On the south side there was a small mill that by its location probably was used for grinding fireclay as it was situated beside the fireclay stove. There was also nearby a much larger stove of unspecified use as well as an even larger drying shed. The presence of a fireclay stove would suggest that fireclay products of a much more sophisticated type than bricks were being made at this time since there would have been no requirement for such drying facilities for fire bricks. There are no records of the range of fireclay products being produced at this time and it is hard to imagine that it was otherwise than extensive when the was a local demand for products of this types It is likely that the products were very similar to the products being produced at the recently opened Works at nearby Tyrie and Grange. These were described as "pipes, gas retorts, and pavement blocks. Ornamental pillars, chimney cans [to new chaste and elegant design] and variegated pavement. Again although not stated it would be reasonable to assume that David[III] had installed machinery to produce pipes by rolling or extruding and tiles. In the Works he would also have produced the "specials" made of red clay such as roof ventilators and water pipes which were glazed internally [sample in KM]. The products from the Works were fired in the three kilns on the south side. These were square in plan and were, probably, those reported in the earlier Railway Court Case. In an engraved drawing made about 1860 for D.M.&S the south most kiln is shown as a circular potkiln which was presumably built out of a squares kilnhouse and may have been the potkiln mentioned in the Titles which was however described as being on the East Wing of the Works. There is no mention of a weighbridge in this area, which would not have been required except for fireclay deliveries as the bulk of the sales were in numerical quantities.

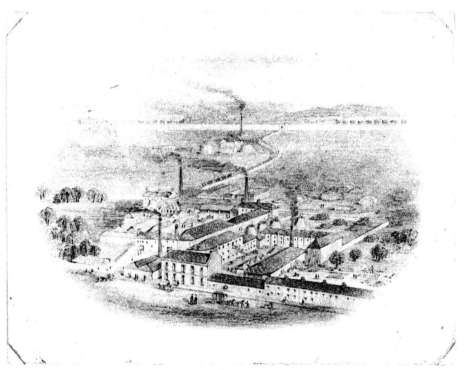

LINKS POTTERY & BRICK & TILE WORKS 1860

The Tile Works House is shown in the north east corner of the site and while this location was very handy for David[III] being so close to his business it could not have been the most pleasant place to live with the associated noise, dust and smoke from the boilers and stoves. Indeed if, as is likely, salt glazing was also being undertaken the atmosphere during "salting" must have been very extremely unpleasant.

The clayfield lay to the west of the Works [outwith the plan] and occupied a considerable area. The southern boundary was the Cloistergutter and footpath, which followed a line roughly similar to Ramsay Road while the western, was Callochy Road [now known as Pratt Street], which at this point ran along the base of the Railway embankment. The clay pit was near to this boundary and clay was transported by a tram road to the Tile Works. The Brickworks with three brick kilns was still near to the clay pit. In the engraved drawing this tramway is shown as being equipped with a railway engine. It is not known if this actually existed or was simply artistic license. However a daughter of William Young, a future owner, recalled playing in the "clay bogies" as a child about 1900. The engraving also shows a large chimney at the brick kilns, which is not indicated on the plan. This addition does seem likely as it would seem only natural to replace the horsemill with steam power as part of the overall improvement

The North Side had been extensively redeveloped perhaps by removing all of John Methven's original Pottery. The new layout shows a truly industrial system of working in custom-built buildings. The clay either from England by ship to Kirkcaldy Harbour and then by horse-drawn carts to the Pottery or local brown clay would be delivered or stored to weather in the "Clay Yard". Deliveries and dispatches could be checked if required on the weighing machine, as could the deliveries of coal from the local mines.

The two clays were processed in separate workshops until firing. These prefiring shops are clearly marked. The "Flat Work Shop" where plates, saucers and perhaps cups were made in white clay. The "thrown" ware was processed on potter's wheels in the 'Brown Throwing Shop" and the "Throwing Shop" for white ware and finally dried in the "Brown Stove" and "White Stove". After firing, in one of the four kilns shown on the engraving, the wares were decorated if required by painting or transferred patterns. It is perhaps indicative of the output the there was a "Printing House" where the paper transfers would have been made as well as a separate section where they were applied to the biscuit ware. After decorating the wares were glazed in the "Dipping House" before being repacked into seggers, also made in the Pottery or Tile Works, before a second firing. Following the practice at that time "green wares" [dry but unfired] would have been packed in flint dust or similar suitable fine material and the glazed biscuit wares would have been separated by stilts or some other form of kilnware. [NB the gardens and beach near to the site of the Pottery show abundant examples of stilts but very few "thimble" dividers for vertically placed flat ware, which suggests that flat ware was placed horizontally in the seggers] After the second glost firing the finished wares would have been taken to the warehouse for dispatch in grates made in the crate shop. The plan also shows that several of the buildings were, at least, two storied. There is no mention of lathe shops or other necessary work areas such for applying handles and it can be assumed these activities would have taken place in the buildings which do not have a defined use.

One other building that is named is a "Bastile" that would seem to suggest some form of secure storage and in part this was true. At that time and for many years later the potters and their assistants were responsible for the greenware they produced and on which their wages depended until it was delivered to the sagger packing shop. This implied that any breakages would not be paid for. However due to the production methods the packers were frequently unable to accept the steady flow of greenware from the potters. On these occasions the greenware could be delivered to the Bastile where it became the responsibility of the Pottery owners. The Bastile must have been fitted out with shelves or racks to store the wares that were presumably carried on wooden boards. The garden ground with a greenhouse was still retained for the use of the owners.

Across Links Street there was the Links Brewery that David[III] had purchased in 1852 no doubt with the view of further expansion. Strangely in 1856 he offered for sale "a brewers copper and copper pump" which was described as "lately in use" [FA 22/3/1856] which might suggest that the brewery had operated for a few years either by Methven or a tenant.

It is worth bearing in mind that although the plan was published in1856 it was surveyed 1853 and the buildings might have changed between the survey and publication of the Valuation Rolls. The picture given of the Pottery is one of rapid development no doubt assisted or even made possible by the windfall of £4318 from the Railway Company.

Although there are only a few commemorative pieces such as "Peace" jugs, celebrating the end of the Crimea War [1856], that can be definitely attribute to this period again the researcher is lucky as there is still in existence [KM] a Price List for March 1855. From this it is seen that that the Pottery produced the full range of Table, Kitchen and Bedroom whiteware that would be expected at that date. Although not stated it appears the prices, in general, would have been for one dozen [in this case 12 pieces]. Most items were offered as "cream coloured, blue edged and sponged, willow, printed and flowing colours". One problem is the reference to Best Printed Plates which would suggest goods to an extra high standard. However they are listed as costing less than the normal printed plates.

This list also shows that sponge decorating only increased the cost by one quarter of the plain ware. On the other hand transfer printing doubled the cost and hand painting trebled it. Caneware is offered for "bakers" [pie dishes] at a price above that of the plain whiteware, which is surprising as caneware would have contained a high proportion of the brown clay.

In addition Carpet Bowls were available at 15p a set. The range of brownware was very much smaller being Rockingham and black jet teapots and coffee pots and accompanying tableware along with special types of pans and basins. The latter appear to be priced individually and may have been lined with white clay slip.

There is also still in existence [KM] a Price List of the same date for Fife Pottery which is so similar in content, layout and prices that they suggest collaboration if not a "Price Ring".

PRICE LIST

DAVID METHVEN & SONS, LINKS POTTERY, KIRKCALDY.

MARCH, 1855.

	Inches.	Cream Colour s. d.	Blue Edged & Sponged. s. d.	Willow s. d.	Printed. s. d.	Flowing Colors. s. d.
Plates	9 & 10	1 3	1 6	2 0	2 0	3 0
Do.	8	1 0	1 3	1 6	1 6	2 6
Do.	7	0 10	1 0	1 3	1 3	2 0
Do.	6	0 8	0 10	1 0	1 0	1 6
Do.	5	0 6	0 8	0 10	0 10	1 3
Do.	4	0 5	0 7	1 8	0 8	1 1
Do.	3	0 4	0 5	0 6	0 6	1 0
Fancy Muffins same as Printed						
Flat Dishes, ...	8	1 6	1 9	2 3		
Do.	9	1 9	2 0	2 6	3 6	4 6
Do.	10	2 0	2 6	3 0	4 6	5 6
Do.	11	2 6	3 0	4 0	6 0	7 6
Do.	12	3 0	4 0	4 6	3 0	10 0
Do.	14	4 6	5 6	6 6	10 0	14 0
Do.	16	7 0	8 0	10 0	15 0	20 0
Do.	18	10 6	14 0	18 0	21 0	30 0
Do.	20			28 0	42 0	50 0
Fish Drainers same price as Dishes they fit.						
Gravy Dishes, ...	16	1 9	2 0	2 6	3 0	3 6
Do.	18	2 3	2 6	3 0	3 6	4 6
Oval Bakers, ...	5	1 0	1 3	1 6		
Do.	9	1 3	1 6	2 0		
Do.	7	1 6	1 9	2 3		
Do.	8	1 9	2 0	2 9		
Do.	9	2 3	2 6	3 3		
Do.	10	2 9	3 0	4 0	6 0	9 0
Do.	11	3 6	4 0	5 0		
Do.	12	4 6	5 0	6 0	9 0	12 0
Do.	13	5 6	6 6	9 0		
Do.	14	7 0	8 6	12 0		
Cane Bakers same price as Blue Edged.						
Nappies, ...	5	0 10	1 0	1 3	1 3	1 6
Do.	6	1 0	1 3	1 6	1 6	1 9
Do.	7	1 3	1 6	2 0	2 0	2 6
Do.	8	1 6	2 0	2 6	2 6	3 0
Round Bakers charged a size higher then Oval.						

Best Printed Plates, 10 8 7 6 5 inch.
2s 6d 2s 1s 6d 1s 3d 1s

	Inches	Cream Colour s. d.	Blue Edged & Sponged. s. d.	Willow s d.	Printed. s. d.	Flowing Colors, s. s.
Soup Tureens, ...	8			1 9		
Do. do. ...	9	1 6	1 9	2 0		
Do. do. ...	10	1 9	2 0	2 6	3 9	4 9
Do. do. ...	11	2 3	2 6	3 0	4 9	6 0
Do. Stands, ...	10				1 0	1 3
Do. do. ...	11				1 3	1 6
Do. Ladies, ...		0 6	0 8	0 9	0 10	1 0
Sauce Tureens, ...		0 6	0 7	0 9	1 0	1 4
Do. Ladles, ...		0 2	0 2½	0 3	0 3½	0 4½
Do. Stands, ...		0 1	0 1½	0 2	0 2½	0 3½
Do. Tureens, complete,		0 9	0 11	1 2	1 6	2 0
Do. Boats, large,		0 2½	0 3	0 3½	0 5	0 6
Do. do. small,		0 2	0 2¼	0 3		
Do. do. Stands,		0 1	0 1½	0 2	0 2½	0 3½
Pickles		0 1½	0 2	0 2½	0 3	0 4
Cover Dishes, ...	6			6 0		
Do. do. ...	7			7 6		
Do. do. ...	8	6 6	7 6	9 0	12 0	15 0
Do. do. ...	9	7 6	8 6	10 6	15 0	18 0
Do. do. ...	10	9 0	10 0	12 0	18 0	24 0
Do. do. ...	11	10 0	12 0	15 0		
Root Dishes, ...	11				5 6	6 0
Salad Bowls, ...					1 6	2 3
Cheese Stands, ...		1 6			2 0	2 6
Do. Covers, ...		2 6			3 0	3 6
Mustard & Peppers,	24	2 9	3 6	4 6	4 6	6 0
Salts & Egg Cups,	36	2 3	2 9	3 6	3 6	5 0
Egg Hoops, ...	36	3 0	3 9	4 6	4 6	5 0
Nest Eggs, Glazed.	12	1 6				

By 1858 the demand for clay from their own workings continued despite being augmented with imported white clay to such an extent that the Links Acres clay pits were worked out by 1858 and the workings were moved to Milton Acres [V.R. 1858]. This was the land beyond the Railway Line and they now made use, for the first time, of the access arch and drainage conduit that George had fought so long and hard for. The narrow gauge tramway was extended into this land which was given a R.V. of £60.35 almost half that of the works. Clay was extracted in small sections and the remainder was farmed by the Methvens assisted by one farm labourer [CR1861]. Surplus crops from this land were sold locally although straw would be retained for use in the packing shed.

As well as considering the various aspects of the business the other important factors must not be forgotten - the employees and the interplay between them and their employers. A general impression can be obtained from the local newspapers.

The working week was normally six days and about 60 hours. Wages were in the region of 2p an hour for skilled men although workers could make more on "piece rates" i.e. paid for output. On a comparative basis this hourly rate was equivalent to the price of a loaf of bread [NB a loaf was twice the present size which until quite recently was correctly known as a "half loaf"]. Wages by today's standards were very low especially as there were no other benefits such as sickness cover, holidays with pay, pensions or a reasonable continuity of work. Workers were "bound" to their master for a fixed period usually one year and could be and frequently were taken to Court if they left their employer during the period of the contract. This contract was very one sided as the employer could discharge an employee at will. For example in 1864 a St Rollox potter [Glasgow] was sentenced to seven days hard labour for leaving his employment without giving nine months notice despite the fact that his wages had been cut from £1.25 to £0.30 per week. Also during any period of trade depression workers regularly had their rates of pay cut without having their hours cut or were "laid off" without pay if trade was very slow. This was all accepted as normal, which it was, and must have given rise to periods of considerable hardship as worker had little or no opportunity to save for such situations on their low incomes. To be fair it can equally be said that conditions were much better than those in 1790 when wages were in the region of £0.35 per week and labour was considered as an "asset" that could be passed from master to master.

The date of this photograph is not known. It is interesting to note the 'willows' and a part of a crate behind the men and of course the tile roof.

David[III] seems to have had a good relationship with his workers when in 1854 he invited 150 of his workers to a banquet to celebrate the wedding of his daughter, Robina, to William Cox [FA 24/2/1854]. The following year the two sons took part in a petition to stop distilling and brewing due to the shortage of grain. There is one strange reference to the Methvens in 1853 when they offered a reward of £5 for information leading to the discovery of the author of threatening letters to one of their employees [FA 14/4/1853].

Despite their long working hours the workers had sufficiently organised their very limited leisure time that in 1855 they formed the Links Pottery Band which made its first appearance at the Links Market. It must have been an impressive sight when they paraded in their "Hussar's Uniforms" The employers encouraged this enterprise and help in the purchase of the instruments. The band was to remain in demand for special occasions such as works outings and parades. Such outings became an annual occasion and in many cases would have been the only "holiday" in the year. For example in 1855 the band led the Pottery workers as they marched to Kirkcaldy Harbour to embark on a steam driven tug at 2.30 am. On arrival at Stirling the band paraded when "it was much admired by the military". Unfortunately Mr Jewson the Conductor was unable to accompany them as his wife was awaiting their child [FA 8/9/1855]. It is hard to imagine the excitement this outing must have made in the life of a potter at that time.

By the time of the 1861 Census there were 61 men, 36 boys and 31 women employed in the Pottery and a further 31 men, 6 boys and 1 woman in the Brick and Tile Works. Among these workers, who mainly styled themselves as potters, were specialists such as kilnmen, turners, teacup handlers, hollow ware and flat ware pressers, sagger makers, engineers, printers, wheelboy, warehousewoman, claymaker, chimney can maker, platemaker, painters and clerks. This range of job descriptions shows that the age of specialisation had truly arrived in the Pottery when a worker's job was so restricted that he only made "teacup handles". Other specialties are worth noting. Firstly the "engineer" showing that the Pottery was sufficiently highly mechanised to justify employing a maintenance engineer. Secondly there were six painters listed which suggests a high output of this type of ware as each painter would have been capable of producing a large number of pieces per day. Thirdly the young children listed such as Alex Gerard and Margaret Longmouth [both age 12yrs.] who are listed as Pottery Workers and at night school and David Heggie [age 9yrs]. These youngsters were presumably augmenting the family income whilst still, hopefully, continuing their education. Fourthly the need for two sagger makers, which again indicates the high output requiring a steady supply of these items, which had a limited life. Lastly A.R. Young [age 22 yrs] is listed as a clerk at the Pottery.

David[III] also employed a living in servant in his house and one workman assisting him to farm the unused land at the clayfield. This land is listed as being 19 acres in area.

The business which had already grown considerably both physically and in productivity under David[III] appears to have continued to expand with no doubt the introduction of new machinery and techniques under the enthusiasm of the Partners. The financial situation was such that in 1960 David[V] was able to feu land at the junction of Milton road and Methven Road [modern names] on which he undertook to build a villa to the value of £800. This house still exists and is bounded by a brick wall with salt glazed cope as required in the feu conditions. There surely can be little doubt that the bricks and copes were made at the Links Works. It is not known if David[V] ever occupied this house as he died on 6th November 1862. Because of the complexity of the business and George Methven's Will David[V]'s estate was not registered until 13th November 1863 and at the low value of £598.08 not including his potential share in the Pottery and Brick and Tile Works. The major item was his "share and interest in the stock and other assets and individual profit in the firm of David Methven and Sons" which was valued at £475. The interest on the unpaid profits was assessed as £19 and assuming the trading year still started on first October this would value David[V] share of the profit at about £150–£175. Since his share in the firm was only 5% this in turn would value the business at approximately £9,500 excluding the property and business profits as being somewhere in the region of £3.000 per annum.

David[V]'s personal Estate was valued at £85 being mainly his household effects and personal items, which appears to be a low sum for a partner in the business. His widow, Ellen Methven [Cox], was left his whole estate along with the expectation of a substantial further inheritance on the death of David[III]. David[V] had also leased land at the junction of Milton Road and Methven Road [modern names] in 1860 on which he built a villa to a value in excess of £800. This property was placed in the names of his wife and himself and was entailed to all children of the marriage.

Whilst these legal and financial affairs were being concluded the business had to continue and since Ellen had no interest in the operations the Partnership was dissolved and reconstituted as being David[III] and James on 4/2/1863 [EG 13/II/1863] The share held by each partner in the Firm, which was still known as David Methven and Sons, is not given although it can be reasonably assumed that David[III] was still the senior partner. To complicate the affairs the partners continued to rent the Brick and Tile Works and Pottery from David [III]. Thus the father received by far the major share of the income of the business

By this time David[III] who was 65 years of age [b 1798] and apparently not in good health went to live in Bridge of Allan in 1863 where he made a new Will in September shortly before his death on 17th June 1864. With this death the problem of sorting out the complications of George's Will had to be faced. Firstly in his Will David[III] left all of his personal Estate to his wife, Janet Izat, although it was to be administered on her behalf by her son, James, and her sons-in-law and their father [Cox]. They were to ensure she had an annual income of £150 and an adequate house along with the full use of all the household items. On Janet's death the Estate was to be divided amongst the children: - James 5/20ths, Widow of David[V] 5/20ths, Jessie 4/20ths, Elizabeth and Florence daughter of Robina 3/20ths each.

When it was examined David[V]'s Estate was valued at a total of £7,857 [SC-20-22-30] as follows

Household Furniture & Personal articles in Dwelling House   £131.60

David Methvens share and interest in the stock and other assets £4,710.85
& undivided profits of the firm DM&S in which he was a partner

Balance Sheet at Death	£8,270.75
Less 5%	£413.55
	£7,857.20

Is the value of the deceased's share due by the surviving partner, James Methven, and includes £2,.227.30 the movable estate belonging to the trust estate of the late George Methven and which the late David Methven had use.

After the deduction of the agreed value of the "Real Value" of the property [£1,800] and other adjustments the final value of the estate was £6,848.25 a far from inconsiderable sum. It should be noted that the total must have included some unrecorded sums.

James now had the problems to settle the financial position regarding the business and family as well as operating the business. Firstly the Business Partnership had dissolved on his father's death and as his brother's widow had no interest in the business the firm was reformed as being James Methven, sole Partner, [EG 29/7/1864] and he had to lodge a Bond of £1,800 against the property with the Trustees of his father's Estate [8/II/1864 GR 3381.23]. This was the earlier agreed notional value of the Property. At the same time James formalised the Agreement with Ellen, David [V]'s widow, that she was due half of the Property [8/II/1864 GR 3381.185] and she and James had to accept [8/II/1864 GR 3386.185] equal share of the debt of £800 to Morgan [15/12/1837]. Further as most of David[III]'s Estate was tied up in the business it was not easy for the Trustees to raise the capital to pay the inheritances due to the sisters immediately and James guaranteed them a future payment of £523.30 each [total £1569.90] using the Property as security [8/II/1864 GR 3386].

The extent of these legal arrangements gives a fair idea of the legal and financial complications brought about by George's Will and the dissolving of the partnership. They did not however place an immediate financial burden on James or his recently acquired business. Indeed he was so confident of his future he purchased a new house, Newton House, in Nicol Street on 15/7/1864 while all of these negotiations were ongoing [15/7/1864 PR344.132]. This purchase was, at least in part, financed by borrowing £500 [15/7/1864 PR 344.136]. At or about the same time James's mother moved to the nearby "Milton House" [V.R.] leaving the Tyle Works House free for David[V]'s widow who lived there until 1867 when she moved to Dundee and eventually San Remo [Italy]. No reason is given for these moves but it can be accepted she must have been a wealthy lady having access to funds other than those from her late husband and that she was not greatly affected by the commercial panics that plagued Scotland between 1866 and 1869.

As if he was not busy enough James was also acting as a Trustee in the Standard Property Investment and Building Society in which it can be assumed he was a reasonably substantial investor [22/10/1863 PR 341.83].

From these very limited details an idea of the difference between James and his elder brother, David[V], can be seen especially when their personal wealth is considered despite the fact that their father took great effort to try and make them equal.

While all of these arrangements were being made, A. R. Young had continued working for the firm. Andrew who was the son of a master tailor was born on 15th May 1837 and spent all of his working life with the firm of David Methven and Sons holding positions from the lowest to the highest. Having started as an office boy he had graduated to the position of clerk by 1861 [CR] and was appointed as a Commercial Traveller by the date of his marriage to Marion Buchanan in 1863. His travels on behalf of the Firm took him far and wide and fortunately he wrote home very regularly so that his routes can be traced [letters in possession of the family]. He mainly covered Ireland [Omagh, Londonderry, Waterford, Limerick, Dublin and Cork] and the north of Scotland [Kirkwall, Thurso, Golspie and Inverness]. As he was one of a team of salesmen including Adam Morrison in London [see Rosslyn Pottery] it can be seen how wide spread the market was for the products. From the letters it can be seen that he was a capable salesman and was obtaining "good orders". He was also an able businessman making private purchases especially flax which he had no doubt he would able to sell at a profit. This "boast" was true as he was to prove to be a superb businessman. Even the pony he bought for his wife "could be sold at a profit if it proved to be too small" [she was heavily pregnant at the time]! The exact position held by Young is difficult to establish as he is again referred to as a clerk in the 1867 Valuation Roll when he was occupying the Tyle Works House which had only a few years earlier been occupied by David[II1] and then his daughter-in-law. This house had a Rateable Value of £12 while Boswall Lindsay, the Tile Works Manager, lived in a house valued at only £4 and James Rough who had replaced McKee about 1867 as the Pottery Manager in one valued at £5. Since all of these houses belonged to the Firm there can be little doubt that A. R. Young performed some function much more than a clerk. In his obituary [FA 27/6/1914] it is claimed "he made himself so familiar with all departments of the work that he became indispensable to his employers". Perhaps his position was as office manager at first and then as business manager by 1871 [CR]. The name applied to his earlier positions are immaterial as certainly he was James's right hand man and he was so "indispensable" that he was taken into the partnership in 1871 presumably after the date of the Census.

The position of Manager of DM&S was one of considerable importance and Andrew continued to occupy the Tile Works House along with his wife and four sons. As would be expected with his status he employed one "live in" servant [C.R. 1871]. The business talents of Andrew cannot be over stressed especially considering that he went from office boy to manager in only twenty years due to his natural abilities coupled with hard work and diligent business studies. He was in addition "lucky" as James was in poor health and although he had several daughters had no son to assist and follow him into the Firm. Perhaps he no longer expected to have a male heir although the working relationship could be easily altered if necessary as Andrew had no share in the Property.

As would be expected when Young's position as clerk became vacant Mr. Herd replaced him. The seniority of the position as "clerk" is shown when workers made a presentation to him and his new wife on the occasion of their marriage they commented, "that they hoped the good relationship between the workers and the clerk would continue" [FA 27/4/1878].

It is only possible to estimate Andrew's influence prior to 1870 but it can be assumed to have been gradually increasing and that at least part of the modest improvements in the Pottery, which increased the R.V. from £190 in 1864 to £215 in 1870, can be attributed to him. These improvements were made at a time of trade depression partly due to the Franco Prussian War. The expansion was not helped by the fire on the 20th February 1869 that destroyed the "biscuit warehouse despite the gallant efforts of Captain Muir and his useful Corps of Fire Brigade" [FA 20/2/1869]. The warehouse was replaced the following year[KTC].

By the Census of 1871 the work force had expanded to 221 workers having almost doubled in ten years. Outwith the decorators, painters, spongers and transferers, most of the workers are described as potters or pottery workers. However this lack of specification in the various types of work can be attributed to the method of recording the information and not any decrease in the specialisation of the workers. Among those listed as specialists one who is interesting is David Clerk who is listed as a "Clay Potter Designer" being the first time such a position was specified and perhaps indicates the continuing expansion in the range of products that would justify such a position that would attract a specialist tradesman from East Lothian.

Links Pottery had always been dependant on Balwearie Mill for most of its ground flint supply. This Mill was operated by Robert Heron and Son [Fife Pottery] and this did not make much sense as Links Pottery was by far the largest user of flint and equally was much nearer to the Mill. This problem was overcome in 1872 when DM&S acquired the lease of the Mill and thus became independent for the supply of that material[V.R.].

The profitability of the Firm had continued and James was able to pay off his debts to his family [12/10/1871 24.149] in 1871 at the same time as clearing the loan on his house [26.9].

The expansion in the Pottery shortly after the formation of the Partnership was spectacular although no details of the improvements are known. They were however sufficiently extensive to increase the R.V. to £315. This increase must have given rise in production as a Large Warehouse was acquired on Sands Road in 1875 [23/11/1875 1929.44]. The expansion continued and helpfully after 1876, when the Links area was incorporated into Kirkcaldy Burgh, plans had to be lodged with the Town Council for approval and the following are developments are listed.

1877 New Printing House and Workshop
1878 New Kiln
1879 New Printing and Sponging Shop
1879 New Jolly Shop
1880 New Packing House and Workshop
1880 New Offices

Sketch of Kiln 1936

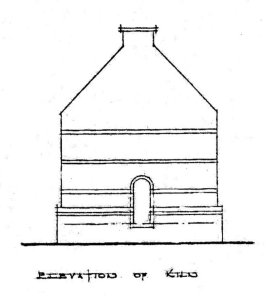

This plan was drawn for demolition purposes after the Pottery had closed but indicates the type of kiln used in the South [Brownware] Pottery. The kilns were contained within kiln houses with only the upper portion protruding through the roofs

It is interesting to note that these works were planned and partly undertaken during the trade depression of 1876-78 no doubt helped by the fact that building costs would have been low.

As part of this last improvement the new buildings in Links Street were set back from the street leaving room for widening. The partners offered this land to the Council free of charge [FA 17.4/1880] an offer that was readily accepted. The following year further property was acquired to the north of the offices so that the Offices could be further expanded and again land was offered to the Council who this time agreed to contribute £25 towards the cost of the street widening. During the Council meetings to discuss these two proposals Young, who was a Town Councillor, not only attended but also voted for the proposals [FA 16/6/1881]. Indeed Young must have been extremely busy as that time he not only was a successful businessman and Town Councillor and Burgh Treasurer he was also a Harbour Commissioner, on the Board of the Links Savings Bank, a Governor of the Philip's Trust and the Fabric Convenor and a deacon of St Brycedale Church.

This further series of expansions was also reflected in the R.V. that increased to £400 by 1881 at a time when James employed 162 men, 79 boys, 86 women and 25 girls. He also employed three servants in his house one of whom was a "Nurse Domestic Servant" [C.R. 1881] perhaps indicating his failing health although at that time he had a two year old son.

The individual Pottery workers listed in 1881 as living in the area around the Pottery can be assumed to have been employed by Methven. Many of these claimed to be Pottery workers or simply clay potters, which only indicates the nature of their tasks. However there is sufficient number who gave their specific tasks to form an indication into the working of the Potteries. As would be expected the individual tasks were specialised such as jigger and jolly men, pressers, handlers, platemakers and turners on the production lines as well as kilnmen and a muffle kilnman. There were also a number of transferers and assistants [usually young girls who cut out the paper transfers] along with spongers, painters and gilders in the decorating shops. Warehouse workers and packers and office staff gave support. The Pottery Manager is listed as Alex Baillie [32 years of age] who was a local man and the Brick and Tile Manager as John Robertson [31 years of age] from Torryburn [West Fife]. David Clark who was still the Pottery Design Moulder suggesting a continuation of the demand for new shapes in jugs and bowls etc.

Although no details are available it is safe to assume that James employed workers to make many of the short-lived accessories such as sagger [approx. 30 firings] and plaster of paris moulds for flat and hollow ware [approx. 40 uses]. He does not appear to have employed a copper plate engraver despite the fact that his requirement for plates must have been high.

During this period the relationship between Methven and Young was being reinforced and purchases of land were made by the Firm and not solely by James. These were for an expansion of the clay field when they took over the Parish Glebe [15/10/1874 72.183] and the remaining land at Old Brewery on the south side of Links Street opposite the Pottery [II/II/1876 II5.99]. This purchase included the frontage onto Anderson Wynd. The Causengutter, which had flowed down this Wynd had been diverted into a culvert. When the Partners proposed to develop Anderson Wynd the Local Authority were considering renaming a number of streets in the now expanded Burgh where there was a conflict with streets of the same name [e.g. there were Pottery Streets in both Links and Gallatown]. As a solution to this problem it was suggested that they revert to the original name for Causengutter Wynd. This suggestion was received with so many objections that it was dropped and the street was renamed Buchanan Street after Young's wife's maiden name when the development of the new "Company" houses was completed [KTC].

Naturally during all of these expansions the output would have also expanded with the associated demand for raw materials until deliveries at Kirkcaldy Harbour were recorded nearly every week [FA]. These loads were clay from Par, Fowley Charlestown and Teighnmouth and boulders [flint] from Dieppe. In the newspaper reports of such deliveries there are a few gaps when no deliveries were recorded but there are no other reports that would give a reason for the gaps and it seems likely that they are more due to the reporting methods than a reflection on the output at the Pottery.

It can reasonably assumed the Young took most if not all of the day to day decisions during the expansions as James's health continued to deteriorate to such an extent that he built an office in his house in Nicol Street. The full extent of his poor health is not known although he apparently could not face the daily journey of some three quarters of a mile to the Pottery. James's son was yet another David Methven [probably the 7th] and presumably due to his father's poor health and as Young had already been taken into partnership the family decided that he would not follow in the tradition of potting and he was eventually trained for the Army where he had a successful career being decorated in the South African Wars. He had been promoted to Captain when he was killed in action in the Great War [FA 31/10/1914].

Abbotsford

Young equally increased in affluence and was able to build himself a new house in Milton Road by 1878. This house was larger [R.V. £60] than James's and was named "Abbotsford" presumably after Sir Walter Scott's house. He appears to have had a special affection for this name as it was also used for a new range of products produced a short time later. As well as building his own home Young purchased six smaller houses in the area, which he rented out to tenants [V.R. 1881]. All of the transactions were undertaken without having to use the properties to secure loans indicating the state of Young's income and standing.

Once Young had moved out of the Tile Work House it was tenanted by James Rough, the Pottery Manager, for a very short time until his death in February 1879[FA 15/2/1879] when he was replaced by Alex Baillie who also took over the tenancy of the house. Thus the Pottery Manager now occupied the house originally occupied by the owner indicating the expansion in the business and especially in the Pottery.

Although there is no doubt that the great emphasis had been placed on expanding the Pottery the Brick and Tile Works were still financially very successful and although there had not been the same spectacular expansion there had been a steady growth in output and the range of products. There is a copy of a Fireclay Products catalogue which although undated appears to be about this period and illustrates a very extensive range of highly ornamental and sophisticated wares as shown it the extracts from a trade catalogue dated about 1870.

LINKS BRICK & TILE WORKS & POTTERY,

KIRKCALDY.

———————◆———————

DAVID METHVEN & SONS

Beg respectfully to call attention to their New Illustrated Catalogue of TERRA COTTA, VITREOUS, FIRE-CLAY, and other Goods of their Manufacture; at same time take the opportunity of tendering their best thanks to their numerous customers, and to state that they have made such improvements in their work by Machinery and otherwise, that they can with every confidence recommend their Goods for quality of material, superiority of workmanship, and moderation in price.

The annexed Illustrations show specimens of TERRA COTTA in VASES, WATER FOUNTAINS, STATUARY, ORNAMENTAL FLOWER POTS, &c., modelled from copies of designs both ancient and modern, and being principally of an embossed character, are well adapted for ornamenting Gardens, Flower Plots, Avenues, &c.

The Engravings also shew a few of their ORNAMENTAL CHIMNEY CANS from Designs by Modern Architects.

The VITRIFIED FIRE-CLAY SEWERAGE PIPES are of first-class materials and workmanship, and are made to any size or shape that may be wanted.

Their VITRIFIED WATERING, CATTLE and PIG TROUGHS, and HORSE MANGERS, now greatly in demand, are much superior, as regards cleanliness and durability, to those made from any other material, and can be had of any size or form.

They also Manufacture STACK PILLARS, WALL COPING, GARDEN EDGING COTTAGE GRATES, VENT LININGS, GAS STOVES, FLUE COVERS any size PAVING TILES, BRICKS, &c., &c., all in Fire-Clay either White or Salt Glazed Common Red Clay Goods of every description; Bricks, Roofing Tiles, Agricultural Drain Pipes, Water Pipes, Paving Tiles, &c.

D. M. & SONS are also Manufacturers of EARTHENWARE in all its variety, in TEA, DINNER, and TOILET SERVICES, for Wholesale and Exportation.

CLAY GOODS of any description made to any Pattern, Sketch, or Drawing.

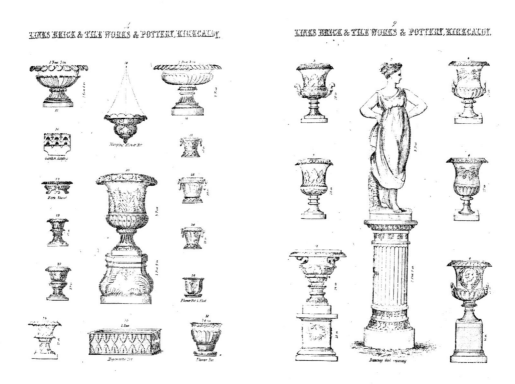

By 1881 the manager of the Works was John Robertson who was 31 years of age and had come from Torryburn. This relatively young age for a senior employee when considered along with A Baillie, the Pottery Manager, who was only 32 years old and a local would suggest the introduction of new "modern" methods which required new young blood to implement

After the birth of his son James finally had been granted the Title to the Brick and Tile Works, Pottery and Clay Field by his brother's children [12/5/1879 170.83]. During these negotiations it was discovered that the Title was not clear. However Munro Ferguson of Raith, the new owner of the former Abbotshall lands, agreed that James did have a clear Title and this problem was readily overcome. Looking to his family's future James continued to purchase property that could provide an income. Although in such poor health that he required to engage a nurse [CR1881] James was able to attend the "Coming of Age Party" for the eldest son of Munro Ferguson [FA 19/II/1881] and would have been in full control of the business as senior partner which enabled him to amass a considerable personal fortune.

James's health continued to decline and Young must have taken over more and more of the running of the business until he was even making the payment of the rates of James's house by 1886 [V.R.]. On the other hand Young went from strength to strength and involved his family as much as possible. He had five sons and two daughters. The eldest son, William [b1864] started work at the Pottery after leaving school in 1881[circa]. He appears to have been employed on the production side. His younger brother, Andrew Buchanan Young, [b1866] who showed academic promise at Edinburgh High School where he gained prizes in 1881/82 and after being dux in 1883 joined his father in the office where he was described as being a clerk when witnessing legal documents in 1885. These young men were also extremely lucky, as by 1887 James's health had so deteriorated that he was unable to undertake the running of the firm even with Young's assistance and the partnership of David Methven and Sons was reformed as James Methven. A.R. Young, W. Young and A.B. Young. The share held by each partner is not recorded but more importantly the ownership of the business property, Brick and Tile Works, Pottery and associated houses in Buchanan Street, were transferred to the newly constituted Firm on a "Survivors or Survivor as Trustees of D. M. & S." [29/76/1887 336.24]. In the associated documents there is no mention of any financial arrangements in this transfer suggesting a very generous gesture by James Methven. This seems unlikely and it must be assumed that there was some private arrangement by which Young would buy the business from his earnings.

James would have continued to receive a considerable income from the business and probably by far the major share. The Youngs must have been delighted to know that they would eventually own the business outright. The new partnership did not last long as James became so ill that he required the full time attendance of a male nurse/attendant as well as a part time female nurse [CR1891] until he died on the 19th April 1892 ending over one hundred and twenty years of Methvens in the Brick and Tile Works and Pottery.

During this period James had continued the expansion started by his father, David [III]. He had also changed the name of the Links Pottery to Kirkcaldy Pottery some time between 1876, when Links became part of Kirkcaldy Burgh and 1879,when drawings were submitted to the Town Council.The name of the Links Brick and Tile Works remained unchanged. This change in the Pottery name was probably a sound business decision but the Pottery continued to be referred to locally as "Links" for many years afterwards. With the exception of red clay all of the other materials were "bought in". White clay and flint have already been explained and other materials such as glazes, enamels and much of kiln furniture probably were acquired from Staffordshire. Another major requirement was for engraved copper plates for the transfer printing as Links/Kirkcaldy Pottery was to become famous for the variety of different designs of transfers. It appears that there was no engraver employed at the Pottery and again these plates must have been acquired elsewhere perhaps from Elay the engraver in nearby Gallatown. Plates could have equally been bought from suppliers in Staffordshire or made by itinerant engravers.

As production increased there was an ever-increasing demand for flint, which was still ground at the Balwearie Mill, and regular loads are reported as being delivered to Kirkcaldy Harbour. These loads are reported as "flint boulders" or simply as "flint" without specifying whether or not it was ground. It is not possible, therefore, to say if ground flint was being imported to supplement that processed at the mill. However this is highly likely as the throughput of the small Balwearie Mill was so limited that by 1884 they acquired the adjoining Hole Mill and converted it to flint grinding [V.R]. The output of these mills is not known. However judging by their physical size Hole Mill must have produced at least ten times as much as its smaller neighbour.

There was also a demand for bone ash but again the source is not known. This material was used to improve the "body" of the products, which were still only earthenware. It appears that the many pieces of chinaware attributed to the Pottery were bought in as finished pieces and decorated overglaze or personalised in gilding by adding a name or message such as William Young's christening mug that says much for A R Young's opinion of the quality of the products of the Pottery.

One of the main essential components of pottery production that always must be considered is water and in an industrial Pottery of this type the quantities required must have been vast. Throughout all of its history there was a possible source from the Causengutter that flowed in a culvert through the site. This ditch may have originally been spasmodic in flow as it did not drain a large area but as it was used to remove the water from the clayfield it is probable that it later flowed fairly continually. Certainly considering the size of the culvert put in by the Railway Company it would appear that substantial flows were anticipated. It is not known for certain that this water was ever used but it is difficult to imagine that such a convenient source would be ignored for production purposes and it is highly likely that the ponds situated in the clay fields were fed from this source. These ponds continued in use until the final closure of the Pottery and were also used to soak the "willows" for the crate shop as well as providing a continual if somewhat dangerous attraction to the local children. There was even a suggestion that they could be used as skating rinks in cold winters but this does not appear to have been officially agreed to. There were also wells and pumps within the Pottery but as the area had been heavily mined for coal many years earlier perhaps the quality was not very high. Drinking water had also been provided by the Town Council by the introduction of the "Lothrie" piped supply. However the pipe sizes were fairly small it is unlikely there would have been sufficient supply to provide all the Pottery requirements.

The Pottery had become over the years more and more organised on a production line basis so that items flowed through the process from worker to worker with each one contributing a small amount. For example a worker might spent much of his working life making or attaching handles and could even be so specialized that he only worked with teacup handles. One worker, John Sim, was to claim that he started as a handler in 1871 and continued in this task for the next forty year [FA 30/4/1910]. There were also dippers, painters, gilders, spongers, jolly men, sagger makers, kiln packers, kiln attendants, turners and other separate skills. In addition there were many support workers such as engineers, boilermen, packers, dispatchers, salesmen and office staff [CR1891].

There can be little doubt that as many tasks as possible would have been mechanised and that the machinery was steam powered although except for the trades mentioned in the Census Returns such as Jollies and Lathes there are no details of the different machines used which were only described as being the "best" or "latest".

The overall impression given is of a highly organized and well-run enterprise well able to take any business opportunity presented. The market had been expanded into England, Ireland, Germany and the Far East as well as throughout Scotland to absorb the great increase in output. Although the late 1880's were not generally a period of business expansion by 1892 the R.V. of the Pottery had increased to £400 and the Brick and Tile Works to £50. This is the first time the two sections had been valued separately and as it can be reasonably assumed that there had been very little increase in the value of the Works it is seen that during the period when Young was a manager the Pottery had more than doubled in value and probably much more in output.

The firm of David Methven and Sons, however constituted, appears to have been reasonable employers by the standards of that time and wages were at or about the Scottish average. In common with most employers they were reluctant to increase wages and were quite willing to reduce wages if economic conditions were not favourable as reported in the Fifeshire Advertiser [22/5/1886]

> "Owing to the depression in trade notice has been given
> of a reduction in wages in Kirkcaldy Pottery"

This gave rise to a strike that was not settled until June [FA 19/6/1886]. The result was not reported but was presumably acceptable to both sides.

An indication of the control the Master had over his employee is given in the Minute Of Agreement between David Methven & Sons and Andrew Elder for his seven year apprenticeship as an enamel painter or gilder in 1883 in which he agreed viz:-

> "....to serve and obey the said David Methven and Sons, and others aforesaid, and any oversman named by them during the said seven years, in their art and trade, honestly and diligently, during the ordinary hours of their factory by day, and less or more per day according to the exigencies of their business, of which they shall be sole judges ...."

For this Andrew was paid 15p per week in his first year rising to 40p in the seventh but only if his output justified such payments. The Agreement was legally binding on Andrew to work for the seven years although the employer waived his right to have a financial penalty on his father who was a kilnman in the Pottery. The document was mainly printed with gaps to be filled in giving the details. This was undertaken by William Young, Clerk to DM&S, and confusingly the date of signing is given as 1886 some three years after the start of the apprenticeship. At that time William must have been gaining all round experience by working in the office.

No doubt the employers were typical of their time and they were usually very powerful. However when trade was better the workers were in a slightly stronger position and more confident. Added to this there was a slow but steady increase in Trade Union activity much to the annoyance of the employers. Thus when Henry Johnstone, a potter, who was engaged in making Cheese Stands at a rate of 23p a dozen was instructed to change to making smaller ones at 15p a dozen it must have come as a surprise when he refused and requested other work. In turn when this was refused he left claiming wrongful dismissal. When this was taken to Court Johnstone lost his case as he was unable to prove a loss of income [FA 16/8/1889]. In the Court Action the Pottery Manager, Alex. Baillie, appeared for the Firm and stated that it was the policy of all the master Potters to keep the wages similar throughout Scotland.

While it is unreasonable to judge the conditions by today's standards there is no doubt the employers had the upper hand and the backing of the "Law". For example when John Neilson who was in his third year of employment as a kilnman gave four weeks notice of his intention to leave the employers were very displeased claiming that he had a four year contract on agreed increasing wages. [This may have been some form of training arrangement although not a formal apprenticeship]. In response the employers refused to pay Nelson his "lie time" of three days being 45p [He earned 90p per week in his second year] and further claimed he was due 50p for "damages". This matter was placed before the Sheriff who ruled that Nelson was due his wages but the employers were entitled to be paid for the damages. He also awarded the employers their "expenses". [FA 19th June & 3rd & 24th July 1886].

Wages for time served tradesmen at this time were about 2.5p per hour giving a weekly wage of £1.25 at a time when a 4 pound loaf of bread was slightly more than 3.5p [FA26/6/1886]. The working week was still five days of 6.30 am to 6.30 pm and the Saturday normally finishing at 2pm. Holidays were still very minimal being usually one or two days at the New Year and perhaps two or three days in the summer. These holidays were all unpaid and no doubt the employers would have taken full advantage of the shut downs to carry out essential repairs and maintenance without interfering with production. In judging these conditions it should be noted that, in general, they were better that those in the English Potteries.

In common with most employers DM&S employed many children as shown in the 1871 Census Returns where there were 56 boys and 16 girls out of a total workforce of 221 listed. These youngsters would have carried out only menial tasks at no doubt very low wages with the hope that they would eventually be trained for more skilled tasks. Unfortunately this frequently did not happen and they were "paid off" either when they could command adult wages or their tasks were replaced by mechanisation [SPHR No 16]

Those lucky enough to become apprentices, on the other hand, were "bound" to their masters for the whole period of their indenture under the Master and Servants Act of 1867-68 which gave the Master the power to take apprentices to Court it the left his employment during the period the apprenticeship. DM&S used this power when necessary although they did not always win the Court Action.

A R Young, who was very much a self made man due to his natural abilities coupled to hard work and studies, admired such qualities in others and was very keen to encourage the workers, at least the males, to copy him. To facilitate this he gave over a small house to be converted into the "Kirkcaldy Pottery Reading Room" and help to finance the provision of books and equipment. At the opening on 2/12/1887 A R Young, as chairman of the meeting, made a speech in which he claimed this new venture was the first of its type in the area and being the combined effort of both Master and employee was an example to the other industries. He also spoke at length of the great progress in the Pottery over the "last thirty years". He also encouraged the workers to make full success of the Reading Room and to enjoy expanding the knowledge of their trade [FA 3/12/1887]. This venture was successful and by the end of the first year under the chairmanship of Baillie, the Pottery Manager, there were II0 members and the library had been helped by a donation of £5 from Mrs. Methven [FA 14/12/1888].

By today's standards working and living conditions were very bad and the workers were definitely exploited when it is seen that the employers could and did make vast fortunes. It would not have seemed thus to the workers at that time as their life style was considered to be and was "normal". It was expected that every winter they would be "laid off" or put on "short time" and their wages and wage rates would be cut if the economic conditions were poor. Since with their low wages there was little opportunity to save for such periods and no form of Social Security such periods must have been very difficult. The newspapers of the time laud the employers because they ran "soup kitchens" where soup and bread was supplied to the needy especially children. The regular donations of food and help by these "rich" people were regularly reported without any comment on the possible social injustice. This is hardly surprising as the newspaper owners would be fully aware of their market.

In an attempt to have some protection some of the potters formed Unions, which the employers although not actively discouraging certainly did not encourage. Approval was given to Friendly Societies such as the "Apron Men" which were not militant. The potters also regularly made collection to help their colleagues who were unable to work and frequently raised funds by holding concerts featuring local talent.

As would be expected the newspapers only report the slightly unusual occasions in the potter's lives such as weddings, accidents, fights, thefts etc. No doubt within the limits of their experience the potters and their families were happy looking forward to annual outings as much as workers today anticipate their annual holidays

By 1891 the Pottery was, probably, reaching its zenith with regards to the size of the workforce, which amounted to about 270 persons [CR1891]. Although in these Returns the precise skills are not as well defined as in the earlier ones this is likely to be due to the methods adopted by Census enumerators and not any significant change in the working methods that would have still been still very specialised

There can be very little doubt that the business was very profitable and they were able to enhance this by selling the Clay Right over 97.5 acres of land and a dwelling house at Southerton to Kirkcaldy Town Council [423.41 12/3/1891] to facilitate the formation of Beveridge Park. With this sale the true value of the clay was seen especially when added to the monies already received from the Railway Company. They still only paid the original agreed sum [£5 per annum] for the Clay Rights. In the same year A R Young expanded his personal holding by purchasing land on the west side of Buchanan Street no doubt with a view to develop it [427.167 8/5/1891].

On his death on 19th April 1892 James left a personal fortune of some £92,000 made up mainly of investments at home and abroad and secured loans to several local businessmen. As well as approximately £1,000 in the bank there was about £30,000 registered as "Mutual access with wife". It is not known if James was a particularly "advanced" husband for those Victorian times or if his health had been such that she required this access. What ever reason his wife, Mary, an American, must have been a strong character as although James named her and several other male relatives as Executors in his Will they all declined to act and she was left in complete control although she was "under burden to clothe and educate their children" who could also borrow from the Estate at 5% interest. This Will had been prepared in Dundee in 1884 by a firm of solicitors, Dow, who were related by marriage to the Cox family. The Dows appear to have been connected to the Kirkcaldy area also as they were to become lawyers in the area and married into the Millie family who were local linen weavers. Judging by the Cox family photograph album James had a good relationship with his sister and sister-in-law as his photograph appears in several family group photographs.

As arranged in 1887 on James's death A R Young with his sons, William and Andrew B., in effect took over control of the firm as well as ownership of the Pottery and Works. There must have also been some form of financial agreement that is not shown in the various Titles as the new partnership did not gain full control until about 1909 [FA 27/6/1914]. It is reasonable to assume that there was a financial arrangement whereby the purchase of the property and James's share in the firm was paid for out of profits.

The partnership was later by expanded in 1897 to include the fourth son, James Methven Young, who had been employed in the Pottery since 1887[circa]. There can be no doubt where this son's christian names were derived.

A. R. Young had thirteen children between 1864 and 1882 of whom three died in infancy or very young and without doubt he was very loving father and husband. Equally without doubt he was an extremely able businessman having worked his way up from office boy to the major shareholder of what at its peak was one of the largest Potteries in Scotland a condition which he had contributed much to. The drive he had already shown was to continue until his death and he was most definitely the senior partner.

Naturally with such a large family they could not all be employed in the business and the other three sons who reached adulthood trained for other professions. John Buchanan Young [b 1867], who was considered to be particularly intelligent, studied for a M.A. degree at Edinburgh University before converting to Law studies at which he was a regular prizewinner. Frank [b1869] was apparently equally clever and added the study of medicine to his Arts Honours Degree. He also was a regular prizewinner who unfortunately died in 1899 before qualifying as a doctor [FA 4/3/1899]. Arthur the tenth child [b 1878] trained as an engineer and died in South Africa of blackwater fever.

On assuming control the Youngs, despite it being a period of trade depression, still looked forward to better times and the future expansion of their enterprises. With this in mind in 1893 A R Young personally purchased 24 acres of the old clay field, Milton Acres, from Ferguson of Raith. Most of the clay had already been extracted and although it still contained the Brick Works and part of the Tile Works the remainder was available for development [497.27 16/5/1893]. Immediately after purchasing this land they sold a strip of the land with the Clay Right to the School Board for the construction of the new Abbotshall Primary School [497.94 14/6/1893].

In March of 1893 when A B Young was to be married the workers held a social at which he was presented with a clock and some silver plate. This occasion was attended by his father and mother accompanied by his brothers and sisters. In reply to the presentation Andrew, who was described as a "junior partner" quoted one of his father's favourite maxims "Do what ever comes to hand, no matter what it is. Do it promptly and thoroughly". A sentiment that surely his father had always followed. Not one to miss any chance to get his message over A R Young also made a speech that was fully reported.

Fifeshire Advertiser   25 March 1893

> I have known the Pottery for over forty years, longer than any other man now about it and I think that there has always been fairly good feelings existing between employers and employed. As much as I venture to say as existed in any other factory. I am very much afraid that we will not have any improvement in trade for sometime to come. Every trade is bad and shopkeepers all over the Kingdom will say "nothing doing". We can only hope that better times will come sooner than we can with confidence look for.

This pessimistic outlook was quickly turned to a business advantage as building cost were equally low enabling the construction of a "new jolly shop fitted out with the latest machines for making tea ware and all sorts of flat plates". Apparently nothing as "trivial" as a national trade depression could deter A R Young from seeing a business opportunity and a reason for expanding.

This large and successful business was not enough for the Youngs and in late 1895 they took over a share in the West Lothian Pottery Co. Ltd. in Bo'ness, which they operated until 1929 [SPHR 20 p49]. The following year they purchased part of the stock from the Possil Pottery, which was in financial difficulties. Although no details are given of the contents of this 'stock' there can be no doubt that they saw a profit in this transaction which cost them £10.

As the economy started to improve later that decade so did the fortune of the Youngs and their business. This was a good reason to expand by building a new Gilding Shop on Sands Road in 1896[FA 21/II/1896] and a new Warehouse the following year [KTC records]. [NB Sands Road is now the Esplanade]. As if expanding the Pottery was not enough they also built a new Brick and Tile Works in 1897 near to the original site. All of these new developments must have represented a considerable financial outlay. It is not known if the funds were obtained from savings or borrowed but if the latter was the case the property was not used as security.

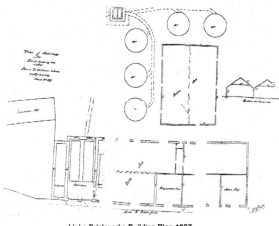

Links Brickworks Building Plan 1897

The decision to build a new brick works no doubt made good economic sense especially as the outlay would have been reasonably low even allowing for new brick making machinery which raised the output per man from about 600 bricks per day to 2,000. Competition however was very strong as the various Coal Companies opened their own Works to process waste clay from the mines to make common bricks which although not visually so attractive were very competitive in price even though DM&S still had the advantage of cheap clay from their clay field in Hutchison Park [now the site of Balwearie High School].

This expansion continued throughout the Works and Pottery and could not be ignored by the local newspapers. The Fifeshire Advertiser reported on June the 31st 1897

Notes from West End

The march of improvement is still westwards. It has emerged from the High Street of Kirkcaldy to Links Street. A R Young of Links Pottery has recently made a purchase at 129 Links Street and is having it pulled down in order to have his new warehouses extended over that space. The property now has a frontage of 100 feet and projects an inconvenient depth into the pavement which is here restricted. By the operation the frontage will be carried back and 3 feet thrown into the street. This is by no means the only improvement that is in progress in connection with the pottery. Vast extensions to the works being in progress. The destruction of the old and the erection of new buildings.

It will be noted that the writer, probably quite rightly, attributes the expansion to the father and not the partnership and still refers to the Pottery as "Links" and not "Kirkcaldy". This old name was to remain in common use locally until the Pottery closed and even later. It is also indicative of the increase in trade that the new 1896 warehouse was considered as inadequate the following year.

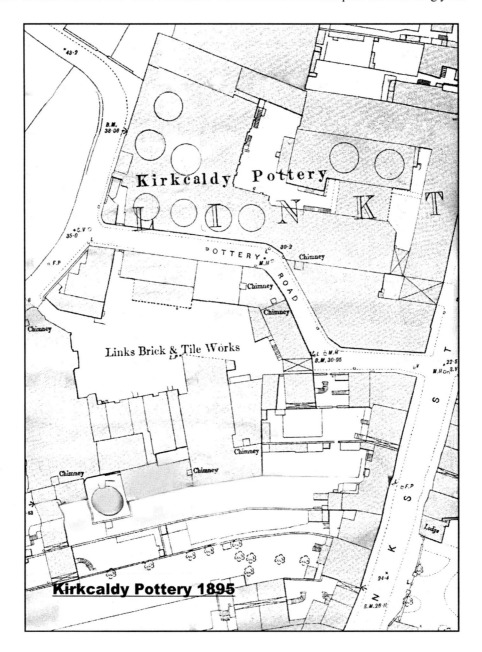
Kirkcaldy Pottery 1895

All of these new buildings with the associated installation of new machinery must have produced a great increase in output. As would be expected it was also reflected by increases in the Rateable Values. When the Youngs took over in 1892 the Pottery was given a value of £400 and the Brick and Tile Works a further £50. These values continued until 1898 when there was a reassessment on completion of the various extensions and a value of £650 was applied to both enterprises this being a total increase of some 40% in six years. Despite the building of the new Brownware Pottery and other improvements this value continued until 1909.

Kirkcaldy Pottery about 1900

The Pottery buildings start at the road leading off to the left [Methven Road]. The main gate is behind the lamppost with the girl in the white apron

As well as the main buildings the partnership of DM&S owned other workshops between Links Street and the sea as well as about 50 houses, which were mainly occupied by their employees. AR Young also personally owned approximately 30 workers' houses while he still owned his own house in Milton Road as well as another substantial villa in the same street, Fairview, which was occupied by William in 1900 having left a company house in James Street.

Strangely after all of these years the was still a doubt about the Titles for the Pottery and Brick and Tile Works but fortunately Munro Ferguson of Raith Estate again agreed that the Youngs did have a good Title [745.174 14/4/1900].

The 1901 Census Returns does not give precise details of the employee numbers but it is reasonable to assume that the bulk of the pottery workers listed as living near the Pottery would have worked. It appears that the workforce had expanded with the various extensions but probably not in the same proportion. Any increase in output would be attributed mainly to the increase in mechanisation. Although the Youngs were in full command they were assisted by various Pottery Managers, Alex. Baillie from 1879 to 1897, Alex. Sutherland from 1897 to 1901 and James Mckechnie from 1901 to 1910. These dates are approximately and are based on Newspapers and Valuation Rolls.

The local newspapers continued to report on small occurrences affecting the potters who married, fought and committed minor crimes such as breach of the peace and trespass or suffered accidents. No doubt minor pilfering from the Pottery continued and workers were still being occasionally caught. The Reading Room continued to be active and by 1894 held 300 books and even allowed female employees access! This facility continued to be popular for a few years more until it became redundant about 1910 as larger and better-stocked free public libraries were opened.

Trade especially to foreign markets continued to expand along with the Pottery and a new Biscuit Warehouse was built to accommodate the increase. After all of this physical expansion of the Pottery there must have been a great feeling of optimism and it was decided to undertake the most ambitious improvement in 1902 when the old Tile and Fireclay Works were demolished to make way for a new Brownware Pottery which was reported as being "probably the best in Scotland fitted up with the latest machinery for making brown and jet wares. The Links Pottery during the last 45 years has grown three times its size and is now one of the finest and best equipped in Scotland". The section of the old Pottery used for brownware was converted to exclusively produce whiteware [FA 5/4/1902].

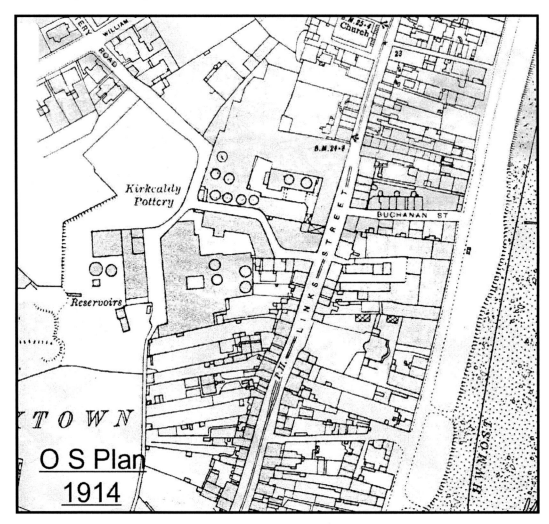

Unfortunately the building plans for this conversion no longer exist and the only details available are those given in the next Ordnance Survey Plan. Although this plan was not published until 1914 it shows clearly the position and layout of the new Brick Works and the Brownware Pottery [South Pottery]. It appears that there were four kilns in this area. It will be noted that the circular kilns at the Brickworks shown on the building plans if built no longer exist.

With the great advantage of hindsight the building of the Brownware Pottery was perhaps the only serious business mistake made by A R Young throughout his long career and for many reasons it is doubtful if this new Pottery ever reached full production.

As part of an extension of the North Pottery a new kiln was added about 1903 and the submitted drawing shows the type of kiln in use which is probably the same type as built in the new South Pottery. It also shows that small square muffle kilns were installed in the same kiln house.

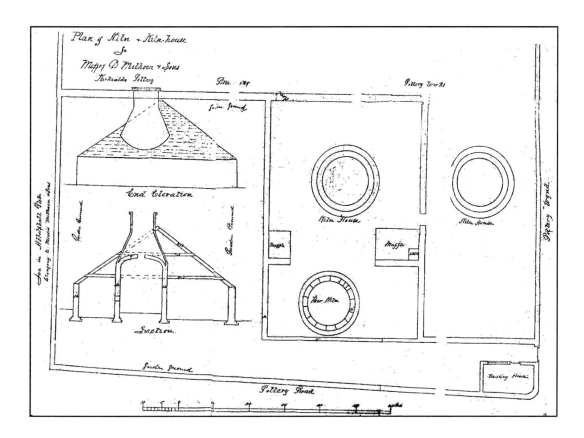

Kirkcaldy/Links Pottery only produced earthenware both red and white, which was generally restricted to low quality mass-produced items with the exception of "Abbotsford Ware". This practice had proved very successful with the increasingly affluent "Lower Classes" who could find within the range of products both "every day" and "best" wares. There was constant competition from other Potteries in Scotland and more importantly from the English Potteries who were producing much finer wares such as "Bone China". The expansion of the Kirkcaldy Pottery shows very clearly that they thought they were very able to tackle this competition despite the number of dealers in the area advertising their competitor's wares and were prepared to advertise this..

Advert from 1908

It is interesting to note that they were awarded a "Prize Medal" at the Paris 1896 Exhibition against competition from many other Potteries.

The market for Kirkcaldy Pottery had been both throughout Scotland, England and Ireland as well as overseas in North America, Far East [especially Burma], Australasia and on the Continent of Europe. From the late 1800s these overseas markets especially in America and Europe were becoming steadily more difficult for British Potteries due to the expansion of pottery production in those areas and their tax laws. If this was not bad enough the foreign potters soon recognised that Britain was a lucrative market due in part to the relative affluence of the British people and they were quick to take advantage of this. By 1910 the British market for pottery and glass was deluged with cheap European [mainly German] wares that were allowed into this country tax-free while British exports were

84

subjected to a tax of 100% in Germany and 60% in the USA [FA 15/1/1910]. This lead to the formation of the "Tariff Reform Movement" which, naturally was supported by many potters and their employers. W. Young was particularly active in this movement and produced a full report explaining his and others views on the situation.

Tariff Reform [F A 15 & 22/1/1910]

There is no branch of manufacturing in this country which has suffered so much from the free importation of goods manufactured on the Continent as the China and Glass trades. During the last twenty years or so a large number of potteries and glass works in Scotland and the north of England as well as Staffordshire have had to be closed down for the want of business. This has been a ruinous affair for manufacturers whose works in which their capital was invested are standing empty. It has been a bad time for the workers. In a Pottery the great majority of the employees are skilled artisans who have served long apprenticeships [between 4 & 7 years]. The want of employment has caused a great displacement of labour. If they can get work at all it is only in other trades as labourers at about half the rate of wages they would have at their own employment. During the past year the value of china and glass imported into Britain was nearly £1,000,000 worth, which means a loss of wages of £300,000.

The absurdity of the present free importation is emphasised by the fact that a very large quantity of raw clay, about 500,000 tons is shipped annually from the south west of England to the Continent. The coal used to burn the clay is shipped from Fife Ports. There is no export duty. Not only do we as a Nation supply the foreigner with his raw material which he manufactures into goods and sends them here at prices which they cannot be made in this country, we are parting with our capital. Every ton of clay exported makes this country poorer in resources. They are the only raw materials we have and they cannot be replaced.

Now how does the foreigner treat British pottery goods sent to his country? On ordinary earthenware the duty imposed by Germany is 8/- [40p] per hundredweight [50Kg], which as nearly as possible doubles the invoice price of it. This shuts it out completely all but the highest grade of semi porcelain and china. The same applies to the USA where the duty is 60%. Here again ordinary grades are shut out and only the highest grades are imported from Great Britain. In both countries the tariff has had the affect of stimulating the pottery industry and many large new works have been built in the last 12 years. The few potteries who are working are not busy indeed short time has become chronic. Some departments there are many empty benches, machines standing idle solely through the cheap goods imported from Germany, Holland, France and Austria. These goods are delivered free of carriage and packing at prices at which workmen here would require for the making them. It is simply impossible to keep up with this year by year as imports keep mounting up. There are dozens of former pottery workers presently employed in the linoleum works who have left on account of short time. They are only receiving labourer's wages but it is steady.

This type of complaint of unfair foreign competition was typical of the time and no doubt was by and large reasonably accurate. It was also a convenient excuse to cover up the basic troubles in the Potteries, which despite all the "improvements" were not producing wares of a quality and at a price which could still command large-scale markets. The complaint about foreign import taxes certainly can be accepted for those markets but does not explain why foreign goods should be cheaper in the British Isles than the comparable British product especially as Young claims that the raw materials were supplied from this country. Perhaps the true answer was that there had been under investment in more productive methods. Similar complaints about foreign competition are still being made today regarding imported cars, motorcycles and electronics etc. that have and still are damaging British industries.

Even accepting that Young would have overstated the situation for effect, the future did not look good for the Pottery. It will be noted that he also claimed that this problem had been ongoing for some twenty years and this must bring into question the viability of building the new brownware Pottery unless this was seen as a way of reducing the costs and becoming more competitive. Bad as things were they were soon to become worse.

Although these pressures had been placed on the Potteries in Kirkcaldy there were still regular importations of flint from Dieppe and clay from south west England including one load of "black clay" in November 1910 presumably to make "mourning ware" for Edward VII's death [FA 26/11/1910]. It is interesting to note that this clay was delivered in a sailing schooner.

Shortly after Young's report was published six long serving workers retired from the Pottery and this was reported fully in the Fifeshire Advertiser on 30th April 1910 giving a good insight into the Pottery. It speaks volumes for both the steadiness and capabilities of the employees and the appreciation of the firm.

> David Stenhouse foreman printer started under old Boswall Lindsay in the Brick and Tile Works and wrought with Sandy Lawson in the Brick Kiln for a season. After the Brickfields stopped the useful Stenhouse went down to the Pottery and wrought as a half timer going to Peter Purves's School for 1.5 hours then up to the work again. He afterwards served his apprenticeship as a printer and for the last 30 years has been foreman of that Department. He worked for 42.5 years.

> John Sim 40 years in the Pottery....., and a handler he has been for 40 years without a break.

> John Smith Crate maker holds the record for long service being in the Links Pottery for 49 years without a break

> William Stark after serving an apprenticeship as a crate maker under the late Sandy Buist. The latter we may mention travelled from Gallatown to Links Pottery for 43 years in the days when there were no [tram]cars and the only convenience Sandy got was a hurl in a cart if he was lucky

> William Stark Packer 2 Buchanan Street worked for the long period of 52 years. He began his working life in the Links Pottery 52 years ago but at one period spent 5 years in Glasgow so strictly speaking his period of service with he firm was only 48 years. He has never had a day off through illness.

> David Herd one of the best known and popular earthenware commercial travellers in Scotland. Represented D.M.&S. for many years. He began commercial training in the office of Links Pottery under the supervision of Mr A R Young now head of the firm

> Robert Stewart a pottery printer who had been employed for 48.5 years without a break replied.

> During the greater portion of this long period Mr. A R Young has been head of affairs in the Kirkcaldy Pottery and everything appears to have prospered under the able guidance of him and his sons. Year by year important improvements have been introduced and extensive additions made to the works. First a large biscuit warehouse and sponging shop combined was built. Then a large pressing shop and mould chamber. Next came a printing shop which was erected on the late Mr. Methven's Garden and this was followed by a jolly shop fitted up with the latest machines for making teaware and all sorts of flat plates. One of the most important improvements was the erection of a substantial range of offices and showrooms with a frontage to Links Street which has since still further extended on the east wing. This formed a decided improvement for that part of Links. It was found necessary to further extend the biscuit warehouse to make room for the greatly increased stocks due to the large and growing foreign trade. Another important improvement was the conversion of the old Tile Works into a first class

> Brownware Pottery, probably the best in Scotland fitted up with the latest machinery for making brown and jet wares. The Links Pottery during these 45 Years has grown three times the size it was when the subjects of our sketch were boys and is now the finest and best equipped in Scotland.

This article is somewhat laudatory which is not surprising as presumably the details were supplied from the Pottery but it is interesting to note that with the exception of the handler these long-lived workers were employed away from the clay and glaze, which were the hazardous materials. There are surprisingly few retirements reported in the newspapers.

In or about 1910 they also closed the Brick Works [V.R.] and the last connection with Adam and the original purpose was severed. It is likely that the Works had not made any profit for some years and indeed may have been running at a loss. With this closure the requirement for local clay was reduced dramatically and although they continued to use the clay in the Brownware Pottery there was no need for the tramway from the clayfield which was closed and the clay hauled by horse and cart and dumped into access chutes off the west side in what is now Saunders Street.

By 1912 the economic situation had not improved much and the worker/employer relations for most industries were so poor that strikes were becoming very frequent. The shortage of coal due to a miners' dispute caused the Railway Companies problems, which in turn affected the Pottery when orders manufactured could not be dispatched nor could supplies be delivered. The Pottery production was so severely restricted that the workers were put on "short time" having their hours and of course their wages cut from 10 hours to 7.5 hours per day although there was still sufficient coal in store to continue full time working [FA 9/3/1912].

The following year the potters having given the appropriate notice came out on strike for an increase in wages of 15%. This does seem to be a large increase being greater than inflation and was probably due to fact that wages had fallen behind inflation over a period of years. This strike only lasted two weeks when a compromise was reached bringing the Kirkcaldy wages into line with those in Glasgow and Bo'ness [FA 19/4/1913]. The warning was given that this increase in wages must raise the cost of the articles and that this would be "bad".

As the A. R. Young was no longer a young man he would presumably be considering retirement and started rearranging his affairs. Firstly he gave the house, Fairview, to William who had lived in it for many years [Lib 1027.69 12/9/1907] and then transferred much of his personal property into the partnership along with a life rent protection for his two surviving daughters, Isobel and Marion [Lib II59.150 9/4/1910, Lib 1290.147 18.8.1913, Lib 1291.77 5/7/1913 and others]. These moves may have been encouraged by his failing health and he supported them by a new Will signed on the 5th July 1913 in which ARY left all of his Estate to his three sons who were co-partners and the forth son, John, an advocate in Edinburgh. The two daughters who were unmarried were to get the life rent of their father's house and all his household goods as their mother had died two years earlier. Quickly after this ARY decided or was persuaded that this Settlement was unfair and he made a new Will on the 22nd July 1913 in which his Estate was divided equally between all of his children. Thus John and his sisters would eventually have a small share in the firm but not the property owned by it which must pass to the surviving partners as agreed earlier. Having settled his affairs to his satisfaction ARY should have been able to look forward to a quiet life but this was not to be as 1914 was to be one of the worst in the Pottery's history.

In June the Rockingham potters [brownware] came out on strike for an increase in wages and with this matter unresolved ARY died on 22/6/1914 after a short illness. As would be expected a full obituary was published in the local newspapers [FA 27/6/1914]

Death of Mr. A.R.Young Kirkcaldy

By the death of A.R.Young senior partner of the firm of D.M.&S. Kirkcaldy Pottery which took place on Monday at Abbotsford Kirkcaldy has lost a public man who served her interests well for two generations. Although failing in health for sometime it is only three months since he was in his office taking an active interest in the business.

Mr. Young was a native of Kirkcaldy and was born in 1837. He went direct from school to the Links pottery in August 1851 when he was 14 years of age. He discharged his duty with characteristic diligence and soon made himself so familiar with all the Departments of the work that he became indispensable to his employers. As Commercial Traveller he did much to build up the business and extend the connections of the firm. 20 years after he first went to the business i.e. in 1871 he was assumed as a partner and in 1887 two of his sons also became partners. Six years ago he and his family finally acquired the business. Mrs. Young predeceased him by three years. He is survived by a family of six, four sons and two daughters - The three sons who were partners with him in the business and Mr. J.B. Young the well known Edinburgh advocate. Although being an exceptionally busy man Mr. Young found time in his leisure to take part in the public life of the Town. He was a member of Kirkcaldy Town Council for 12 years the last 5 of which he was Honorary Treasurer of the Burgh For about 40 years he was a member of Kirkcaldy and Dysart Water Commission and most of that time was Treasurer - only resigning that office last year when failing health prevented him from discharging his duties. He took a keen interest in Educational affairs. He was for many years a member of Kirkcaldy School Board and for several years chairman. As Governor of the Philp's Trust he also gave good service his business acumen and knowledge being of valuable assistance in dealing with the various properties belonging to the Trust. He was a trustee of the Kirkcaldy Savings Bank and one of the original directors of the Fife Electric Power Company. He was also a member of the Chamber of Commerce, while numerous private companies considered they had acquired a valuable asset when they secured Mr. A.R.Young as one of their directors.

In Politics Mr. Young was a keen Unionist and sometime acting as Chairman for of the Association. He was an enthusiastic member and office bearer of St Brycedale Church and one of the oldest members of Session. as a deacon and member of the Building Committee Mr. Young rendered valuable service in the erection of the present handsome edifice. The funeral took place on Thursday and was attended by a large number of all classes of the Community including representatives of public bodies. A service was conducted in the house by Rev. William Todd of St Brycedale and Rev Francis [Raith] and a short service was conducted at the grave in Abbotshall Church Yard by Rev William Todd. The chief mourners were Messers William, Andrew, John, and James, sons, Andrew Ramsay and Andrew Francis, grandsons, John Buchanan and Mathew Ireland, nephews, Alex Balfour, Glasgow, and James Wishart, friends.

The following month there was further tributes from the church and the Water Commissioners [FA II/7/1914 & 18/7/1914].

This obituary is truly a story from the Victorian Age of the office boy eventually owning the business. His success is borne out by his Estate that was registered [8/8/1914] at almost £83,000 excluding the value of the Pottery and its associated properties. This is even more remarkable when it is noted that at that time a potter would consider himself very lucky if he made £100 per year. Recalling the funeral many years later his granddaughter spoke of being lifted by a maid up to the window to watch the cortege "which seemed to go on for ever" and the maid explaining that there would probably never be another funeral that would be so grand. It is rather nice to see that Alex Balfour who had been a rival salesman for many years had still remained such a good friend. James Wishart was a former employee who had left many years earlier to become the manger at Pollockshaws Pottery and for a short period was manager at Fife Pottery.

It is interesting to speculate how many of the Pottery workers attended the funeral of their long time colleague and employer especially as many of them were still out on strike. The strike continued throughout July when the whiteware potters decided to join the brownware workers and served the required three weeks notice [FA 18/7/1914] with a request for a 20% increase in wages. A few days before the notice expired events were overtaken by the outbreak of the First World War. Despite this the potters still came out on strike leaving only the women and girls at work. The Youngs, never ones to miss an opportunity, called a meeting with representatives of each department in the Pottery, which was out on strike at which they offered

> In spite of the War the firm offered to provide work even though orders were being cancelled or execution indefinitely postponed for about four days a week as long as the clay lasted, which might be 2-3 months. In short it was proposed that the question of wages should be left as it is, without prejudice to either side, and when affairs returned to their normal condition they could be taken up if the men so desired. The representatives agreed to put this offer before their comrades and promised to give their reply by 10 am on Thursday. No communication was received by the firm and their offer was accordingly withdrawn. In this particular Pottery it is chiefly men to the number of 65 who have left their work but about 200 women and girls will ultimately be thrown out of employment. As far as possible they are being kept employed but in a week or two they will be idle also.
>
> [FA 15/8/1914].

This strike only lasted about one more week when it was abandoned and a temporary continuation agreed [FA 22/9/1914]. The biscuit and glost kilnmen returned immediately and the remainder of the workers in stages thereafter.

From these reports it is seen that there were only 65 skilled men in the Pottery and 200 women and girls plus no doubt a number of unskilled male labourers and boys making a total of about 300 persons. Many of these females would have been employed on the "women's" work such as decorators, gilders, spongers, transferers assistants and in the ancillary sections of storekeeper, packer and office workers. All of the former group, with the exception of some of the gilders, would have worked in the Whiteware Pottery which had only been on strike for about two weeks and it can be assumed there was enough biscuit ware available for them to continue their work and that the muffle kilns did not require the skilled men to fire them.

It must be remembered that in most of these actions the potters in Kirkcaldy Pottery would be acting along with those in the other Potteries in Kirkcaldy and Scotland in general.

It also seems that both sides of the dispute considered that the War would not last long, maybe not even for 2-3 months, an assumption that was far from correct. Within a few weeks of the start, Captain David G Methven the only son of the late James Methven, a regular officer in the Seaforth Highlanders, was killed in the trenches [FA 31/10/1914].

The Pottery continued in production and importing white clay although production had to be restricted since the home market was very depressed and the overseas markets virtually non-existent. Although it is hard to imagine that pottery could be considered as an essential product for the war effort potters were exempt from service in the early years of the war. Despite this many of them did volunteer following the "patriotic" advice from the "Church" and in the newspapers. Many such as the two Farmer brothers enlisted immediately for service as they were in the Reserve Army. The partners were not liable for service due to their age as James M. the youngest was 46 years old at the outbreak of hostilities. James had been an officer in the local "Volunteers". William did join the local Special Constabulary and was prepared to help if possible.

Trade did continue all be it at a low level that was boosted by occasional but large orders of mugs for the Royal Navy at the opening of the Rosyth Dockyard and smaller orders from hospitals and railways. The range of decoration was extended to include themes of a patriotic nature. Life in the Pottery would have been fairly quiet punctuated by regular collections especially for the "Belgium Fund" which was well supported in the area due to the presence of a very active local lady from that country.

Over the first year of the war the only report concerning the Pottery in the local newspapers was a very minor fire involving one haystack in 1915 [FA 3/7/1915]. By the end of 1915 the Pottery must have been reasonably active in proportion to the numbers still working as the potters felt confident enough to request and increase in wages [FA 6/11/195]. This claim was apparently unsuccessful and the outcome was not reported. Later in 1917 after negotiations between the Union and the Scottish Pottery owners it was agreed to raise the wages of the Scottish Pottery workers by 10% in February. This was refused by the Kirkcaldy Pottery owners. The matter was quickly solved by the workers coming out on strike and after the intervention of the General Secretary of the Male and Female Pottery Workers Society the employers quickly agreed and backdated the rise to the national date of 7th February 1917. This rise was given in the form of a "War Bonus" which could be removed at the end of hostilities [FA 3/3/1917]. This unusual form of wage increase had been introduced by the Government and remained in use up to 1921. The individual increases were not reported but the "bonus" appears to have been in the region of 50%-60% by 1918.

These increases would have been very good if full time working was available. However it was far different as the Pottery was mainly on short time and examples have been quoted of workmen enlisting simply because they could not maintain their families on the "take home" wages available and would be paid more in the "Trenches of France"

In September David Herd completed fifty years service with the firm and although his long service had been recognised only a few years earlier he was presented with a gold watch in recognition of his service as a commercial traveller for the firm covering the North of England and the whole of Scotland. In his reply Mr. Herd noted the tremendous change there had been in trade over his fifty years and cited Edinburgh as an example claiming that there was not one dealer left who was working when he commenced travelling about 1875. He, of course, remarked on the lack of business at the time and hoped it would return to normal after the war [FA 22/9/1917]. It appeared that this wish would be fulfilled by June of 1918 when trade was very brisk and there appears to have been a shortage of labour [FA 22/6/1918]. This mini boom was short lived.

Compared to their father the sons were not so active in public life. William was a chairman and very active participant in the Kirkcaldy Naturalist Society and a Special Constable. James was a Town Councillor. Any comparison would however be unfair.

The end of the war in November 1918 did not bring the hoped for prosperity or provide the promised "Land fit for Heroes". The increase in trade appears to have been slow and the labour market was very disturbed by the returning servicemen. There is a local tradition that many of the Pottery Workers having seen the "outside world" were not prepared to return to the low wages and poor conditions in the Pottery.

There was also a major worldwide influenza epidemic [1918-1919] that killed more people than the war. This is a truly horrific statistic. This epidemic, which spread through Scotland and Kirkcaldy, had a major effect on production in all industries including the Potteries. No specific reports were made for the Kirkcaldy Pottery although the situation was so bad that one of their smaller local rivals was closed for a few weeks at the Armistice due to illness within the workers

1919 did not fare much better even though the influenza was abating and trade improving as there was a major fire in the Pottery in August. This started in the early hours of the morning in the throwing and drawing departments and quickly spread to the old painting, gilding and dressing flats which were completely destroyed when the roof and floors fell down bringing down "machinery and piles of delft". It was estimated that there was about £2,000 worth of damage and 700 lbs[300Kg.] of "colours" to the value of £280 destroyed. The offices and showrooms which were near by were protected by "double iron fire doors" which held although reputedly "red hot". The Youngs who had help to fight the fire with their managers were able to report that the damage was covered by insurance and that there was sufficient spare workspace for the displaced workers to be accommodated else where in the Pottery. It has to be assumed that the Insurance Company paid the claim but it appears the damaged buildings were not replaced as no new plans were submitted to the Town Council.

This was a period on general labour discontent and the first attempt at a National Strike was tried with very limited success in October 1919. The Scottish potters had their own problems and the Rockingham potters managed to negotiate an increase in the "War Bonus" from 71% to 80% on the pre-war rate in August making Scottish rates slightly higher than the English ones. The English potters also made a similar agreement shortly thereafter. As the English rates had been higher than the Scottish before the war this meant that the English rates were again higher and the Scottish potters requested parity with a further increase of 7.5%. The employers through the Rockingham and Caneware Manufacturers Association accepted this for the Glasgow potters but not for the Kirkcaldy potters who came out on strike in early December. Feelings became more heated and the Glasgow and Rutherglen brownware potters soon joined their Kirkcaldy colleagues. Most strikes have peculiar aspects and this one was no exception as for some reason the Scottish whiteware potters had little difficulty in obtaining the same settlement although their employers, the Scottish Earthenware Manufacturers Association who in many cases employed both classes of potters and were members of both Associations. No explanation is given for this attitude but it was thought locally that there was a conception that the whiteware potters were more skilled. To complicate matters the whiteware potters decided to come out on strike in sympathy with their colleagues. After this move the Rockingham Manufacturers were at least prepared to discuss the problem provided the whiteware potters went back to work immediately. The workers again refused this. The strike continued into 1920 and appears to have petered out as no further reports were made.

In the earlier reports of the strike it is reported that the two whiteware Potteries in Kirkcaldy [Kirkcaldy and Fife Potteries] employed 160 workers between them. No subdivision of this number is given for each Pottery nor is the number of brownware potters given. This number is for males and females together and presumably for production workers only. As the proportion at each Pottery was probably the same as in 1881 it would suggest that there were about 100 workers in the Kirkcaldy Whiteware Pottery.

It is difficult to estimate the profitability or otherwise of the business throughout the early 1900s but it would be fairly safe to assume that the profits when made would not be very high even in the best times. Losses could be minimised simply by laying the employees off as labour costs were approximately one third of the overall cost of production and material cost were virtually nil if production was reduced or stopped. There would have been other overheads that could not be avoided along with the cost of capital tied up in materials and unsold stock. The partners did have considerable assets mainly land outwith the Pottery which they started to realise as early as 1916 when the started feuing land in William Street on the original clayfield [Lib 1370.33 15/4/1916].

The three brothers continued as partners in the business with their sisters having minor life interest shares business that they had inherited from their father. The partners still wholly owned the Pottery.

James, the youngest of the partners, having other ambitions or perhaps driven by the economic necessity of providing a future for his family started his own wholesale and retail china merchants business in 1919 with a warehouse in Sands Road. The location of this warehouse is not given in the Valuation Rolls and it appears he must have used the Pottery Warehouse on the Esplanade [formerly Sands Road] that was surplus to requirements by the firm. As his general health was poor he was presumably assisted by the eldest of his three sons, Andrew Francis Young, who had been working in the Pottery for a number of years and was referred to as "Frank" to avoid any confusion with his grandfather. To confuse matters James registered himself as a "China Merchant" in the 1920 municipal Elections, which would suggest that this was his principal occupation although he was still a partner in DM&S No doubt he would have retailed Kirkcaldy pottery wares but also dealt in pottery imported from England and elsewhere. Perhaps he arranged for the English bone china, which was personalised with gilding at the Pottery. In making this move to selling pottery James had returned to the type of pottery business that had started with David[I] and John Methven more than a hundred years earlier.

In the early 1920's the Town Council started a "labour relief scheme" by converting the Sands Road along the foreshore into a paved road, The Esplanade, with a large sea wall. While such work would have been very welcome to the unemployed it placed a further burden on the Pottery, as they were no longer allowed to dispose of the "wasters" onto the sea beach. As the amount of red clay being dug at that time did not provide sufficient capacity they were obliged to find other dumpsites. This problem was over come by renting the obsolete Inverteil Quarry, which was about one mile away [V.R.]. Although this problem was only a minor matter it did increase the costs of production at a time when the situation was poor.

James died on the 15th June 1922 after an unsuccessful operation in Edinburgh and in his obituary he is only mentioned in connection with the Pottery and there is no reference to his china business. His Estate was registered as being valued at £16,565 a not inconsiderable sum but not remarkably high considering the inheritance from his father only eight years earlier. Frank as his father's heir continued the china business and inherited the family house, Rowandene, in Milton Road [Lib 1598.II3 12/10/1922]. He also continued to work at the Pottery for a few years but could not become a partner under the old agreement that ensured that the property and business passed to the two remaining partners, William and Andrew.

Perhaps James had made a wise decision by diversifying into dealing while still a partner in D M & S as the financial affairs in the business continued to decline until in 1923, less than a year after James's death, they had a massive financial burden which they could only relieve by borrowing £20,000 from the Commercial Bank of Scotland using the Pottery as security [Lib 1606.159 21/3/1923]. This injection of cash and a slight upturn in trade helped the business for a short time, as did the sale of plots of building land in William Street and Milton Road. There was ongoing importation of flint and clay for the Pottery but assuming that all of the loads received were reported in the newspapers the total quantities were fairly small. These reports are somewhat confusing as certain loads do not have specific customers and the local Linoleum Works also received occasional loads of china clay at that time. The two brothers must have had some concern for their two sisters whose future and part of their income was tied up in the fortune of D.M.&S. Having now acquired adequate working capital the brothers "bought out" their sisters' Life Rent on the business and transferred their late father's house, Abbotsford, into the sisters', ownership [Lib 1710.179 24/4/1926]. This concern for their sisters was well founded as trade had sunk so low by 1925 that they were forced to close the Brownware Pottery and transfer all of the work available to the main Whiteware Pottery [FFP 9/1928].

By this closure the overheads should have been cut except the Town Council would not accept that the rates should be substantially reduced unless the kilns were demolished. Just why they adopted this stance is difficult to imagine as in England the Rates could be reduced to a peppercorn level simply by bricking up the kiln. No doubt this must have equally been a difficult time for the Local Authorities as many commercial premises were being closed and there were regular appeals for similar reductions by other manufacturers in the same position. All closures would reduce the Council's income from rates

Since the War orders had been very hard to find and this was not helped by the regular highly discounted sales of "bankrupt stock" from English Potteries many of which were making wares of a higher quality than those from Kirkcaldy Pottery. The situation appeared to be helped when a large order was received [circa 1925] from a dealer in New York for hand decorated earthenware which was given the trade names of "Auld Heatherware" and "Dundee". This order, which was obtained despite the import tariff imposed by the USA authorities, gave a slight boost to the business that probably accounts for the delivery of larger loads of clay and flint

The Youngs had continued with their Hole Flint Mill and still employed two flint millers [Whittam and Wardlaw] who occupied the mill houses [V.R.]. The cost of running these would have been very low amounting only to wages, small quantities of coal and raw materials with very few overheads. It may have been possible to sell ground flint to the other Potteries and the Linoleum Works if the price was kept competitive

The slight upturn in 1925 continued into 1926 when further small loads of flint were delivered in the first few months. This upturn was short lived as the social and trade conditions were so bad that in late April the miners were "Locked Out" because they would not accept the general reduction in wages and conditions being imposed by the mine owners. A General Strike was called on the 5th May to support the miners that was generally backed by the workers in most industries. It was not reported which individual industries in Kirkcaldy took part but it appears to have been very extensive. Although this General Strike only lasted a few days the miners stayed out on strike until the end of the year.

This strike must have had devastating effect on the Pottery as they depended on regular supplies of coal from the local coalmines. They also depended on the railway for the delivery of materials such as glazes and more importantly to deliver their products to the customers. The trading situation in the

92

Pottery were so bad that the partners were forced to borrow a further £3,000 secured against the feu duties on lands in Pratt Street and Methven Road [Lib 1714.56].

The legal papers for the two major borrowings do not give the rates of interest charged but even assuming a rate of 5%, which appears to have been common a few years earlier, the annual interest charged would have been in the region of £1,300. This sum added to the annual rates bill from the Burgh Council, which was in excess of £1,000, must had been a great strain on the resources of the business.

Thus when the continuing lack of coal severely restricted the operations of the Pottery they were in an extremely awkward position with production reduced to a very low level. This lack of production is reflected in the lack of reports of clay imports in the second part of the year. Despite all of these problems the workers did have a successful works outing in June when they went to Dundee [FA 12/6/1926].

Production did continue at some low level as a young female sponger suffered severe burning while cleaning out the ashes from an oven in October [FA 23/10/1926]. She was saved by Frank Young, who was nearby, and put out her burning clothes with his apron and hands.

No indication is available of the level of production that appears to have been dependant on supplies, when available, of coal from the few "black leg" miners who continued to work. There is also a local tradition that supplies of sea coal were used being bought from local collectors but it seems reasonable to assume that this, if true, could only have amounted to a very limited amount and not sufficient in quantity or quality to fire the kilns.

The restrictions in production were such that they were unable to complete an order for New York on time and it was cancelled, leaving the Pottery with a large amount of finished wares which they were unable to sell except at a substantial loss and with the possibility of a "penalty clause" for non delivery. Members of the Young family recalling the situation some forty years later spoke of the local "gentry" buying large quantities of this pottery at prices well below that of production which they donated to local charities for sale at fund raising bazaars. This in turn must have reduced any possibility of selling the wares at a reasonable price.

1927 did not start any better when the partners' brother, J. B. Young, the advocate, died in January [FA 22/1/1928] and perhaps conditions were so bad as to cause the suicide of a local potter [FA 5/3/1927]. There were a few deliveries of clay although the larger, which came by steamer, were delivered to the Linoleum Works. It may be that the smaller loads delivered by sailing schooner to Kirkcaldy Harbour for unrecorded purchasers were for Kirkcaldy Pottery.

By the start of 1928 the conditions were terminal and their creditors were no longer satisfied by the actions of the Firm and forced them to sign a Trust Deed for the whole of the property and business in February [Lib 1768.192] in which the situation was fully stated.

DEEDS OF TRUST 8/3/1928 for Creditors

DM&S and William Young and James B Young individual partners considering our affairs become embarrassed and that we are unable to pay several debts due in consequence we have resolved to grant a Trust Disposition and Assignation for behoof of our creditors as underwritten hereby Dispone, Assign, Convey and make over to A W Robertson CA the whole means, estate and effects heritable and movable of what so ever pertains and belongs or due and indebted to us.............
[CS318 - BT2   Vol 5205 p409]

The Trustee [A W Robertson] was given powers similar to those of a Sequestration under the Bankruptcy [Scotland] Act, 1913 and could [1] pay his own fees, [2] pay all taxes and wages and [3] collect all debts due to the firm and pay in whole or part. By this act the Youngs gave up financial control of the business but the Trustee had to depend on them for the day-to-day operations for which they might have been paid some form of salary or fee.

The financial situation was further complicated as much of the major asset, the property, was already committed as security for loans. The remainder of the property did have a commercial market and houses in Links Street and Buchanan Street were quickly sold in June, which enable a repayment of £940 to be made against the debt of £20,00 [Lib 1767.27]. This was followed by other transactions later in the year that reduced the debt by £448.

Although there were many factors that affected the decline of the business the loss on this major order was virtually the final blow and most of the north side pottery was also taken out of production [FA 15/9/1928] leaving only a small section in production as and when orders were available. However the partners still hoped to reopen later when conditions improved and tried to minimise their liabilities by requesting the Town Council to give them relief on the payment of Rates. This request was refused and the matter was taken to Court.

In making his case William Young followed the Assessor's method of subdividing the property into three distinct sections, North, South and Pottery and Warehouse [133 Links Street]. The first and last units are in total the whole area on the north side of Methven Road, which had prior to 1914 been considered as one unit under the name of "North Side". The reason for this split is not clear, as the Plans of that date do not show any physical demarcation line within the site. The O.S. plan does show that there were two kilns separate from the main range near to the warehouse and it appears that these must, for working reasons, have been considered separately

Fifeshire Advertiser   15/9/1928

> Messers D. Methven & Sons appealed against the valuation of their potteries. On the pottery and warehouse at 133 Links St. the Assessor placed a valuation of £615, and the firm appealed for a reduction to £100. On the Potteries on the south and north sides of Methven Road the assessor placed valuations of £293 and £158 respectively, the firm asking that they should be assessed as nil for these subjects. Mr. Young who supported the firm's appeal said that the firm had had to close the pottery on the south side of Methven Road entirely for three years. Two years ago he had appealed personally to Mr. Jinks [Assessor] and on that occasion Mr. Jinks instanced a local firm which had been settled in the Court of Session where the firm was not using the buildings. The whole pottery was not being used, and the whole of the other premises were in the same condition and it was absurd to pay the full rate of assessment and he suggested that the assessor write to the assessor in the pottery district of north Staffordshire. He [Mr. Young] had been there recently and a manufacturer had been quite surprised to learn that they paid the full amount of the assessments. There, whenever they ceased one kiln, they built up the doors and the assessor made allowance on £75 assessed on each oven. He [Mr. Young] had quite a number of ovens which were not burning a piece of ware as a result of the war and the coal strike. As regards the pottery on the north side of the road, neither it nor the one on the south side were used for anything, and up till now full rates had been paid. In reply to a question, Mr. Young said that not a wheel was being turned in any of the two potteries. He [the assessor] said that he had walked through Messers Methven's warehouses, in which there was pottery of every description. At that date, he understood, that two kilns were being fired so that the firm had not definitely ceased to manufacture. He could not find any evidence that the firm had advertised for a tenant for their buildings and they not only owned their buildings but occupied them.

After making this claim the Assessor must have changed his mind very quickly as he listed the Potteries and Offices as not being in use in the Valuation Roll for 1928/29 although he still gave them a full valuation. . This report also supports the suggestion of a gradual section-by-section closure of the Pottery until only a small portion remained in operation. Perhaps eventually the "two kilns" were all that were still in production until some time early in 1928 when they were finally closed. At the time of the report the Pottery was no longer in production although, no doubt, it was hoped it would soon restart. The hopes for the rest of the Pottery were much lower if not zero. It can be assumed that no production on any scale was restarted by D.M.&S. when the following month the local newspapers reported that "three Potteries had closed down that year" and that must have included the Kirkcaldy Pottery [FA 20/10/1928]. Also this was confirmed by the Assessor who in 1929 listed the Pottery as "Silent" and the Warehouse as "Empty" and gave the whole property the reduced value of £342. The Pottery was listed as being "owned by the Trustees of David Methven & Sons" and was never to reopen although sections were rented out for various other non-pottery purposes on occasions.

Kirkcaldy Pottery North Side Kilns

This photograph was taken after the Pottery had closed and is looking down from Saunders Street.

It was obvious that the properties had some value that must be realised if any repayment of the debts was to be made. They were placed on the market in 1933.

PROPERTY IN KIRKCALDY

THERE WILL BE EXPOSED FOR SALE,

by Public Roup, within the Chambers of Messers BEVERIDGE & AITKEN, Solicitors, 220 High Street, Kirkcaldy, on the 7th Day of December at 3 o'clock afternoon the following Propertied in Kirkcaldy, viz:-

1. That PROPERTY, consisting of two Dwellinghouses, No 156 Links Street, and Stores, Workshop, Stables, etc. behind, and Large Warehouse with frontage of 101 feet or thereby to the Esplanade.   Rental, £137. No Feu-duty
UPSET PRICE, £1,000

2. The SUBJECTS situated on the West side of Methven Road, Kirkcaldy, recently occupied as a Rockingham Pottery, with relative Warehouse and other appurtenances. No Feu-duty.
UPSET PRICE, £1,000

3. The SUBJECTS situated on the North side of Links Street and West side of Methven Road and having a frontage of 245 feet or thereby, recently occupied as a Whiteware Pottery, with relative Warehouses and Offices. Feu-duty £11 12/-
UPSET PRICE, £2,000

For further particulars apply to A. W. Robertson Durham, Esq., C.A., 33 Charlotte Square, Edinburgh, or Beveridge & Aitken, Solicitors, Kirkcaldy, who hold the Titles and Articles of Roup.
Kirkcaldy, 11th November 1933

It will be noted that the description of Subjects No 3 is incorrect as they should have been described as being on the "West" side and not on the "East" side of Methven Road and that the confusion of orientation in Kirkcaldy still existed some two hundred years after the original Titles. When it is considered that the Partners had borrowed £20.000 against the property the upset prices seem remarkably low being only a total of £4,000. Despite this the sale was unsuccessful and part of the Whiteware Pottery was rented to Fife County Council Education Department. It will also be noted that there is no mention of any equipment, machinery or materials and it must be assumed that this had been already disposed off confirming that there was no expectation of restarting the Potteries.

The partners and the Trustees did manage to sell parts of the clay field, Links and Milton Acres and the Glebe, which was acquired by the local Town Council who demolished the Brick and Tile Works to make way for Local Authority houses. This area was developed in such a way to avoid building on the recently infilled clay pits. This was in general successful except for Scott Street, which suffered from subsidence in the late 1990's.

Three years later in 1936 the properties were sold. The house and Warehouse on the Esplanade [Subjects No1] were purchased by Robertson, a local scrap dealer [1936 1929.44]. The Whiteware Pottery and Warehouse was sold to J C Rolland [Painter] and subsequently demolished to be replaced by a Cinema. The Rockingham Pottery was bought by P K Livingstone [Yarn Merchant] who demolished the kilns and some of the buildings [1936 1933.56].

Following these two sales of the remaining assets the Commercial Bank of Scotland and the other creditors accepted some form of payment and the Bond and Deeds of Trust were discharged removing all burdens from William Young the only surviving partner bringing to an end one of the largest Potteries in Scotland which at one time had been a very prosperous enterprise.

Chapter 8   FIFE POTTERY   1837 — 1930

As would be expected the history of the Fife Pottery over this period matches that of the Links Pottery as they were both subjected to the same pressures such as the economic conditions and the growth of Trade Unionism. Also it should be remembered that over much of the period the owners were related and although competitors were willing to help each other. Fife Pottery did not, however, have the same spectacular expansion in size or output but did produce what was to become one of the most highly prized and priced of the Scottish Potteries products, Wemyss Ware. It is also worth noting that the lack of detail from "official" and newspapers of the Fife and other Potteries in the area is due at least in part to the fact that for much of the period Gallatown was separate from Kirkcaldy both administratively and physically.

As explained Mary and Robert Heron inherited all of Mary's father's estate and debts on his death in 1837 and to clear the most pressing debt with the Commercial Bank they sold the Links Pottery to Mary's uncle George for £1500 and cleared the loan from Stocks secured on the Pottery. At that time the loss of the smaller brownware Pottery would not have seemed important as they were left with the more important Fife Pottery although it was still mortgaged under two Bonds to the "Gray's Trustees" with the "Lions" which was mortgaged to Stocks and the shop in Cupar which was also mortgaged. They also owned several small properties in Links and more importantly they held the lease of the Balwearie Flint Mill.

The Herons had little interest in their property in the Links and treated them as "assets" which they tried to realise starting in 1839 when the sold the Garden of the "Lions" [25/5/1839 PR 235. 228]. This lack of interest is not surprising as although the "Lions" was a much larger house than the Fife Pottery House it was not a convenient place for them to live being so far from Gallatown. Robert and Mary continued to live in the Pottery House along with their two children Robert Methven [b1833] and Mary [b1834]. Two older children had died before baptism and a third child, Janet [Jessie] Campbell, was born later in 1844 [DPR]. Although the property and business were jointly owned by Mary and Robert it is likely in these early Victorian times that the business was run by Robert who by that time must have been well versed in the operations of a Pottery including production as well as the sales and office requirements. In running the Pottery Robert was assisted by James Beaton who died later in 1852 while still working as the manager [FA 6/II/1852]. It will be recalled that James had held a position of some authority with the Grays and probably had continued to work at the Fife Pottery under John Methven.

Shortly after taking control and before 1840 Robert appears to have required further assistance and he entered into some form of partnership with John Goodsir under the name of Robert Heron and Co. trading as the Fife Pottery Company. They also used the name of "Heron and Goodsir" on their products. John acted as agent for the Company in the sequestration of Thomas Thomson of Perth on 19th June 1840 [CS276/2] which may suggest that he was mainly involved in the non-production side of the business. No details are available for John but he may have been some relation as Robert's mother's maiden name was also Goodsir. Certainly their relationship must have been strong when Robert asked John to be his son's godfather. There is only one "John Goodsir" listed in the 1841 Census Returns as a potter [age 25 yrs] but it is uncertain if he was the partner. The reason for this Partnership is unknown but the most likely suggestions are either to get an injection of capital or simply the need for specialised assistance or indeed both of these. The date of the termination of the Partnership is also unknown, as it was not advertised in the usual newspapers. The partnership was included in the Rosslyn Estate records of 1841 in the "List of Farm Tenants and their Rents" when "R Heron and Co. at a rent off £16-3-2 [£16.16]". Also in 1884 they are recorded as producing a pattern, Sultana [SPHR 15]. The Company had been dissolved by 1850 when Robert was again acting on his own. It may be significant that in 1843 property owned by a "John Goodsir" was judicially sold to pay off debts [FH 15/6/1843].

The only newspaper report connected with the Pottery at this time is in the Fife Herald of 15/2/1840 when the workmen at Fife Pottery raised £3.30 in support of the Anticorn League.

Little is known of the Company and Pottery until the Census of 1841 in which there are thirty four persons listed in the area as working in a Pottery although no total number of employees is given for the Fife Pottery. By this time the "Grant" Pottery was certainly closed and as there is no evidence that there was another Pottery then it can be assumed that the pottery workers listed in the Gallatown area were employed at the Fife Pottery as at this time of poor transport it is unlikely that many workers would have lived far from their work place. Thus it is no surprise that all of the pottery workers lived near to the Pottery with the exception of six who lived nearby in Boreland Village. Of those recorded 24 were journeymen potters while the remainder comprised 3 apprentices, 2 male labourers, 2 female labourers, 2 boys and 2 girls the youngest of who was only nine years of age. Of this total two were born in England and five in Scotland but outwith Fife while the remainder were born locally. Most of the Journeyman potters who were born locally had started their apprenticeships between 1815 and 1830 with concentrations about these dates, which coincides with the expansion in Pottery activity in the area. The oldest locally born potter recorded is James Ramsay [age 65 yrs.] who would have started his training about 1790 and one would assume in the Gallatown Pottery. Whilst it is always dangerous to attempt too read to much into statistics such as these, it would be safe to assume that the very low number of labourers employed must imply that the power source for the machinery such as wheels and lathes was not manual and was steam as there is no suitable water supply to drive a wheel.

These tradesmen are simply described as "Potter Journeyman" a term, which suggests that they could cover all aspects of the trade except perhaps high grade decorating. This need not imply that they did undertake all types of work but only that they were capable of doing so, as even at that date there would have been a fair amount of specialisation. The only other trade specified was James Dawson a 25-year-old "Porcelain Painter". This is a somewhat unusual description since as far as is known Fife Pottery never produced porcelain. However as he was born locally perhaps he had learnt his trade elsewhere and continued using this description even though he was decorating earthenware. There are no "Transferers" listed and it must be assumed the potters undertook this work. Also a John Boppie age 25 [born out with Scotland] is recorded as an "Engraver". Although not stated it seems unlikely that there was sufficient demand for this skill except at the Pottery.

By the 1851 Census the Pottery work force had expanded and Robert employed 78 hands in the Pottery as well as 6 on his 127 acre farm. This farm was in the Overton Mains area about one mile to the west of the Pottery [VR & KM notes]. This farm would have been the one described earlier as being leased from the Rosslyn Estate primarily to extract clay for his brownware production. He would have farmed the rest of the land including growing straw for his packing shop and breeding horses [FA 7/10/1860]. It is not known when brownware potting was introduced into the Pottery.

Assuming that the figures suggested for the employees at the Pottery in 1841 are reasonably correct it is seen that in the ten years to the 1851 Census the number of employees had approximately doubled while the proportion of female workers had increased to nearly 20% of the work force. The term "potters labourer" had virtually disappeared and the majority of the work force was simply listed as "potters". Plainly this is incorrect if a potter is considered to be a "time served" tradesman as several of the potters listed are children, one being a girl of eleven years. It would be interesting to know if this description was decided by the Census Enumerator or by the worker as it certainly debases the trade of potter. As was the case at Links Pottery by 1851 the age of specialisation had arrived and skills such as presser, turner, kilnman, packer, wheel driver, transferer and crate-maker were used. This is well illustrated in the case of Thomas Boyd who in 1841 was an apprentice potter by 1851 had specialised as a Presser. Strangely no decorator is listed although the skill of hand painting must have been available at that time.

In this Return the place of birth is given in more detail and as would be expected the non-locals mainly came from other recognised areas such as Prestonpans and Leith [e.g. James Beattie the new foreman potter was born in Prestonpans]. Also it can be seen from the family details that some of the potters had lived part of their lives in other Pottery areas. This would be expected as even as early as this workers commonly moved round the country seeking employment. There were also a good number of "tramp potters" who moved very regularly and rarely settled for long in any area. It is also seen in the Return that the age span of the workers had increased when the older hands were joined by younger workers as the business expanded.

Fortunately a Price List for 1855 still exists and is held in Kirkcaldy Museum. This list shows a remarkable similarity in layout and pricing to the Links Pottery Price List of the same date. From this list it is seen that Fife Pottery produced a comprehensive range of domestic white ware pottery offering the majority of the products in cream coloured, blue edged and sponged, Willow, printed and flowing colours. Although it is not stated it is probable that the milk pans, stool pans, K pans and plunge basins were red ware made from local clays perhaps with a coating of white clay slip while cane bakers were made from a mixture of red clay and flint with perhaps a small amount of white clay.

PRICE LIST

ROBERT HERON, FIFE POTTERY.

MARCH, 1855.

	Inches	Cream Colour s.	d	Blue Edged & Sponged s.	d.	Willow s.	d.	Printed s.	d.	Flowing Colors s.	d.
Plates	10	1	3	1	6	2	0	2	0	3	0
Do.	8	1	0	1	3	1	6	1	6	2	6
Do.	7	0	10	1	0	1	3	1	3	2	0
Do.	6	0	8	0	10	1	0	1	0	1	6
Do.	5	0	6	0	8	0	10	0	10	1	3
Do.	4	0	5	0	7	0	8	0	8	1	1
Do.	3	0	4	0	5	0	6	0	6	1	0
Fancy Muffins same as Printed.											
Flat Dishes, ...	8	1	6	1	9	2	3				
Do.	9	1	9	2	0	2	6	3	6	4	6
Do.	10	2	0	2	6	3	0	4	6	5	6
Do.	11	2	6	3	0	4	0	6	0	7	6
Do.	12	3	0	4	0	4	6	8	0	10	0
Do.	14	4	6	5	6	6	6	10	0	14	0
Do.	16	7	0	8	0	10	0	15	0	20	0
Do.	18	10	6	14	0	18	0	24	0	30	0
Do.	20					28	0	42	0	50	0
Fish Drainers same price as Dishes they fit.											
Gravy Dishes, ...	16	1	9	2	0	2	6	3	0	3	6
Do.	18	2	3	2	6	3	0	3	6	4	6
Oval Bakers, ...	5	1	0	1	3	1	6				
Do.	6	1	3	1	6	2	0				
Do.	7	1	6	1	9	2	3				
Do.	8	1	9	2	0	2	9				
Do.	9	2	3	2	6	3	3				
Do.	10	2	9	3	0	4	0	6	9	9	0
Do.	11	3	6	4	0	5	0				
Do.	12	4	6	5	0	6	0	9	0	12	0
Do.	13	5	6	6	6	9	0				
Do.	14	7	0	8	6	12	0				
Cane Bakers same price as Blue Edged.											
Nappies, ...	5	0	10	1	0	1	3	1	3	1	6
Do.	6	1	0	1	3	1	6	1	6	1	9
Do.	7	1	3	1	6	2	0	2	0	2	6
Do.	8	1	6	2	0	2	6	2	6	3	0
Larger sizes same price as Bakers.											

	Inches.	Cream Colour s.	d.	Blue Edged & Sponged s.	d.	Willow s.	d.	Printed s.	d.	Flowing Colors s.	d.
Soup Tureens, ...	8					1	9				
Do. do. ...	9	1	6	1	9	2	0				
Do. do. ...	10	1	9	2	0	2	6	3	9	4	9
Do. do. ...	11	2	3	2	6	3	0	4	9	6	0
Do. Stands, ...	10							1	0	1	3
Do. do. ...	11							1	3	1	6
Do. Ladles, ...		0	6	0	8	0	9	0	10	1	0
Sauce Tureens, ...		0	6	0	7	0	9	1	0	1	4
Do. Ladles, ...		0	2	0	2½	0	3	0	3½	0	4½
Do. Stands, ...		0	1	0	1½	0	2	0	2½	0	3½
Do. Tureens, complete,		0	9	0	11	1	2	1	6	2	0
Do. Boats, large,		0	2½	0	3	0	3½	0	5	0	6
Do. do. small,		0	2	0	2½	0	3				
Do. do. Stands,		0	1	0	1½	0	2	0	2½	0	3½
Pickles, ...		0	1½	0	2	0	2½	0	3	0	4
Cover Dishes, ...	6					6	0				
Do. do. ...	7					7	6				
Do. do. ...	8	6	6	7	6	9	0	12	0	15	0
Do. do. ...	9	7	6	8	6	10	6	15	0	18	0
Do. do. ...	10	9	0	10	0	12	0	18	0	24	0
Do. do. ...	11	10	0	12	0	15	0				
Root Dishes, ...	11							5	0	6	0
Salad Bowls, ...								1	6	2	3
Cheese Stands, ...		1	6					2	0	2	6
Do. Covers, ...		2	6					3	0	3	6
Mustards, ...	24	2	9	3	6	4	6	4	0	6	0
Peppers.	12	2	0	2	3	2	9	2	9	3	3
Salts, ...	36	2	3	2	9	4	0	4	0	5	0
Egg Cups, ...	12	0	10	1	0	1	3	1	3	1	6
Egg Hoops, ...	12	1	0	1	3	1	6	1	6	1	9

	Cream Colour s	d.	Sponged s.	d.	Painted s.	d.	Printed s.	d.	Flowing Colors s.	d.
Bowls, ...	2	6	2	9	3	3	5	0	6	0
Do. Pudding, ...	3	0								
Do. Sprouted, ...	3	6								
Do. Cullender, ...	3	6								
Do. covered & handld.	6	0	6	6	8	0	11	0	14	0
Stands for do.							14	0	15	0
[illegible]			2	9	3	3	5	0	6	0
Triffle Cans, ...							2	9		
Jugs, Common, ...	3	0	3	6	4	0	5	0	6	0
Do. Pressed, ...							8	0	9	0
Do. Embossed, drab, 10s										
Do. do. pearl white 9s										
Do. Turquoise, ... 14s										
Do. Covered, price of half										
Do. Toy embsd. 6/, 4/6, 3/										
Plain Basins & Chas. 4 6 9s	2	6	3	0	3	6	5	0		
Do. do. do. 12s	2	9	3	6	4	0	5	0		
Do. Ewers, ... 4 6 9s	3	0	3	6	4	0	5	6		
Do. do. ... 12s	3	6	4	0	4	6	6	0		
Pressed Basins & Chas. 6s							7	0	8	6
Do. Ewers, 6s							7	0	8	6
Do. Basins & Chams, 9s							7	9	9	0
Do. Ewers, 9s							7	9	9	0
Soaps and Trays, ...	0	7					0	10½	1	0
Round Soaps, ...	0	4	0	5			0	6		
Sponge Trays, ...							1	6	1	9
Spitoons, ...							1	3	1	6
Foot Pails, ... 16 in.	5	0					8	6	10	0
Do. do, ... 18 in.	6	6					10	6	12	6
Supply Jugs, for 16 in.	3	0					4	6	5	6
Do. do. 18 in.	4	0					6	0	7	6
Bed Pans, 1s 9d and 2s.										
Sick Cups, ...	0	5					0	8		
Nursing Bottles, ...	0	5					0	8		
Carpet Balls, 3s ℔ Set.										
Jelly Cans, ...	1	10								

	Cream Colour s.	d.	Sponged s.	d.	Painted s.	d.	Printed s.	d.	Flowing Colors s.	d.
Hd. Evening Teas, plain,			2	0	2	2	2	6	3	0
Do. do. French,							2	9	3	3
Do. do. Greek,							3	0	3	6
Do. Breakfast do.,			3	6			5	0	6	0
Uunhandled do. ...			1	6	1	8				
Creams, plain, ...							6	0	7	6
Do. pressed, ...							9	0	10	6
Bread Plates, ...							4	0	5	0
Toy Teas, unhandled,			1	0	1	2				
Do. handled,					1	6	2	0		
Do. Teapots, ...					0	4½	0	5½		
Do. Sugar Boxes,					0	3½	0	4½		
Do. Creams, ...					0	1½	0	1½		
Do. Slop Bowls, ...					0	1	0	1		
Do. Bread Plates, ℔ pair					0	2	0	3½		
Do. Tea Set, complete,					1	6	2	0		
Covered Sugars, ...			6	0						
Butter Tubs, ...			6	0						
Punch Bowls, ...							8	0		
Urinals, each, ...	0	10								

Stoolpans	5	6	7	8	9	10	11	12		
	4	5	6	7	8	10	1s	1s 3d.		
K Pans	5	6	7	8	9	10	11	12	13	14
	4	5	6	7	8	10	1s	1s 3d	1s 6d	2s 3

C. C. Plunge Basins	15	16	17 inch.
	1s 3d	2s	3s
Milk Pans	12	14	16 inch.
	8	1s	1s 6d.

Straw and Cord to be charged at the following rates, ***and no allowance made for it even if returned—***

10	12	14	16	18	Bar Crate.
1s 6d	2s	2s	2s 6d	2s 6d	Nett.

TERMS.

15 ℔ *Cent for Cash settlement.*
12½ *do* „ *Bill do.*.

All of these items would require the addition of flint. It is also worth noting the large increase in cost of items as the quality of the decoration improved. For example an undecorated ten-inch plate is listed at 1/- [5p] per dozen and goes up in price to 3/- [15p] when decorated in flowing colours an increase by the factor of three. Since all of this decoration was under glaze it only required one further firing after the biscuit stage similar to the cream colour this increase in cost is solely attributable to the decoration. It should also be noted that Willow printed patterns were usually cheaper than other designs. The pricing system is not fully explained and care must be taken when considering each item for example plates and flat dishes are specified by their diameter in inches and priced in dozens while other items such as tureens are priced individually. There are no teapots or coffee pots listed except under "toy teas" nor are there any black glazed or Rockingham wares. This might imply that there were no wares of these types being made at that time or simply that this list does not cover the full range of products. Perhaps the range of these other products was sufficiently large to justify a separate list. These details are the same as seen in the Links Pottery Price List of the same date.

So little is known about Fife Pottery under John Methven and under Robert Heron until 1841 that it is impossible to judge if there had been any change in the output or types of products. It can be assumed however that there had been a gradual but small increase in the output at least as "modern" production techniques were introduced and the Pottery expanded [see later]. Perhaps the number of employees increased despite the trade slump in 1836 when weavers' wages fell to about one third their normal. This increase would be similar to other Potteries in Great Britain and might have been accompanied by a small deterioration in the quality of the wares that were aimed at a lower income bracket as limited affluence moved down the social scale. There are so few authenticated pieces pre 1836 to compare with the later periods to be definite with regards to quality. However after 1841 it can be safely be assumed that with the continuation in the "improvements" in techniques that the production increased at a greater rate than the increase in the number of employees and was perhaps accompanied by a deterioration in quality of product. This will be considered in more detail later when the "Wares" are considered.

It is also difficult to estimate the profitability of the business but no doubt it fluctuated greatly dependant on the national economic conditions. The situation must have been reasonable in 1843 when the £600 Bond held on the Pottery was reduced to £450 [GR 2161:282 13/12/1842].

The family relationship between the Fife and Links Potteries continued presumably amicably as at that time they were not fully competitors since Links Pottery was not producing whiteware. George Methven must have still had some regard for his niece, Mary, as he left her property known as "Barnyards" in Heggies Wynd near to the "Lions" in his Will [13/10/1845]. This property was a number of small houses, which would have produced a small income for the Herons as they were unable to sell them. They were considered to be of such little importance that the change of Title was not made until 1863 [13/10/1863 PR 341.4].

Gallatown 1856

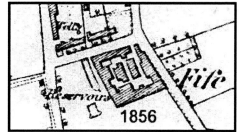

1856

This extract from the Ordnance Survey Plan of 1856 [surveyed 1854] shows the location and general shape of the Pottery but is not in sufficient detail to establish the individual buildings or their use. In the enlargement it is interesting to note that there were two reservoirs adjacent to the Pottery and that at least the nearest one was on land owned by Robert Heron. Since any Pottery requires a good water supply it would seem reasonable to assume that this was the source of the water for the Pottery

During this period Robert's manager was James Beaton who had worked for the Grays and probably John Methven. Robert. James died in 1852 [FA 6/II//1852] and was replaced by John Young of Glasgow who was engaged at the comparatively young age of 32 years [CR 1861]. Another death reported was of a young painter from Musselburgh who had been working at the Pottery for two years. He died of tetanus in 1856 [FA 20/12/1856].

In the first Valuation Roll issued in 1855 the Pottery was given an assessment of £60 showing clearly that even as early as this the once smaller Links Pottery had overtaken the Fife Pottery in size and probably output. [Cf Links Pottery and Tile Works R.V. of £115]. The apparent affluence of the owners is also seen by comparing the Rateable Values of their houses as David Methven [V], a junior partner in Links Pottery, occupied a house valued at £35 while the Fife Pottery House was only valued at £15.

This Valuation remained the same until 1861 and it is likely that there were no significant alterations to the buildings thus increasing the difference in size between the two rival Potteries. It is equally likely that during this period of ever improving technology the working methods would also have improved thus increasing the output. Certainly by the 1861 Census Robert was employing 92 workers [68 men and 24 female] in his Pottery, an increase of some 20% in ten years. The proportion of females had increased to nearly 30% and as would be expected they were employed in the more menial jobs except for the decorators. There were seven females employed in the warehouse, which is indicative of a reasonably large output and certainly a substantial increase since 1851.

The 1861 Census Returns also shows that there had been an even greater move towards specialisation as more separate trades are listed including packer, turner, cratemaker, transferer, warehouse worker, thrower, kilnman, painter, printer, wheel driver, presser, smokehouseman and treasurer. There were, as before, many workers who are simply listed as "potters" who could not all have been fully trained tradesmen [e.g. Ann Millar who was only nine years of age]. Surely in these cases this can only mean that they worked in the Pottery and on the production side. There was also one pottery paintress and one young girl listed as a sponger

One other worker listed was James Wishart, Smokehouseman, who presumably worked in the boiler house of the steam raising plant. This is the first time this term is used and although steam power must have been used for many years perhaps it was on such a small scale that it did not justify a dedicated worker. Certainly to accommodate the increase in employees, especially in the warehouse, there must have been an increase in the power driven machinery for processing clay and other raw materials as well as producing the pieces. There are only a few "wheel drivers" listed for the wheels and lathes, which required a finer control of speed than was available at that time. It can be assumed that Jollies and Jiggers were all steam powered.

The overall picture of Fife Pottery of the Pottery at this time is one of ever increasing output related to the number of employees coupled with ever increasing specialisation and mechanisation. The owner in full control as he had the facilities and workers to undertake the whole process from the purchasing of the raw materials through production to dispatching in crates made by his own workers packed with straw, which he grew. There was also the required office and sales staff including a "Treasurer" [bookkeeper/accountant], which also indicates the increase in turnover to justify employing such a well-trained and expensive employee.

Robert was still renting the Balwearie Flint Mill [RV £22.50] from Ferguson of Raith Estate, which was operated by Robert Henderson [flint miller] and his assistant Charles Levack. This would have supplied him with all his flint and perhaps also supplied the Links Pottery with part if not all its flint requirements. The raw materials would have been white and ball clays, glazes and, perhaps, china stone, which along with kiln furniture would have been purchased from England. The red clay was available locally as were coal and fireclay for seggers, which could have been made at the Pottery or acquired from the Links Fireclay Works or elsewhere. Bone may also have been used in the body.

Some short time before 1860 Robert's only son, Robert Methven, [aged 27 yrs] returned to the Pottery from his art studies in Edinburgh and Paris and was appointed "manager"[CR 1861]. No doubt Robert who was sixty one years of age would have been glad for this extra help from his son who presumably undertook an executive position over the whole business while James Young retained his position as works manager restricted to the production side.

Before continuing the story of the Fife Pottery it is well worth considering the other very important factor, the workers, who would naturally have had a life style very similar to their colleagues in the Links Pottery. Of the few details available perhaps the most significant is found in the Census Returns where it is seen that generally the only workers who were older than fifty were the kilnmen. Whilst this can be explained in part by the expansion in the workforce since 1830[circa.] it is no doubt attributable in part to the fact that kilnmen's work kept them at least partially clear from the dangers of working with finely ground powdered clay, flint and lead glazes. This sad fact is echoed in the Links Pottery and was to continue as long as the details are available. The other details available are in themselves fairly trivial but do add to the overall picture of the conditions at that time. Thus when it is seen that Robert gave his workers a holiday without pay on the second of January as the first was a Sunday [FA 10/12/1853] and the next year that work would cease at 2 p.m. on Saturdays although the working week was still 69 hours [FA 28/1/1854] it is hardly surprising that this was a period of large scale immigration. To be fair Robert was probably typical of employers of that time and no doubt conditions had improved gradually under his control. Certainly the details written in 1836 for inclusion in the 1845 Statistical Account [p157] for another local factory in the area shows clearly the working conditions at that time and the attitude of the employers.

> At the mill where flax is spun the work people are employed from half past five in the morning until eight at night, a half hour being allowed for breakfast and dinner. The female spinners earn from 6/- to 7/- [30p to 35p] per week. It is deserving to note that the proprietors of the Mill are of great respectability and that they take an interest in the morals of the young people and also they will not allow the least immorality.

This report, which was written by the Parish Minister, is easier to understand when it is remembered how powerful the Employers were in the local community and that they along with the local landowner would control the minister's "Living". When working conditions such as these are read it is not surprising that there was a high incidence of drunkenness and a correspondingly active Temperance Movement.

When considering the small villages within the Gallatown area it should be noted that the total population was only about one thousand and allowing for the normal family conditions approximately three hundred persons would have depended on the Pottery. It is seen that Robert Heron was by far the largest single employer. Thus in 1862 when the Pottery was "on short time for a good while" it is easy to imagine the relief when the Pottery became "much brisker" [FA 1/3/1862].

Whilst operating the Pottery Robert also had interests in lands near Dunfermline. This interest may in some way be connected with his family but also it may be significant that the lands contained coal, fireclay and red clay. The first land he acquired was the farm of "Headwell" which he bought from Janet Mudie of Headwell [relic of William Campbell, surgeon, Dunfermline] [GR 2595.765 22/6/1852]. To make the purchase he borrowed £700 from Janet Mudie on 22/7/1852 [GR 315.II 29/5/1861]. He also borrowed £2400 from the Commercial Bank of Scotland using the land as security [GR 2595.171 30/7/1852]. He placed this land in the names of Mary and the children [GR 2595.277 31/7/1852]. In the Title Deeds he described himself as "of Headwell, Potter at Gallatown". Further adjoining land, Dawsondale, was acquired in 1858 again from Janet Mudie [GR 2938.156 27/8/1858]. In making these purchases Robert borrowed significant sums, implying that his financial affairs were on a very sound footing.

At first Robert was recorded as occupying the land although presumably only on a part time basis. Later in 1857 he rented it to Robert Milne when the land and buildings were given a RV of £200. For some reason Robert paid off his debt to the Bank in 1858 [19/8/1858 GR 2938.156] and immediately borrowed £5000 from two sisters, the Misses Roy of Perth [1/9/1858 GR 2938.163 & GR 2938.169]. This appears to be simply a change of creditor.

Although there was a Fireclay Works on or near to Headwell Robert is not recorded as owning or operating it. Just why Robert was so interested in this land is a mystery as are his reasons for changing the loan and perhaps borrowing more money. It may however be significant that shortly afterwards he did open a Fireclay Works in Gallatown. Also if it is accepted that this venture into land ownership and farming was only a business venture, why would Robert choose Dunfermline so far from his home and Pottery? Perhaps part of the reason was family connections. This is supported by the fact that Robert's daughter was christened Janet Campbell, the married name of Janet Mudie and later Janet Mudie took over part of Robert's debt to Stocks for the "Lions" [II/II/1861 345.149]. This Headwell land was to remain in the Herons' ownership until 1873 when it was sold and the loans discharged.

As well as this interest in Headwell Robert continued to administer the property that Mary and he had inherited from John Methven. This involved trying to sell the small houses in Links. Firstly a small house near the sea that he suggested would be suitable for "bathing quarters" in 1855 [FA 15.3.1855] and then "a small park with houses in Heggies Wynd" in 1860 [FA 10/3/1860]. The main property was still the "Lions" which was heavily mortgaged to Stocks. At first Robert tried to sell part of the garden ground near the mouth of the West Burn as industrial ground in 1855 [FA 1/9/1855]. This sale was unsuccessful and later in 1860 & 61 Robert repaid a total of £910 of the debt against the property showing that his business ventures, especially the Pottery, were reasonably profitable, Needless to say a house of this size was not available to manual workers and the tenants included Mr. Mould the local School Teacher [FA 17/10/1863]. A further attempt was made to sell the "lower half of that Park at Lion House" in 1864 at an upset price of £800 along with the lower flat of the house which was offered for sale or lease [II&19/7/1864]. Again the sales were not successful. Later the whole property was sold to John Stocks of Abden [GR 3383.187] whose family already held the property as security for the remainder of the loan. Stocks much later built a linen mill on much of the site and the house was finally demolished as it was in a ruinous condition about 1901.

Although there had been a substantial expansion in the Pottery up to 1860 Robert had not shown the same entrepreneurial spirit as his relatives the Methvens at the Links Pottery that had expanded from a small Brownware Pottery to an enterprise that was much larger than the Fife Pottery. Whilst it is easy to criticise Robert in this way it must be remembered that although he was a man of substance he was never on the same financial footing as the Methvens as he and Mary had inherited very substantial debts from John Methven. However if he had not put so much effort and time into his enterprise in Dunfermline perhaps much more could have been made of the Fife Pottery. It appears that Robert was very content with his small but successful business until his son, Robert M., joined the business about 1860. After this Robert assisted by his son sought to expand and diversify.

This expansion took a strange form for a mainly whiteware Pottery as they built a Fireclay Works within the Pottery site. This is even more surprising when it is remembered that Robert M. had trained extensively in art. The construction of the works started in 1861 and completed by 1862 at which time the property was given a new RV. being Pottery £65, House £15 and Fireclay Works £20 giving a total valuation of £100 [c.f. the Links Valuation of £170]. Also at this time Robert took his son into the partnership and the firm was reformed as "Robert Heron & Son" [VR 1861/62]. As it was built within a fairly restricted site the new Fireclay Works must have been small although they were able to offer for sale specialised products as illustrated by their advertisement for "Firebricks, Fireclay, Chimney Cans and Ground Fireclay" [FA 22/3/1862]. In doing this they were trying to compete with the very well established and much larger Links Brick and Tile Works, which already carried a very extensive range of fireclay products as well as other suppliers from further afield who delivered regularly to their local agents via the railway. This new venture was a failure and the new Works were closed by 1865 and the buildings converted to pottery use and described as "Kilns, Warehouse and Workshops" which retained the valuation of £100 [VR].

The Pottery and house increased in RV from £100 to £115 in 1866 perhaps as minor extensions were built or a new house was built [see later] It remained at this level until Robert died of influenza in 1869 and the property passed into the ownership of his widow and co-owner, Mary Methven, under the terms of her father's Will. The business continued under the control of her son, Robert Methven Heron as "Sole Partner" although he was assisted by his sister, Janet [Jessie] especially on the design and artistic side. The other sister, Mary, had died earlier.

By the Census of 1871 the number of employees had dropped from 92 to 66 and since there are no unemployed pottery workers listed it must be assumed that this reduction was not of a temporary nature. Of the 66 listed 31 were men along with 8 women, 20 boys and 7 girls. This break down of the labour figures does not suggest a workforce of particularly high skill, as generally only workmen could become tradesmen. However by this time a second Pottery, Sinclairtown, had opened in the area and it is not possible to allocate any worker to a specific Pottery except perhaps the decorators who would have worked exclusively at the Fife Pottery. This reduction in the workforce from 92 to 66 in ten years suggests a significant decline in the Pottery especially as over the same period the work force at the Links Pottery had increased. This does not necessarily imply a corresponding reduction in output as changes in the working methods could have increased the output. No explanation for this reduction is given in either the official papers or newspapers but it is significant that the recently opened Sinclairtown Pottery seems to have absorbed the surplus labour as the total number of pottery workers in the area remained roughly the same. It may be that Fife Pottery suffered a decline due to the failure of the Fireclay Works or because the labour was "poached" by Sinclairtown Pottery by offering better wages. Perhaps a mixture of both of these reasons is the more likely.

In this Census Returns the details of the various workers show that specialisation had become even more pronounced and in addition to the job descriptions given previously there were also plate maker, cup maker, stove man, spout maker, bowl maker, handler, muffin maker, cutter, sales woman, joiner and engraver. Of these new "jobs" the last four are worth noting. "Cutter" is a new trade and was a transferer's assistant who cut out the individual patterns on the paper transfers. The sales woman and joiner are trades that do not require explanation but do show the expansion in the Pottery output that now required these skills. The Pottery engraver listed was James Eley who was from England had been in the area in 1861 [CR] when he was listed only as an engraver so may have been working independently at that time. Assuming that the expression pottery engraver is accurate then he would have been employed at the Fife Pottery and if this is correct the demand for engraved transfer plates must have been large to keep a workman in full employment unless of course he also made plates for other Potteries. Some of his tools are now in Kirkcaldy Museum.

Despite this apparent decline in the labour force at the Pottery, Robert M. did not lack ambition and assisted by his manager, Robert MacLauchlan, who had replaced Smith in 1870[circa] strove to improve the business. Robert MacLauchlan [b1836] had been working at the Pottery for about thirteen years as a potter preferer, a skilled worker, prior to his promotion. He was born in Portobello and presumably trained there before coming to Fife and setting up home. Robert M. chose not to expand in the same manner as Methven at Links Pottery and he started to improve the design and decoration on selected items.

As well as making that decision he decided that he no longer required the use of his flint mill and that it was more economic to grind flint at the Pottery using a steam mill and buying in ground flint when required. He therefore passed the lease of the Balwearie Mill to James Methven [Links Pottery] who had probably been taking some of the output of the Mill for many years. It is likely that Robert M. would have made some arrangement for the supply of flint as required. It is worth remembering that Robert M. Heron and James Methven were related although by this time fairly distantly and, although competitors were still willing to help each other. The decision to improve the decorative quality of the wares appears, with the advantage of hind sight, to be obvious since Robert M. who had been formally trained as an artist and having toured the "Continent" would have been well aware of the various types of decoration in use there. It was perhaps on one of his foreign trips that Robert M. acquired the services of August Parsche, a German pottery printer, who joined Fife Pottery about 1880. [CR 1881]

Whilst the wares in general will be discussed later it should be noted now that about 1870 Robert M. introduced or more probably improved the black glazed jet wares and adopted the trade name of "Rosslyn Jet" for the cheap red ware body which had a high quality black glaze finish which was frequently decorated in over glaze enamels or gilding. This type of black ware was very popular at this period helped greatly by the long period of mourning undertaken by Queen Victoria on the death of Prince Albert in 1863. The choice of "Rosslyn" after the local titled landowner was no doubt a good marketing ploy.

A separate, but in some ways similar, style of hand painted under glaze decoration was developed for whitewares. This usually featured flowers, fruits, and birds, especially cocks painted in a "French" style. Many of these whiteware pieces were "improved" by over glaze gilding. The quality of these decorations suggests that they were aimed at a slightly higher market especially with the use of overglaze decoration that involved more than the normal two firings, with the associated increase in the cost of production. These firings also had to be at a relatively low temperature and the kiln had to be packed in such a way to achieve a suitable range of temperatures. The gilding also had to be hand burnished to expose the "gold" finish.

The increase in these types of decoration is well illustrated in the Census Returns for 1871 and 1881. In these it is seen that while in 1871 there were no gilders and only one paintress, Anne Heath of Glasgow, by 1881 there were six painters and three gilders. These new workers were mainly recruited locally except one gilder who was born in Bohemia. This worker, William Starich, was only twenty-four years of age in 1881 and therefore had only arrived in Gallatown within the last few years. It seems likely that Robert M. would only bring trained and skilled workers from the Continent and Starich must have been particularly skilful. Perhaps he was employed to introduce a new style and method of gilding. This suggestion is based on a very strong local tradition that Robert M. recruited talented workers during his frequent journeys to the Continent and that they usually returned home after a few years. Certainly Starich and the other foreign worker August Parsche who were listed in 1881 had left the area before 1891 [CR 1891]. It must be remembered that although there were no gilders listed in the Return for 1871 this does not necessarily mean that this type of work was not undertaken at that date as this work could have carried out by the paintress. It does however mean that the quantity, if any, must have been very small.

As stated earlier much of the credit for these developments must go to Robert MacLauchlan, the business manager, who managed the business during Robert M's absences. Indeed a few years later a report appeared in the Pottery Gazette [1/10/1883] leaving little doubt about MacLauchlan's contribution.

> "This ware [Wemyss], if I am not mistaken, had its inception from some distinguished local amateurs and under the fostering care and attention of the late manager of the firm, Mr. Robert McLauchlan it has reached its present commanding position."

As well as being a talented manager MacLauchlan was also well respected in the community being a leader in the "Free Church Mission" [FA 19/6/1869].

This reference to gifted "amateurs" is very remarkable. There are no supporting references and attractive as the suggestion is it must be treated with caution. It must also be noted that some types of decoration such as birds continued to be used after Wemyss Ware was well established suggesting that the artists were still at the Pottery. There was, however, a strong local tradition that Jessie took a very active part in the development of both the new decoration and in the design of the shapes of many new items and is credited with working "along side" the established mould maker John McKinnon. Robert M's contribution, as owner and an artist would have been very large as he was very much the driving force behind the whole expansion. While there can be no doubt that Robert M. had a reasonable knowledge of potting it is not known if he actually undertook any practical work in the design or decorating fields. However it is hard to imagine that he could have resisted the temptation to at least dabble if not gain expertise in both. There can be no doubt he would have taken a very intense interest in all of the designs for decoration and shapes even though he may not have been capable of producing the final product.

By 1881 the number of employees had returned to the 1861 level of ninety three of which forty eight were men and fifteen women. The remainder were children. Unfortunately by that time there were two other Potteries in the area and with very few exceptions it is not possible to allocate the workers to a specific Pottery nor can the balance between the trades and skills be established. Similarly there are so few reports in the local newspaper that little is known of the day-to-day life of the Pottery or the potters except that they made regular donations to various charities and enjoyed their annual "works outings". The Fife Pottery Band that had been active in the 1860s seems to have disappeared [F A 11/8/1866]. It is likely that the Pottery had been steadily improved by the introduction of new equipment and by that time the majority of the machinery would have been steam powered. Certain types of wares would have remained solely handwork such as moulding which remained such until the Pottery finally closed although the technique did change.

The Pottery was progressively more organised on a production line basis continuing the change that had started many years earlier. This style of production as seen at the Links Pottery and in other industries led to extreme specialisation with frequently a drop in the quality of the products which was perhaps not so marked at the Fife Pottery. There was, more importantly, a marked fall in the prices of the wares, which as the Pottery had many competitors both locally and within Great Britain, must have been unwelcome. By this time the railway system was so extensive and efficient that goods could be easily moved throughout the whole of the populated areas of Britain as seen in the advertisements in the local newspapers [E.G. FA 22/10/1881].

> "Extraordinary sale of highly decorated China and Earthenware - by Auction - owing to the great depression in the Pottery Industry."

Robert M. still had complete control over the whole process, which he expanded by making his own frit glazes in a newly constructed kiln and mill. This change to frit glazes was perhaps not greatly welcomed by Robert M and the other master potters in the area as it was a government requirement. By this process the glazes, which were inherently dangerous, were rendered much safer. All of the moulds were made at the Pottery and frequently the masters for the moulds were also designed and made at the Pottery. Robert M. also employed his own sagger makers thus extending his control. Coal and red clay were very readily available locally but all other raw materials [white clay, blue clay, flint, china stone, colours for glazes etc.] were still all imported, mainly from England, and sailing ships with clay were a common sight in Dysart Harbour. Kiln furniture was also purchased from England. The market for the wares was very extensive covering much of Britain and Ireland along with the Continent, USA, Africa, Far East and Australasia. There is a strong but unsubstantiated local tradition that for a long period under Robert M. and his father the bulk of the output went especially to Australasia. Robert M following on from his father still exchanged pottery for scrap from itinerant traders a practice that was to continue until the Pottery closed.

In early 1880's this enthusiasm to improve the quality of the special wares continued and it is thought that Robert M. while on one of his many tours to Europe met and persuaded several more "German" tradesmen and artists to move to Gallatown to work for him. Most of these immigrants were Roman Catholics who did not find Calvinistic Scotland to their liking quickly returned home with the exception of two, Anton Weber and Karel Nekola. Both of these were talented artist in the conventional sense and, more importantly, as ceramic decorators. Weber remained for a few years until he left in 1884 after being Nekola's "best man" at his wedding. However it is Karel Nekola who must be considered.

Karel Nekola was born in Bohemia 1857 [circa.] where he learned his trade and skill in ceramic painting. It is thought he also worked in Dresden, Germany, where he might have met Robert M. It is not known precisely when he came to the Fife Pottery. In his obituary [FFP 4/12/1915] it is suggested that he arrived "some thirty five years ago" [i.e. about 1880] but as neither he nor Weber are included in the 1881 Census Returns it is unlikely that his arrival was before mid 1881 unless they were both, for some reason, away from Gallatown over the Census taking period. Nekola was probably in Gallatown by 1882 and certainly well established in the area by 1883 when he painted the two plaques illustrating local scenes [WW p16]

At or about the time of Nekola's arrival at Fife Pottery and by 1882 Robert M. had found the higher quality product he was seeking to produce and he proceeded to market it under the Trade name of "Wemyss Ware". This was at first mainly single coloured items as described in the Fife Free Press on 28th October 1882.

The "Wemyss Ware"
We have had the opportunity this week of examining the new ware, manufactured by Messers R Heron & Son at Fife Pottery, Gallatown. The designs are taken from very old wares in the possession of the Wemyss Family of Wemyss Castle, the most of the pieces come from various parts of the Continent before the ceramic art had reached such a point of excellence in this country. Some of the pieces now being made for Wemyss Castle are of

considerable size one huge cup measuring 90 inches [2.25 metres] in circumference, a splendid receptacle for a palm or other growing plant for internal decoration. On a rather smaller size, there are many specimens of the ware for similar purposes some being of the most curious antique shapes imaginable - round, square and diamond shaped. The vases of the same ware are of light and graceful outline, others rounded and more like the remains of Tuscan Pottery, while others still resemble no vessel with which we are familiar. All the shapes are quaint but exceedingly pretty. The articles are made in two colours - a deep fleshy red and yellow, each piece having one colour only. The ware is sure to be a great favourite with people of taste, as few could be more beautiful for decorating a main entrance. Messers Heron have also tried the ware with great success for smaller vessels of different kinds such as various sorts of vases, bowls, candlesticks, cups and other ancient looking articles which although somewhat doubtful as to their particular use are extremely effective. These are made in the two colours, the pattern being copied from old wares from Wemyss Castle. A few of the vases for flowers are embellished with local views by the firm's own artist. The new ware is likely to be as great favourite as the black and hand enamelled ware for which Messers Heron are so famous."

It seems probable that this "artist" was Nekola and at that time he was only painting local scenes on Wemyss Ware. Assuming he was in the Pottery at that time then, no doubt, he could also have been decorating the "hand enamelled" wares [Rosslyn Jet] and the "pre Wemyss" ware with flowers and birds already described.

Sadly in or about the time that the new Wemyss Ware was being launched Robert MacLauchlan died in mid 1882 and he was never to see the fruition of his long developments as Robert M's Business Manager. Although there had also been a Pottery Manager, Peter Weepers, working under MacLauchlan for a number of years he was not considered to be suitably experienced to be promoted to Business Manager.

Weepers [b1847] had followed his father [David] into the Pottery where he also trained as a potter before becoming a pottery printer and eventually promoted to Pottery Manager taking control of the production side of the business. The vacancy for Business Manager was filled by the appointment of J K McKenzie who had been working in Glasgow.

Wemyss Ware was an immediate success and was quickly on sale in London and throughout Britain as well as being mentioned twice in the "Pottery Gazette" in 1883. For reasons that will be fully explained later it is far from certain that it was a long-term financial success.

The improvement in trade at the Pottery that started in the early 1880s was several years ahead of the national trend due, in no small way, to the popularity of Wemyss Ware. The later national improvement allowed producers in general to command higher prices and to pay higher wages thus stimulating further demand. The potters who were never paid wages commensurate to their skill would have especially welcomed this increase in wages. Indeed the potters in Scotland were paid even lower wages than their compatriots in England both on day and production [piece] rates [PG 1/12/1893]. It also provided profits surplus to requirement and the two Bonds were paid off in 1885 [21/5/1885 289-178] and 1890 [30/7/1890 408-161].

In 1887 Mary died and her children, Robert M. and Jessie, inherited the Pottery although the Title was not transferred into their names until 1890 [29/8/1890 410.74]. This transfer of ownership would have had no effect on the running of the Pottery and it is doubtful if Mary had made any practical contribution to the business.

Using the profits due to the upturn in trade Robert M. started to carry out much needed repairs to and extend the premises. The main repair was undertaken in 1889 when the large chimney stack was straightened as it was nearly three feet off the vertical and reported as being "at nearly at the tumbling down state". This work was undertaken by Mr Burns a specialist contractor from Glasgow [FA 6/12/1889]. The improvements continued the following year by building a new warehouse and showroom [FA 24/10 1890]. The report on this extension, which included a reference to a "Royal Visit" illustrates the popularity of Wemyss Ware.

Gallatown - Visit of Royalty to Fife Pottery

Inhabitants of the third ward were, on Friday afternoon honoured by a visit of the Princess Louise [Marchioness of Lorne] the guests of Mrs. Wemyss at Balfour House. Arriving with a large party of Ladies and Gentlemen including Mrs. Wemyss, Mrs. Paget, Mrs. Hugo Wemyss, Mrs. Campbell and others the distinguished visitors called at the Fife Pottery belonging to Messers R. Heron and Son. The party went over the works and visited the different Departments through which the wares pass before reaching the saleroom. Her Royal Highness was particularly interested in the beautiful glaze on the brown teapots. Princess Louise expressed thanks for the pleasure the visit had afforded and gave orders for the supply of the beautiful Wemyss Ware to be forwarded to her.

The enterprising firm are making large extensions to the ware room and when finished will add greatly to Messers Heron's increasing trade. The building is 100 feet in length and two storeys height and the work has been entrusted to Mr Masterton builder, Mr Thomson joiner, Mr Hutchison plasterer and Mr Robb plumber.

Over the period 1880/90 Robert M. had paid out not inconsiderable sums of money to clear his debts and develop the Pottery. It is suggested in "Wemyss Ware" [page16] that these had been funded "not from the profits of Fife Pottery [nor from Wemyss Ware], but probably as a result of a substantial legacy". Although no explanation is given for this suggestion there is no reason why this could not have been true. It is now impossible to know how Robert M. and his father had operated but it is certain that he was an affluent man and his life style was supported by an adequate income from the Pottery especially when it is remembered that he made frequent trips abroad and to London where he was "well known... and as much esteemed as in his native town as an able and artistic potter" [Scottish Pottery p. 198]. Also as his father had cleared the bulk of the inherited and personal debts from the business it appears that Robert M. could have paid off the debt secured against the Pottery at any time he chose. It appears more likely that the interest arranged was fairly low and there was not much to be gained in clearing the debt.

Whatever the financial position this must have been a very proud time for the Herons who had been for so long in the shadow of their relations at Links Pottery as their new product, Wemyss Ware, became ever increasingly popular with the titled and rich middle classes. This popularity was in part due to the support of the local Wemyss and Rosslyn families through whom it was fashionable for "gentry" visiting the area to view the Pottery especially after the visit by Princess Louise.

As well as these triumphs Robert M. had his troubles some of which at least were self-inflicted. In common with many employers in Scotland, but contrary to the other local Pottery owners, he was particularly "anti-union" and would not accept the principle of collective wage bargaining on a National scale. Thus in 1891 when the Potters Union negotiated a National agreement for an increase in wages of 2.5p per day he would not accept it. After local negotiations also failed and "serving notice" the kilnmen and some of the potters came out on strike in September claiming that their wages were "under the Glasgow rate". After prolonged discussions Robert M. was prepared to accept the raise provided the Potters left their Union as reported in the Kirkcaldy Mail on 3rd November 1891.

The strike at Fife Pottery Kirkcaldy

In connection with the strike at Fife Pottery, Kirkcaldy which has continued for eight weeks, a mass meeting was held in Gallatown Free Church on Saturday evening. The hall was crowded. Mr Wallace, president of the Union, occupied the chair explained that the men had come out on strike for an increase of 6d per day in order that they might be put on an equal footing with their fellow workmen Since the commencement of the strike the employer had offered the increase on the understanding that they sever their connection with the Union. This they refused to do ....

This strike was settled soon after the meeting and the workers granted the pay increase. Having lost the battle Robert M. did not give up his struggle against the Union and shortly afterwards he sacked the Union representatives in the Pottery. This action so annoyed the workers that they threatened to come out on strike again [KM 9/2/1892]. This threat was sufficient to have the men reinstated. The other Pottery owners in the area who would not have been happy at the thought of their workers coming out on strike to support the men at the Fife Pottery did not support this action by Robert M.

Despite this and no doubt other setbacks the Pottery continued to flourish and further extensions were built in 1894 [FA 5/5/1894] and further land acquired opposite the Pottery [6/6/1894 528.190]. There was a small house on this land that was demolished and the area turned into a garden with a tennis court for the owners' use. They may well have occupied this land well before this time.

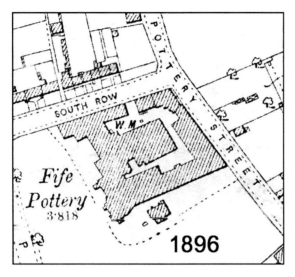

In 1899 the RV. of the Pottery and house was raised from £120 to £140 and it can be assumed that this increase was for the Pottery only and was due to the various extensions. This compares very unfavourably with the Kirkcaldy Pottery [formerly Links] that was valued at £600. It would be unkind to be to critical of Robert M. by comparing the expansion of the two Potteries as James Methven and especially A. R. Young had exceptional business talents. In addition they started on a very much more sound financial base. It must be assumed however that Robert M. never had the business drive of his rivals. Certainly it is impossible to imagine James Methven or A.R. Young going abroad for a lengthy period and leaving the business in the hands of a manager. This lack of drive was only partially compensated for by his artistic nature because popular as it was Wemyss Ware did not continue to be the financial success it promised when it was first produced indeed it may have made the Pottery less profitable as a whole.

Naturally the working and living conditions of the Fife Pottery workers were similar to that of their fellow workers at Kirkcaldy Pottery with the ever awakening of socialism which was reflected in the various trade disputes as the workers gained more confidence and felt able to challenge their "masters". These challenges were partially successful and as trade improved the potters realised that their lives could and should be better. Although the weekly wage for good tradesmen in the Pottery rose as high as £1.50 by 1889 there were many occasions when the wages were cut by substantial amounts simply because trade was "slack".

Having achieved this improvement in their working life many of the workers in the Potteries and elsewhere also sought to improve their social lives by setting up various "self improvement" societies and leisure clubs such as The Gallatown Mutual Improvement Society, Ambulance Classes, Working Man's Institute, Bowling Club and Boys Club. Of course the Church still had a very strong hold on the community. Robert M. does not appear to have participated in these organisations except by his membership of Pathhead Parish Church although he was prepared to make small donations where appropriate. He regularly gave a pair of silver mounted bowls as prizes to the Bowling Club and also gave copies of Punch, Fun, Judy and Daily Scotsman to the Liberal Institute [FA 21/3/1874]. It is probable that he read Punch and the Scotsman but why he should have the other two or consider that the Institute would require them is problematical. Within this self-improvement movement one of the prime movers was Karel Nekola surely a tribute to his general attitude and his knowledge of English [see extract from one of his notes on the following page].

Notes written by Karel Nekola for a talk on his homeland

I feel that I have undertaken rather too much
when I agreed to tell you something about the
country that gave me birth, but not wishing
to be a block in the way & wishing to induce
others to come forward & do better, I will
do my best to show you where land &
people differ from you here.
I shall arrange it in such a way as if you
were on a visit to Bohemia
yourselves and I to act as your cicerone.
And I beg you to understand that when
I am bound to say anything derogatory
about existing facts & usages I am not
doing so with any feeling of disrespect
or trying to draw ridicule &
contempt upon land, people or manners.
The country of Bohemia as it appears on the
map is a quadrangle
each corner of which points to the four
cardinal points of the compass, its four
sides are flanked with ranges of mountains
& hills & the interior is of an undulating
character, & its geological formation is such
that it gave rise to the theory that at a certain
remote time it was an inland sea.

The workers regularly contributed to various charities and especially the local Cottage Hospital as well as raising money to help their work mates when they were ill as there was no form of Social Security to compensate for the loss of income or pay for hospital treatment. A few employees were reported as being involved in accidents at work or fighting with their fellow workers and ending up in court for assault. Indeed they were typical of most workers. In considering the working conditions care must be taken not to judge by today's standards and Robert M. would have been a typical Victorian employer and considered to be "reasonable" by the standards of his day.

One improvement the workers did not achieve was holidays with pay, and any short holidays taken would be at home with the exception of the annual Works Outings which were usually subsidised by the employer. Judging by the local newspapers these outings, were happy and occasionally riotous affairs. The workers were transported to a local beauty spot in horse drawn carts usually accompanied by some form of music such as a local brass band or small section of fiddles that would entertain the crowd and play for dancing until they drove home in the evening. As would be expected these outings were highlights in the potters' year although not without incident nor were they alcohol free as reported in the Fifeshire Advertiser 2/6/1894.

Gallatown Potters Trip
Annual outing from Fife Pottery to Glenfarg some of the party were so highly pleased with the beauty and liquids of Newburgh that they forgot to attend when the time was called to leave for home and were left behind. They arrived home the next day none the worse of their long walk [approx. 20 miles].

Robert M's sister, Jessie, died in 1895 and this must have been a severe blow to him since they had lived together for most of their lives as both were unmarried and she had taken a great interest in the artistic side of the Pottery. It is difficult to assess Jessie's contribution to the Pottery but certainly local tradition credits her with designing several of the Wemyss shapes well as being a skilled painter. Neither her Will or Estate were registered as presumably her affairs were so closely linked with her brother's on a "survivor" basis that the longer living would automatically become the owner. There was no change in the Title Deeds at this time.

The new twentieth century and the end of the Victorian Era did not bring about the much hoped for improvement in trade and Fife Pottery was subjected to the same pressures as the others as the country was flooded with cheap foreign pottery. Through this difficult period they continued to produce the "ordinary" lines along with Wemyss Ware, which maintained its popularity if not its profitability. Royal patronage continued with a visit by the Grand Duchess Michel-Michelovitch in 1904. She was shown round the Pottery by Mr McKenzie and bought some Wemyss Ware [FA 17/9/1904]. Perhaps as McKenzie organised the visit Robert M. was on one of his many travels!

Also the start of the new century was marked by the death in June 1901 of Mr Robert Duncan, "Mr Heron's trusted Manager who was highly respected in the district" [FA 22/6/1901]. The precise nature of the managerial position held by Duncan is not given but as there was already a Business Manager and a Pottery Manager it can be assumed that he must have been the Commercial Manager responsible for all the office work including accounting as well as sales and dispatching. He would have worked under McKenzie. There is no record of who replaced him although a Mr Forester held this position some years later.

The Census Returns for 1901 unfortunately do not indicate which Pottery the individual entrants were employed in or the total number of employees in each Pottery. The individual types of occupations are much the same as those in earlier Returns except for one an "Underhand Shingler (pottery)". No explanation of this term has been found. Also listed is James K. McKenzie [age 45 years] a Commercial Traveller in Earthenware [born Glasgow]. Although not stated it is reasonable to assume that this is the son of J. K. McKenzie the Pottery Business Manager at the Fife Pottery.

After being in control of the Fife Pottery for upwards of thirty five years Robert Methven died on 23rd June 1906 in his seventy third year following a short illness which was diagnosed as "Angina Pectoris" [FFP 30/6/1906]. With this the long line of master potters descending from David Methven[1] came to an end. His death is described as "...with startling suddenness . Mr Heron laid aside a newspaper he was reading when he heaved a sigh and expired"[FA 30/6/1906].

Fortunately for the researcher Robert M's Will [dated 23/6/1904] and Inventory were registered as required by law on 14th August 1916 and give a very good insight into the Pottery and the trading position. The Estate was valued at £25,334.72 of which £9500 was cash or lodged in the bank. He also had a small portfolio of shares mainly in local companies such as linoleum and coal mines. The business debts were individually small and as would be expected mainly with pottery dealers. These were distributed throughout Scotland on a basis approximately the same as the population distribution and it is a tribute to the quality of the products that they were able to trade in other Scottish "pottery" towns such as Prestonpans, Portobello, Clydebank, Bo'ness and Glasgow. Local debtors were the "gentry", Ferguson of Raith, Oswald of Dunniker and the Wemyss family. Equally Heron had also traded with the Co-operative Societies in Kirkcaldy, Dysart and Cowdenbeath. Presumably the gentry had bought Wemyss Ware whilst the "Co-ops" had purchased more basic wares. Also listed were

Morrison and Crawford probably for white "flat ware". The debts amounted to some £1500 in Scotland of which executors expected to recover only £1200 due to "bad" debts giving an indication the state of the economy at that time.

There were also a few debts in England of which the £317 owed by Goode of London was by far the largest and would have been for Wemyss Ware. The others were fairly small and in the Newcastle and Carlisle areas except for several "titled" ladies in the south. These last were, probably for Wemyss Ware. Surprisingly although Robert M. had traded extensively in Ireland there are only a few debts listed in Athlone, Killarney and Dublin. Whether this indicates the amount of trade or only the level of credit given to the Irish is not known. The trade in Dublin was with the Royal Irish School of Needlework and may have been for Wemyss Ware as embroidery was often copied from this ware. It is worth noting that the Wemyss family operated a "School of Needlework" in Coaltown of Wemyss.

To these debts were added the assets in the house and Pottery

Asset	Value £
Hay at Pottery	10.62
Household Furniture etc.	470.00
Pottery Materials and Machines	2709.80

The contents of the house were given in remarkable detail and suggest that Robert M. had lived a convivial and cultured life. Certainly there was no shortage of drinking glasses and he had a fair supply of whisky and champagne.

The Moveable Estate totalled approximately £14,000 and the property that consisted mainly of the house and Pottery was valued at some £11,000. The whole Estate was valued at £25,334.77, which was to be distributed to a long list of benefactors including friends and workers along with various charities. Among the workers were J. K. McKenzie [£500], and Peter Weepers [£100] who were described as "managers" and were to retain their positions until the Pottery was sold. The list also contained D Barrie, crate maker at the pottery [£100], Ann Barrie, table maid [£20], Carlo Nekolo, artist [£50], John McKinnon, mould maker [£50] and Bella Turner, housekeeper [£100]. The friends listed had no apparent connection with the Pottery except indirectly Mary Methven, the widow of James Methven of Kirkcaldy Pottery, who was left £50 to purchase a mourning ring and somewhat surprisingly two rockingham vases.

[NB this spelling for Karel Nekola is not considered by his family to be an alternative but simply an error by the lawyer who prepared the documents. The same mistake were copied by the local newspapers]

These bequests although apparently small would have been significant sums at that time compared to a potter would be very lucky if he earned £100 per annum. It is thought that both Nekola [artist] and Mckinnon [mould maker] earned about £5 per week making them by far the highest paid workers and that there was an on going argument about which "skill" had the greatest value to the Pottery. Robert M. surely gave his answer to the question - they were equally important when he left them both £50. However Barrie the crate maker was left £100, which is perhaps explained by the fact that he had worked in the Pottery for some sixty years [FA 29/12/1917]

After all of the bequests, which amounted to approximately £4000, had been paid the remainder including the Pottery was left to Robert M's friend, William Williamson.

The Executors, who included J. K. McKenzie, submitted the Confirmation of the Inventory to the Cupar Sheriff Court on 14th August 1906. In these papers McKenzie was described as "sometime Business Manager at the Pottery" which seems to suggest that he had retired sometime between the date of the Will [1904] and Robert M's death. Similarly in the local newspapers he was described as "former manager" [FA 15/9/1906] that might confirm this suggestion. However as the Will had been prepared only two years earlier and Robert M protected his position there must be doubts. If indeed he had recently retired his retiral was short lived.

In making this condition of continuing employment for the managers Robert M. must have expected Williamson to sell the Pottery fairly quickly as it would have been an unreasonable condition to expect the new owner to offer unlimited continuing employment. Although William Williamson as a Yarn Dealer would have had little or no knowledge of potting he had other ideas and decided to continue operating the Pottery at least on a reasonably long-term basis. As he required technical assistance to operate the Pottery and he was also, within the term of the Will, to employ Weepers and McKenzie as managers [if they had not already retired] until the Pottery was sold the solution to his problem was easily solved when he handed over the running of the business to J. K. McKenzie and appointed him overall Manager. He was probably on some "profit sharing" scheme and his position was sufficiently high for him to leave his family home in Windmill Road and move into the Pottery House [VR 1908].

Peter Weepers was also retained until he died suddenly later in 1906 leaving McKenzie without the managerial backup he was used to. As there was no obvious replacement in the Pottery McKenzie had to find a replacement quickly. Fortunately for him James Wishart who had been manager at Pollockshaws Pottery for thirty-eight years was due to retire. Wishart, who was a native of Kirkcaldy and had been trained at Kirkcaldy Pottery, was easily persuaded to return to his birthplace and to continue working for a short period. Although it is not known for certain that McKenzie and Wishart were acquainted it is unlikely that these two "senior" potters had not met when they both worked in the Glasgow area.

Wishart was in his late sixties when he came to the Pottery but was still an active man working long hours as he was a "key holder" and expected to turn out when ever required. To achieve this he lived nearby in Miller Street. Having helped the Pottery through this management problem Wishart retired in 1908 and although he had only worked there for two years the workers presented him with a clock that was inscribed "Presented to Mr Wishart manager of the Fife Pottery by the employees as a mark of respect and appreciation. Nov. 1908" [FA 14/II/1908]. During this short period he also had the honour of a visit by the Grand Duke Michel of Russia [FA 19/10/1907]. Having had time to plan for James Wishart's retirement Mckenzie was able to recruit James Gardiner from Alloa Pottery as a replacement. This was organised to provide a short overlapping handover period. James continued to live in Kirkcaldy near to the Kirkcaldy Pottery and he attended A.R. Young's funeral as a "friend".

As in the case of the other Potteries in Great Britain Fife Pottery continued to suffer greatly under the mass importation of cheap pottery from the Continent. The employers and workers were naturally in favour of the proposed "Tariff Reform Bill" which was designed to control what was seen as unfair competition. The Gallatown potters and linoleum workers apparently felt more strongly about this and formed their own branch of the "Tariff Reform Party" in 1908 [FA 5/12/1908]. This Bill was never passed much to the detriment of the Potteries

Although the Pottery continued to work and Williamson continued to exploit Wemyss Ware, the works were seldom at full capacity and by 1910 many workers were leaving the industry for personal and economic reasons. This entailed skilled workers seeking employment elsewhere such as the local linoleum works where the smaller wages were compensated for by more regular work. Other workers had so little faith in the future of the Pottery and even the country that they emigrated to seek a better life abroad. The loss of these workers was a blow to the Pottery especially as in many cases it was the skilled men who left. This is well illustrated by Joseph Nekola, the eldest son of Karel Nekola. Joseph had been trained by his father and was a talented decorator. His strict upbringing by his now Presbyterian father and his socialist tendencies were such that he was considered to be a "pacifist and sort of a Communist" [this description was given many years later and would have referred to his general attitude]. Popular as he was with his fellow workers he apparently had difficulties with his employer over working conditions and wages. It was also claimed that he did not try for a high output, as there was no bonus available. He left the Pottery in 1910 to go to Canada [FA 2/4/1910] and eventually found work in Buffalo USA where he worked successfully for two years before returning to Kirkcaldy due to family commitments. He was fortunate in being re-employed at the Pottery but left soon thereafter to work as a "wagon painter" in the nearby Thornton Railway Workshops.

Joseph was far from unique in seeing little future in the Pottery but his employer who had already seen the trade expansion in the late 1880's following a cyclic depression did not share this view. This more optimistic view was, in part, justified when in 1911 they were able to offer almost full employment to the workers and in 1912 they were able to expand the work force to about one hundred despite a period of "short time" due to coal and railway strikes. This increase in trade continued into 1913 and was repeated all over Scotland to such an extent that when the Potters Union felt confident enough to request an increase in wages of 15% the potters at Fife Pottery were willing to join in this claim and to win an increase in wages.

Trade disputes of this type were far from uncommon in most industries during the first half of the twentieth century as the workers had a continual struggle to improve their conditions, a struggle that fortunately was eventually to bear fruit. One small but typical example was David Colville the kilnman at the Fife Pottery who was the subject of an industrial accident at his work that caused him a significant loss of wages [FA 24/5/1913]. To obtain compensation for this he was forced to take his employers to court because there was no Government help at that time. He won his action

Despite complaining that the potters' increase in wages would raise the cost of the wares to an uneconomic level the Williamson still thought it was worth while investing in the Pottery and he improved the warehouse in 1913 and built a new bisque kiln and a frit house in 1914.

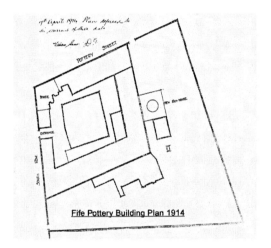

Fife Pottery Building Plan 1914

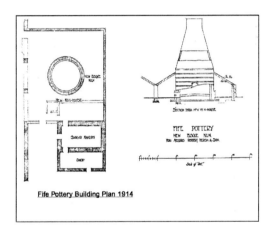

Fife Pottery Building Plan 1914

After these alterations the RV was increased to £127 in 1913 and £145 the following year. With all of these alterations and improvements the Pottery reached its peak in size but it is doubtful if it ever reached its full potential output for any sustained period.

At this stage it is worth considering the many improvements that had been undertaken over the life of the Pottery. To illustrate this the available maps are reproduced together and although they are not of the same scale the do show the progress reasonably well.

The Development of Fife Pottery

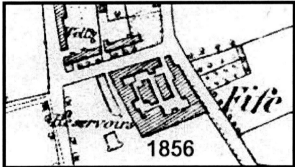

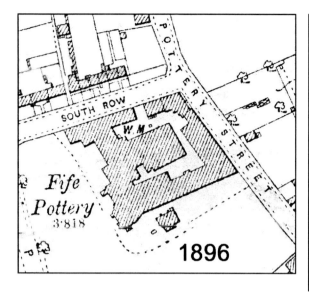

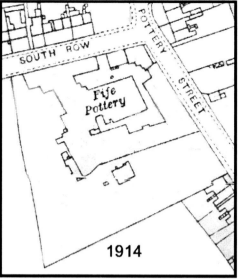

The first map [1828] can be considered as being reasonably representative of the layout while the originals of other three are accurate being from the Ordnance Survey. The full extent of the site as shown on the 1914 map was not occupied by buildings and was, at least in the last years, used for storage of clay and other materials.

It is seen clearly that the general outline of the buildings was established by the Grays and indeed many of their buildings remained in use throughout the whole active period of the Pottery. The original outline was in the form of an open square with no buildings on the Pottery Road frontage. It is not possible to be sure where the entrance was nor if there was a house or not. By 1856 this frontage had been complete and separate buildings erected in the centre of the square. The access was off South Row and it appears that the house was to the west of the entrance. The kilns were built into the south range of buildings and the other buildings would have been used for the various processes as required. It is seen that there were two reservoirs immediately adjoining the Pottery buildings and it seem reasonable to assume they were part of the Pottery. In this location they must have been supplied by underground water, as there is very limited surface water in the area.

Over the next forty years the redevelopment continued including building a new Pottery House in the northeast corner and a new entrance off South Row. The buildings in the centre were joined to the west wing. The garden for the House was opposite on the north side of South Row. Once established by 1896 the basic layout remained the same until the end. There can be no doubt that there would have been internal alteration as described in the general text and that new machinery would have been introduced where required.

The optimism shown by Williamson and his manager, Mckenzie, during this period of expansion was smashed by the outbreak of the Great War which started when the potters were yet again on strike for an increase in wages of 20% [FA 22/8/1914]. The war reduced the production to almost a token amount at first but it increased slightly later. To add to the problems Karel Nekola who had been in ill health for some time died in 1915.

In Kirkcaldy and elsewhere there has been an on going argument about the importance of Karel Nekola to Fife pottery and especially for Wemyss Ware. This has varied from considering that Wemyss Ware would not have existed if Nekola had not come to Kirkcaldy to almost dismissing his input. Ken Mckenzie expressed this latter view long after the Pottery had closed when he claimed, "it was the potter that mattered as you could always get a decorator". Both these views are, obviously, incorrect and the truth must lie some where in between. What is certain is that he was a very intelligent man and an extremely talented painter both on ceramics and on the normal artist's mediums on paper and canvas. His work on ceramics will be discussed later when the wares from the Pottery are considered. Fortunately several of his pencil sketches, water colours and oil paintings still exist which show his undoubted talents especially his views of "Pan-hall" in Dysart which seems to have been a favourite subject as he did several versions both in oils and on ceramics.

While there maybe some argument about his artistic and decorating ability it would be difficult to challenge his intelligence. Karel was born in Bohemia [then part of Hungarian Empire] in 1857 the son of a carpenter with whom he trained and worked until he had a serious accident when still a very young man. This prevented him continuing in that trade and he retrained as a ceramic decorator. He must have shown a natural aptitude for this art and became sufficiently highly skilled by his mid twenties that he and other decorators were persuaded to come to Gallatown to work for Robert M. It is thought that he was able to speak a little English when he arrived but even so he quickly achieved a very good command of the language when compared to his compatriots at work. He was soon very involved in the local community and very interested in "self improvement" organisations as well as getting married [1884] to Isabella Thomson, Robert M's housekeeper, and raising a family.

In his early days he was very active being a keen walker and cyclist as well as the gym instructor at the "Boy's Institute" but it was at the "Gallatown Mutual Improvement Association" that his ability with English came to the fore. He joined the Association in 1897 and was President by 1990 as well as being a regular lecturer. The subjects he chose were to say the least challenging: -

1899   Cremation in preference to burial [NB he had been raised as a Catholic and changed to Presbyterian in Gallatown]
1900   Sacrilege in religion
1901   Tomorrow
1902   Evolution
1903   Evolution
          Hugh Millar
1904   Can we take humour seriously?

While these subjects may show his mental ability they can only hint at the standard of his English. However there also still exist the notes for a lecture [undated] he prepared which shows clearly his command of English [page 109]. He is reputed to have been fluent in other European languages as well.

As time passed he became more crippled in his lower limbs and was unable to make the short trip from his house in Bandon Avenue to the Pottery and a small studio with a muffle kiln was built in his garden where he could continue decorating pots that were carried to him every day in specially designed baskets. He continued working until shortly before his death when he was greatly missed by the pottery workers and the local community. His obituary in the Fife Free Press [4/12/1915] is probably the longest and most appreciative printed except for the major landowners and businessmen

The Late Karel Nekola   An appreciation
Death with "impartial foot" and indiscrimatory sway has again crossed many thresholds in our midst and removed from our ken the form of many well known citizens plunging into mourning communities and families.
Among those who have within the last few days fallen asleep there is one, comparatively unknown maybe outside the Gallatown District but to the inner circle of friends who were privileged to visit and love him, a man of noble character, one whose life was an inspiration to good deeds. We refer to the late Karel Nekola and offer our humble tribute of sympathy to his surviving widow and family.
A Bohemian by birth he came to the district some 35 years ago to fulfil an important position as designer, painter and decorator in Fife Pottery [R.H.& S.]. Besides doing general work of an excellent kind he was mainly responsible for introducing and popularising the well known Wemyss Ware. In the early years of more vigour and activity he was an untiring pedestrian and there are few beauty spots in the County within a radius of 15-20 miles from the "Lang Town" he did not explore. He extolled the scenery of Fife, its hills and fertile straths, its pleasant fringed shores. To the present writer he once said that few fairer scenes could be found anywhere than the prospect across the Forth on a Summer evening. Always cheerful with a love of humanity he played his part in schemes for the welfare of youth. We will only name one - The Boys Institute in Hill Street. It will surprise those who have known him only since his bodily strength began to fail in more recent years when he was unable to walk beyond his garden and workshop to learn that he was drill instructor and teacher of

gymnastics to the young lads.

Other bodies he took a deep interest in were the Society of Free Gardeners and the Gallatown Young Mens Association. To the latter of which he was a tower of strength. The members valued highly his contribution to debate since his opinions were so just and carefully thought out and anticipated with unfeigned pleasure. When it is remembered that English was to him a foreign language his diction and clear flow were alike remarkable.

Incapacitated in his lower limbs and denied the pleasure of walking he was a patient sufferer. His unselfishness and natural courtesy no physical weakness could affect. He would rise from his chair or couch - though racked with excruciating pain to greet a visitor making thoughtful inquiry as to the visitors well being.

How we shall miss his presence and consideration of his well informed mind.

Even accepting that such tributes will normally be over laudatory there can be little doubt that Nekola had made a great impression on the writer and the local community. His death must have left a serious gap in the decorating section at the Pottery that was never going to be easy to fill with a worker of sufficient ability, especially during the war period when so many workmen including Carl Nekola, K Nekola's artist son, had joined the services.

Pencil Sketches by Karel Nekola drawn in 1898

Fortunately this vacancy was filled early in 1916 when Edwin Sandiland was discharged from the army due to ill health. His discharge was granted whilst he was stationed at Perth, which was very convenient for both the employee and his new employer.

Sandiland had trained as a potter with his father who owned the firm of Sandilands Ltd. in Hanley. As well as this training he had studied at the Art College in Stoke on Trent and this type of work was very much his first choice. Prior to joining the army he was a director in his father's business but, apparently, he was very prone to worry and as he did not enjoy the stress associated with that position he was very glad to work at the Fife Pottery as the Chief Decorator. No doubt the owner of Fife Pottery was delighted and surprised to fill this vacancy so quickly and more so when Sandiland turned out not only to be a talented decorator but also a very quick worker whose output was about twice that of Karel Nekola.

As Sandiland must have been very aware of the range of colours and glazes available for ceramic decorating in Staffordshire and their use he would have be surprised at the on going problem with the glazes on Wemyss Ware. Nekola had developed most of the "Wemyss" colours and judging by his logbook [KM] they were mainly very dangerous containing lead, arsenic and other hazardous ingredients. To add to this to maintain the bright and vibrant colours the wares had to be glost fired at a relatively low temperature [900 c], which produced a final glaze that did not amalgamate with the body. This gave rise to the characteristic crackled finish that was not a seal against liquids such as ink or preserves that soon marked their containers. To add to this problem the low temperature of the biscuit firing required to produce a body suitable for the type of colours used also produced a relatively soft body, which was prone to chipping. Sandiland introduced a new type of colours, which enabled the firing temperature to be raised to about 1080 c, and produced a harder body as well as a better glaze. He was also able to extend the range of colours. This must have been a welcome change for the potters as there had always been a problem firing Wemyss Ware with general wares as they required different kiln temperatures and there was a limit to the difference in temperature that could be achieved by packing the Wemyss Ware in the cooler parts of the kiln [KM files notes J.K. McKenzie]. This new technique was not a recent improvement in the industry and it is difficult to imagine why it had not been adopted years earlier except perhaps simply because sales had been successful despite the obvious defects.

The arrangement of Mckenzie undertaking the running of the Pottery continued for a few years with him in full control except perhaps for major policy or financial matters. This arrangement was extended in 1917 when the firm of Robert Heron and Son was reformed as a partnership of William Williamson, his two sons, James and William [jun], and J.K. McKenzie [Company Records 4724]. The individual shares in the business are not specified but as the arrangement was further extended in 1919 when the partners were taken into co-ownership of the property it was probably on the same share basis. McKenzie's precise share is not listed but since it was valued at £1250 and the property was valued at about £12,000 his share would have been about 10%. It is not known if McKenzie paid for his share in the Company but if he did his share in the property was a significant investment. However, it may have been part of a general financial deal set up so that he would continue as manager. It does show his confidence in the future of the Pottery that would have been based on his past experience with the business and the optimism at the termination of the War.

Having gained this extra control in the business McKenzie quickly promoted his son, J.K. McKenzie [Ken], to Pottery Manager. Ken it will be remembered had trained as a potter although he had been employed as the commercial traveller [VR & CR1901]. The local tradition from former employees claims that Ken had been "working the farms", which suggests a sort of door-to-door salesman. This suggestion is unsubstantiated and perhaps a little unkind. Also it is claimed that the Pottery Manager, Gardiner, was "frozen out" so that Ken could get his job. How much truth there is in this claim is conjectural. It is further claimed that Gardiner had introduced slip casting to the pottery and as he had not given the details of the mixture for his slip to either of the McKenzies this process had to stop when he left until it was reintroduced a few years later. This claim appears to be less likely since by that time the method of slip casting was reasonably well known. It is however a very nice story and would have been only justice if the rest of the claims were true.

Under the management of father and son the Pottery continued in production all be it on a reduced scale due to the decline in the National Economy. Their attempts to retain if not improve their share of the market were not helped by the decline in the popularity of Wemyss Ware. Although the sales were limited due to the War the common ware was still reasonably popular throughout Britain and they continued sending wares especially teapots to Ireland as well as flatware through Morrison and Crawford to the same market. Irish loads were easily recognised as they were packed in wood shavings instead of straw for Public Health reasons [KM files]. This relatively low level of trade must have presented David Mathews, the traveller, with many problems as he sought business throughout Britain from Manchester to Inverness and in Ireland from Dublin to Ballamena. They even tried to export to Iceland but with little success [Mrs. C Nekola].

At the end of the War [1918] Ken and his father continued the improvements started by Sandiland to the wares and changed the kilns from up draft to down draft firing and raising the firing temperatures to 1190 c. This method of firing reduced the coal costs by a significant amount [perhaps by as much as 50%] as well as producing a better body while still maintaining the quality of the colours.

In 1922 William Williamson [sen] retired from the company although he retained his share of the property. His place was taken by J.J. Greenaway, a cashier, who had worked for Williamson in his yarn and linen business [Company Records 4724 28/6/1922]. Greenaway had previously been employed one day per week as cashier at the Pottery and would have be conversant with the office side of the business. The details of the number of shares held by each partner was not given but it is thought that Greenaway was a junior partner although still having a substantial number of shares [Greenaway Family].

Also in 1922 Carl Nekola who had worked at the Pottery since he was a boy, except for his war service, left to work for Morrison and Crawford at the Rosslyn Pottery [Mrs. C Nekola]. The loss of one of the principal decorators would not have been very important as trade was fairly slow and as stated before Sandiland was capable of a very high output. Despite this decline Wemyss Ware still amounted to some 20%-25% of the output on a financial basis but very much less on a production basis as individual pieces of Wemyss Ware were about fifteen to twenty times dearer than the similar common ware.

As experienced throughout British Industry the 1920's were in general a period of strife and depression starting off with short periods of minor boom alternating with longer periods of depression when sales were low. These problems came to a head with the National Strike of 1926. Although this strike only lasted a short time the coal miners continued and the lack of coal for the boiler and kilns brought the Pottery virtually to a complete standstill. It is doubtful if it ever reached anything like full production again. During this period they also stopped using the local red clay in the manufacture of teapots and associated wares presumably as it had become uneconomic when compared to buying processed white clay [N.B. this also happened at the Kirkcaldy Pottery]. The clay lease was given up in 1925 [VR 1925]. Also that year the RV of the Pottery was raised to £213 due only to a general revaluation of commercial properties.

They did not simply accept the situation and McKenzie tried to maintain if not expand trade by introducing new wares. Wemyss Ware had lost much of its original popularity and attempts were made to improve its popularity by changing the background colours and varying the subjects. They also introduced a new range, Langtoun Ware, using a more "modern" Art-Deco style of decoration mainly on the existing range of shapes. These variations had very limited success. They had also acquired a number of moulds and transfer designs from J & MP Bell of Glasgow a few years earlier which they continued to use. Many years later Ken McKenzie claimed that even earlier than this they had manufactured wares with the Bell's design "Blythswood". He claimed that this pattern was numerically second only to the ubiquitous "Willow" although he did not confirm or deny that it was marked as being made by "Bells". Certainly there are very few marked as "Heron".

After the National Strike J K McKenzie wished to retire and his son Ken either because he was not considered suitable for the senior position or because he had a better offer left to take over the tenancy of Rosslyn Pottery from Hunter in 1927. J K McK. ceased to be a partner on 1/8/1927 [Company Records]. As part of the agreement the remaining partners had to buy his share in the business. This would not have been difficult for the two Williamsons who were relatively affluent men but it was a strain for Greenaway who had to mortgage his house in Abbotshall Road to raise the necessary capital. It is thought that J K McKenzie retired some months before the partnership was altered.

Being deprived of both the managers with the required technical experience assistance had to be acquired and a new manager was engaged from England. The first choice was singularly bad as he completely ruined his first two firings by using the very high temperatures he was accustomed to in England, which were unsuitable for the conditions at the Fife Pottery, despite warnings given by the local tradesmen. He made such an impression on the employees that none of those interviewed many years later could remember his name although they certainly remembered that the kilns had to be emptied using picks and shovels. Not surprisingly he was quickly replaced by John Huntbatch, again from England. Huntbatch had trained as a "modeller" and had been employed as a manager in Staffordshire for thirteen years. [Notes written about him perhaps at an interview are shown on page 27 of "Wemyss Ware"]. No doubt he would have been a good manager if he had been given the chance however trade was so bad that the Pottery was totally uneconomic and the kilns were left unfired in 1928 [VR 1928]. This "closure" was not considered at first to be permanent and when Sandiland died also in 1928 he was replaced as the chief [perhaps only] decorator by Joseph Nekola. The kilns were apparently never refired and the Pottery can be considered as having closed in 1928 although the company was still in existence.

With end of production there was no need for production staff or indeed Huntbatch, the business manager who left by early 1929 [VR]. By then it must have been obvious that it was highly unlikely that production would ever restart and it has to be assumed that the owners were only interested in disposing of their few assets which were the remaining stock of pottery, the property and the trade name "Wemyss Ware". To have some form of continuity J Nekola was appointed "manager" although there was little to manage.

There is also at least one piece of Wemyss Ware decorated by J Nekola and dated 1929 which appears to contradict the claim of the Pottery closing in 1928 but from the other evidence available it appears unlikely that a major kiln would be fired to complete a very limited amount of this type of ware and surely if the works had gone back into production during this period of extreme depression it would have be reported in the local papers. It seems reasonable to assume that J Nekola would have had a large stock of biscuit ware blanks to use and indeed may have operated within the Pottery perhaps using the small muffle kiln. It will also be remembered that Joseph's mother still owned the late K Nekola's workshop and muffle kiln. The glost firing is more problematical and perhaps this was done outwith the Fife Pottery. If this suggestion is accepted then Rosslyn Pottery is the only near by possibility as McKenzie had the necessary facilities and the required skill. Similarly the wares could have been sent further afield. About this time Joseph Nekola also decorated overglaze a number of china plates that may have been personal presents or commissions.

As important as it is the history so far of Fife Pottery is mainly about the owners and the more senior workers. This had to be as very little is recorded about the workers except the occasional social event and the periodic industrial disputes. The only source regarding the workers were the recollections of the workers collected many years later [over thirty] mainly from retired female workers and these were very similar to those from the other Potteries both local and national. These, as one would expect, paint a fairly glowing picture of the life of a pottery worker, as it is natural for people to try to forget the "hard times". The conditions were poor by modern standards but at that time would have been accepted as normal. The working week was about 59 hours and the working day was 6 am to 6 pm on Mondays to Fridays. Saturday was usually a shorter day with work ceasing about 2.30 pm. The working day as long as it was could be extended by overtime when the demand justified the additional expense. Similarly wages and hours were reduced if trade was slack and workers would be sent home for any reason such as shortage of materials or orders without any compensation.

Wages were considered to be low although the opportunity to work on "piece rate" was usually available for skilled workers. By this means one lady claimed to have earned £2.50 per week compared to her husband's £1.60 as a miner in the early twenties. To achieve this she worked overtime to 10 pm. on a regular basis. Although there is no doubt that she could have earned such wages this must have been fairly infrequent as when Pottery closed because of the lack of orders the local unemployment level had reached 32.6% [FA 18.2.28].

One other worker was, perhaps, more accurate when she wrote later of the life in the Pottery with its hard, cold and heavy work which she undertook only as she was unable to get any other work. Another lady who agreed with her still considered that the Fife potters were "superior" to those at the Links Pottery and she still was aggrieved when recalling the times when she was sent down to the Links to work when the relative workloads justified it. One of her complaints was that the Links potters made their tea with the water used to boil eggs. This seems a strange occurrence to remember after some forty years.

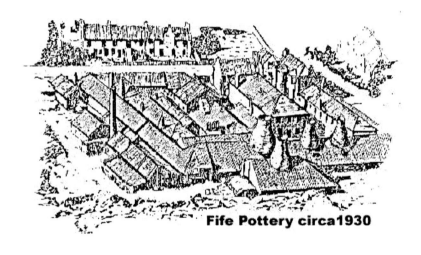

Fife Pottery circa1930

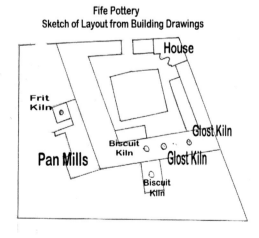

The above sketch of the buildings was drawn from an aerial photograph taken about 1930 before the Pottery was demolished, in conjunction with the Ground Plans show how the Pottery looked during the final period. From these it is seen that although Ken McKenzie considered it to be to a good design the Pottery had developed over the years in a piecemeal way which although no doubt was adequate compares unfavourably with the second Sinclairtown Pottery which was designed from scratch on a green field site.

The company had to stay in existence, as there were very large business debts and very few realisable assets. The Pottery including all of the machinery and equipment had little value and the large stock of wares including Wemyss Ware was virtually unsaleable except at very discounted prices and a small amount of biscuit ware to decorators. Some of these blanks were impressed with the Wemyss mark, which has raised many problems for collectors! A small section of land was sold in 1929 to Buist who had made the crates for the Pottery. The only moveable assets they were able to realise were the Trade Name and the designs and moulds for Wemyss Ware. These were sold to the Bovey Tracy Pottery in 1930 and J. Nekola was fortunate enough to be offered a position as decorator at Bovey Tracy where he was to remain for many years continuing to decorate in the Wemyss Ware style.

FIFE POTTERY,

KIRKCALDY,

SCOTLAND.

We beg to advise you of the closing down of our works and we take this opportunity of informing you, that in our desire to keep alive the name of Wemyss Ware, we have disposed of the rights of the name and goodwill, including all the moulds for our well known shapes, to the BOVEY POTTERY CO. LTD., BOVEY TRACEY. Our head artist has gone to Bovey Tracey and you may rest assured that the decorations will be carried out as before.

We thank you for past favors, and solicit a continuance of your orders for the Bovey Pottery Co. Ltd.

Yours truly,
R. HERON & SON.

BOVEY TRACEY,

DEVON.

We are pleased to take advantage of Messrs. Robert Heron & Son's kind introduction to invite your enquiries and continued orders for WEMYSS WARE.

By acquiring, together with the name and good-will, all the Moulds of the original shapes, and engaging the services of the artist who is the " soul of Wemyss," we shall be in a position to satisfy your needs in the decorations and models hitherto produced.

There is little doubt that the selling qualities of Wemyss Ware will be considerably enhanced by reason of its being made of our exceptionally White body and on which the decoration will show in capital relief after being covered with our brilliant and durable glaze which is free from crazing.

After studying the specimens we already have finished we are confident that the demand for this attractive ware will considerably increase, if you extend your display with our productions.

Yours faithfully,
THE BOVEY POTTERY CO., LTD.

Notices regarding the closure of Fife Pottery and transfer of Wemyss Ware

Thus was the sad end of Fife Pottery, which for over a hundred and ten years had sent its products throughout the world and had been so renowned for its wares. It was an even sadder time for the partners who were left with large debts which they were personally responsible for. This was especially difficult for Greenaway and placed a great strain on his limited capital. The Pottery was left abandoned to vandals who quickly broke into the works and stores and destroyed all of the remaining wares including hundreds of pieces of Wemyss. The property was rented out in separate parts including the house and sold several years later.

Consideration must now be given to the other Potteries in the Gallatown area and the following plan gives an indication of their location.

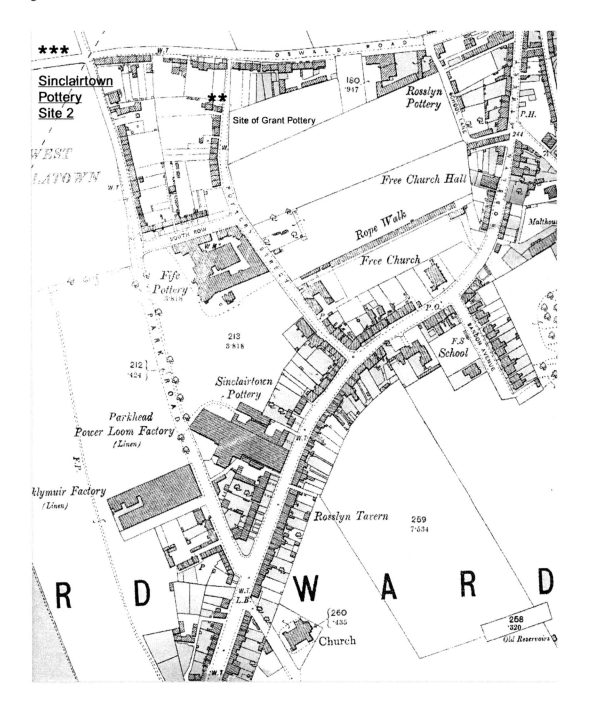

Plan of Gallatown Area Showing the

Location of the Potteries

Chapter 9   SINCLAIRTOWN POTTERY   1868 to 1928

As well as the two major Potteries still in operation in the Kirkcaldy area two other Victorian entrepreneurs took the opportunity to exploit the locally available materials and talents. They both started in 1868 although there were several years between the actual dates for the start of production. George McLauchlan was the first to open at the Sinclairtown Pottery in Rosslyn Street fairly near to the Fife Pottery.

Although there were several families of McLauchlan listed in the 1861 Census at least one connected to the Fife Pottery George McLauchlan appears to have moved to the area after that date and before his third son was born in 1862. George was born in Prestonpans [1830] and later moved to Glasgow where he married and his first two sons, Robert [1857] and William [1861] were born. His other sons Robert [1862], Charles [1865] and David [1868] were all born in Dysart Parish. While it is not certain it appears that George was the son of James McLauchlan of Clyde Pottery who certainly had a son of that name.

As there was a period of some six years between George coming to the district and starting his Pottery it is likely that he worked locally and possibly as a clerk as that was his training. What ever he was doing at the end of the slump caused by the American Civil War George bought a small section of land from Robert and Janet Cameron on the 4th. Nov. 1868 [P.R.377.159]. In the legal documents he described himself as "clerk residing in Parkhead" [part of Gallatown]. On this land he quickly built a small Pottery, which was in operation the following year when it was given a R.V. of £25. It was described as having "a kiln" which was, no doubt, an accurate description Although no other details of the Pottery appear to exist it seems that there was hardly sufficient time between November and March [say] to build even a small Pottery suggesting that George had some form of lease with the Camerons prior to purchase. It may even be that Robert Cameron built the Pottery as he was a mason. The start of production must have been successful as the following year George required more space for expansion and on 12th April 1869 he fued an adjoining strip of land from the Earl of Rosslyn. On this occasion he described himself as "potter" confirming that his status had changed and he was now in production [P.R.337.147].

With hindsight it is now easy to see that the late 1860s was not a good time to start a new business venture as the short lived slump of 1865 was quickly followed by another in 1870 which was mainly due to the Franco-Prussian War. This financial situation was so bad that George admitted that he was in financial difficulties within a few years of starting business. He was never to recover from this situation. Despite his financial problems he still took a very active part in local life and was held in sufficiently high esteem to be appointed Chairman of the Gallatown Young Men's Improvement Society and the local School Board [F.A. 21/3/1870].

Ignoring the poor trading conditions George attempted to overcome his financial problems by expanding the works in 1871 by borrowing £400 from the Kirkcaldy Property Investment Society which he agreed to repay at £1.99 a fortnight [15.192]. With this capital he built a second kiln and probably other workshops, which increased his R.V. to £37.33. His work force also increased to 12 men, 12 boys and 9 women [CR]. The similarity in the number of boys and men would seem to suggest that boys were used to power the wheels and lathes. In the following year the expansion was complete and the R.V. was increased to £40. Thus in a few years his business had grown to be approximately half of that at the Fife Pottery both in work force and in "value".

The future should have appeared brighter for George and his staff as they left for the works outing to Largo in the summer of 1872 [F.A.6/7/1872], however as time was to tell it was not to be when later that year his financial state continued to decline and he was forced to borrow the somewhat unusual sum of £221.99 from John Mclauchlan of Clyde Pottery [his father?] and the Bank of Scotland through their local agent James Galloway [42.86 18/11/1872]. This further loan may have helped a little but George slipped even deeper into trading debt until in 1873 he was forced to enter into an extrajudical arrangement with his unsecured creditors for a payment of 38p in the pound to be paid in three instalments. By this ploy he managed to fend off his creditors for a short time until he was unable to make the third payment and had to attempt to sell the Pottery by advertising in the local papers [F.A. 14/3/1874]

124

POTTERY FOR SALE.

There will be exposed for sale by public roup within the George Hotel on Saturday 21st March at 2pm. SINCLAIRTOWN POTTERY presently occupied by Mr George Mclauchlan together with machinery, moulds, utensils, etc.
The buildings are mainly new and the whole in good working order. To ensure a sale the whole will be exposed at the upset price of £700.
Although built specially as a Pottery the buildings could with little expense be adapted for other purposes.
The ground extends to 2 roods 26 poles or thereby. Feu Duty is £13-14-1.For further particulars apply at the works or to Messers Harrow & Johnson Writers.

This sale was unsuccessful and his creditors quickly moved in and sequestered his Estate on 27th. March 1874 as his debts amounted to £951.03 while his funds only totalled £30.98 and the balance was not even covered by his valuation of the property [C.S.318/19;202].

The creditors are listed in the extract from the sequestration documents and give a partial insight into the Pottery. He was using imported white clay from Devon, which he could have made into whiteware or more probably mixed with the local red clay to form cane ware. No doubt he would have used red clay on its own as well. The glazes and kiln furniture came from Staffordshire whilst coal and perhaps fireclay were obtained locally from the Begg Colliery. He also had a surprisingly high number of debts at other Scottish Potteries:- Alloa, Clyde, Verreville, Rosebank [Portobello], Port Dundas, Callender [Falkirk] and Portobello. Whilst he probably obtained some form of fireclay goods from Callender it is highly unlikely that he obtained pottery materials from the others and more likely that he was acting as an agent for the products of these Potteries. He also appears to have been acting as an agent for the Glass Works in Edinburgh and Newcastle although he may as well have obtained flint from Newcastle as none of his creditors appear to be suppliers of that essential material. The other creditors, excluding those who lent money, were local and would have been for services and goods both personal and for the business.

There are, apparently, no "marked" pieces from this period and insufficient evidence to be certain of the types of ware produced. The best clue is given in the book "Industries of Kirkcaldy and District" published in 1872 when the Pottery was in production. In this it is claimed that George only made baking dishes and teapots and that the latter were made in brown and white ware. The output was sold mainly in Scotland and Ireland with occasional loads to Hamburg and other German towns. It is also claimed that George made 700 dozen teapots per day and that he employed 30 men and boys. Also that the Pottery had started "three years ago". The last two claims are reasonable allowing a period between writing the book and publishing. However the suggested output seems to be rather ambitious.

Having taken control of the business [22/3/1874 65-61] the creditors put it up for sale and advertised it in the newspapers [F.A. 4/4/1874] but "at the much reduced upset price of £400". On this occasion the Pottery was simply described as "lately occupied by G. McLauchlan" and it can be assumed that they were aiming at local purchasers.

This sale was successful and the Pottery was sold to the partnership of David Kirk [senior] and his three sons David [junior], Andrew and Robert. There was apparently some form of competition at the sale as the price was £775, almost twice the upset price and more than George's original upset price. The selling price was made up of £375 in cash and by taking over responsibility for the bond for £400 held by the Kirkcaldy Property Investment Society for which the partners took equal shares [30/5/1874 67-58].

The full financial arrangements are not given in the legal papers but presumably the Kirk's bought all the movable estate [stock, materials, tools, etc.] as the Trustee was able to repay the bond to the Bank of Scotland and James McLauchlan [1/6/1874 67-56].

The closure of the Pottery was reported in "Ceramic Art in Great Britain" in 1883 after the sequestration when the firm is reported as "G. Mclauchlan and Son". This use of the "& Son" may have been the trading name as George did have a son, George, working in the Pottery as a "pottery presser". He was, however, still a youth [b.1857] and was not mentioned in the legal documents associated with the sequestration.

The Kirk family having purchased the Pottery set themselves up as a partnership under the name of "Kirk Brothers" which would suggest that the father was a silent partner only having a financial interest. Indeed the same may be true for David [jun] as they both continued to work as mole catchers [VR]. It should be remembered that at that time it was common for workers to have more than one seasonal trade. The other two brothers did have definite connections with the Potteries. Andrew who was twenty three years of age when the partnership was formed had been registered as a mole catcher in the 1861 Census but in 1871 he was a "kilnman". This latter occupation was highly skilled which would suggest that he had earlier experience, even if only part time in one of the local Potteries. It can hardly be doubted that he was the kilnman at Sinclairtown Pottery when he was part owner. Robert on the other hand had trained as a "pottery clerk" [C.R. 1871] and worked locally perhaps with George McLauchlan. To continue the family interest in "potting" their sister, Elizabeth, married Robert McLauchlan the manager of Fife Pottery. It is not known if George and Robert MacLauchlan were related although they both were born in East Lothian.

Although the precise details of the partnership are conjectural there is no doubt that the business was successful and that it flourished apparently under the control of Robert. This success enable them to expand in a somewhat unusual way in 1874 when they purchased "power" from the neighbouring linen factory owned by McLaren. This power could have come in the form of a steam supply to drive an engine or more probably as a drive shaft passing between the two premises. This improvement was significant and was given a R.V. of £10 compared to the R.V. for the Pottery of £40 [V.R.]. This development must also indicate a substantial increase in the output. This requirement for power also indicates that the Pottery was mainly manually powered before that date.

There can be little doubt that Robert was the driving force behind this expansion especially as in the 1881 Census he styled himself as a "Master Potter" and Andrew is still a "Kilnman" although a partner in the business. The two Davids were still mole catchers and it is probable that they contributed very little, if anything, to the running of the business. The most obvious explanation to the partnership is that Robert had provided the funds to purchase and run the Pottery and the other Partners simply stood as guarantee for the bond. This is, in part, confirmed in 1883 when the Davids and Andrew withdrew and left Robert in complete control [8/10/1883 276-62]. In this Robert took over full responsibility for the loan against the property and would have paid the retiring Partners for their share in the partnership. These sums of money, if any, are not given in the associated legal papers but this does show that Robert must have been on a very sound financial footing as he did not appear to require any additional funding.

Additional funding was required two year later and Robert used the increased value of the Pottery to raise a further loan of £300 from the Bank of Scotland [27/12/1886 322-126] and a smaller sum by selling the Pottery House to John Herd. The loss of the house would have been of no significance to Robert as he was unmarried and did not require it as a family home. This extra funding would have been for the development undertaken by Robert who greatly expanded the range of the products as well as the overall output. Indeed he was so successful that within two years in 1888 he was able to pay off the loan from the Kirkcaldy Property Investment Society [10/5/188 353-88]. From these details it can be seen that during the period of "Kirk Brothers" the Pottery had steadily and substantially expanded.

At that time it was common for businesses to be family affairs and for son to follow father in his trade. However this did not apply to Robert. Thus when Lawrence Buist. a part time potter/weaver married Robert Kirk's sister, Isabella, it is not surprising that their son, David Kirk Buist, also became a potter and worked for his uncle Robert. As David K. advanced he was eventually given some form of preferential treatment and eventually a managerial position [K.M. Files].

Although he was obviously successful Robert had other ambitions and wished to immigrate to Philadelphia USA where he had the opportunity to acquire another business. To achieve this he tried to sell the Pottery, which was advertised on the 18th January 1889 [F.A.].

POTTERY FOR SALE AT KIRKCALDY
Tenders will be received by the subscribers for the purchase of the long established business known as Sinclairtown Pottery situated in Rosslyn Street

Kirkcaldy presently carried on by Messers Kirk Bros.

The works consist of warehouse and offices, straw and packing shed. throwing, turning. pressing, moulding and gilding shops; two glost & biscuit kilns; two enamel kilns, biscuit ware & dipping house, drying stove, storeroom etc. and machinery including engine and boiler, two throwing machines, four turning lathes, pugmill, claymill etc. also about 1/4 acre of vacant land. There are two entrances one from Rosslyn Street and one from Park Road. The business only disposed off because the owner takes up a larger business in another town. This is an unusually favourable opportunity for acquiring an established business and one capable of a large extension.

Tenders to be lodged by 9th Feb.

J. & J.R. Herd Sol.

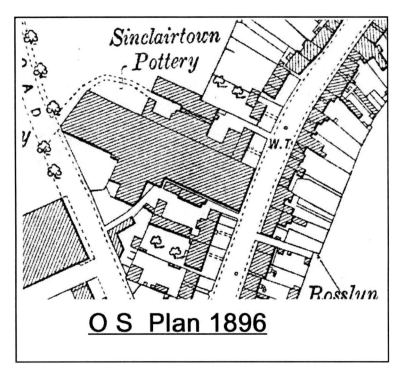

The Pottery was the buildings immediately below the name but did not include the large rectangular building, Mclaren□s Mill

The details in this notice compared to that on 14/3/1874 show clearly the considerable expansion that had been undertaken by Robert. As Sinclairtown Pottery now had two major kilns as well as two enamel kilns and a gilding shop the range of wares produced must have been much greater than those when it was purchased. By this date the Pottery was an extensive operation capable of producing as wide a range of products as its larger and much older competitors in the district. Unfortunately there appears to be no "marked" pieces and those few with reasonable attributions are all made in Rockingham Ware so it is impossible to know if whiteware was made as gilding or enamels could have been applied to glazed brownware.

The sale was not immediately successful and Robert left for the USA where he was to remain for some fifteen years. To facilitate this he either entered into or continued an existing agreement with his nephew, David Kirk Buist, to operate the Pottery in his absence. This agreement was sufficiently strong that David had to agree to the eventual sale. David would naturally have been keen to acquire the Pottery but apparently did not have the capital of credit to do so. This problem was overcome by seeking help from his family and especially his eldest brother James [born 11/8/1856]. James had trained as a draper in Kirkcaldy where after surviving a near drowning accident on 2nd. January 1869 he moved to Glasgow and established a successful drapery business. It is interesting to note that James was serving his apprenticeship when he was only twelve years of age.

James purchased the Pottery in 1890 with the consent of David and The Bank of Scotland when he took over the existing bond against the Pottery for £300 [25/2/1890 399-41]. Although the total price is not given nor are the details of the funding there can be little doubt that the major, if not only contributor, was James as he took the Title to the property. James as he was operating in Glasgow would have taken little part in the operation in the Pottery, which he leased to the new Company of "Lawrence Buist and Sons". Later the same year James transferred the debt of £300 from the Bank to the Dysart Provident Deposit Society [16/5/1899 706-78].

This new company was formed by the partnership of Lawrence Buist [senior] and his three sons James, David and Lawrence [junior]. Lawrence [sen] also borrowed £100 at this time secured against his house [II/6/1890 1018-59] that could have been used to fund the company. Lawrence [sen], according to the Valuation Rolls, had two trades, which he moved between as the conditions dictated. Firstly he was a Master Weaver owning his own loom shop with five looms and secondly he was a potter. Not surprisingly in 1890 he decided he was a potter although he still owned the loom shop, which was rented out. David as has been explained was already operating the Pottery although he had originally trained as a pottery clerk while Lawrence [jun] had trained as an engineer at first and retrained as a potter in the 1870's [CR 1871/81]. Although it is not stated it is reasonable to assume that David and Lawrence [jun] had learned their trade as potters at Sinclairtown Pottery as did their younger brothers John [born 1872] a clerk and Robert [born 1875] a pottery warehouseman.

The partnership was very successful and two years later in 1892 the partners all took equal shares in the property and the debts against it [2/10/1892]. The Title was set out on a "Survivor or Survivors" basis thus ensuring that it stayed within the partnership in the future. Throughout the 1890's the partners led quiet life styles living in relatively small houses in Rosslyn Street near the Pottery and in Aitken Street that were only given R.Vs. of £9. Lawrence [sen.] continued to lease out the loom shop to hand weavers. It appears that any profits made were ploughed back into the business.

It appears that they mainly made rockingham teapots and coffee pots and pie dishes for which there must have been an extremely large market. Surprisingly when the Possil Pottery had financial difficulties in 1896 L Buist was listed as one of the creditors and it can be assumed that this debt would have been for wares i.e. teapots. Business was such that they wished to expand and probably modernise but unfortunately their site was fairly restricted. Fortunately they in turn restricted the expansion of their neighbours, Mclaren [weavers]. This was easily overcome to their mutual satisfaction as the Buists were able to lease 0.75 acres of land at Oswald Road from the Rosslyn Estate. This was a "green field" site that may also have been the site of their clay pits judging by the quantity of wasters found during more recent roadworks adjoining the site. Having come to some form of agreement with both Rosslyn and Mclaren they submitted plans [shown below] to Kirkcaldy Dean of Guild Court in February 1898 [K.T.C. plan No. 237] and were given permission to build. Having started building they sold the old Pottery to Mclaren the following year [27/4/1899 706-80] and cleared the debt of £300 with the Dysart Provident Deposit Society [15/5/1899 706-78]. The timing of the hand over allowed them to pay off the debts and finance the building of the new Pottery. To facilitate a relatively smooth transition between the two Potteries the Buists continued operating the old Pottery until mid 1900 [V.R. 1900] when they were able, at least on a small scale, to start production on the new site. Also during this period they had been able to change their lease of the new site into a feu from Rosslyn thus giving them full control of the site [18/9/1899 718- 49]. The partnership forming Lawrence Buist and Sons remained the same.

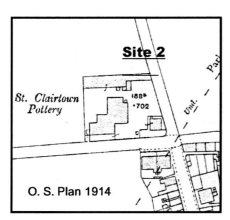

St. Clairtown Pottery

Site 2

O. S. Plan 1914

The new Pottery was at first given a R.V. of £100 being the same as the Fife Pottery. This was reduced to £75 on appeal and the two associated houses were valued at £12.50 each. These notional valuations give a good comparison of the relative sizes of the two Potteries. However as the Sinclairtown Pottery had been built from scratch it is likely that it would be to a much more efficient design with modern machinery than the Fife Pottery which had developed on a much more piece meal fashion. The new Pottery was designed to give the work flow necessary for a production line style of operation. Red clay was obtained nearby and flint and any white clay required imported, probably through the local harbours. This clay was processed in a steam driven mill and taken into the adjoining store and workshop for processing into greenware that again was taken to adjoining room for drying. Once dried it was packed into seggers and taken across the yard to either of the two coal fired kilns for firing. After firing and cooling the successful biscuit ware was glazed, dried, repacked in seggers and refired. When complete the final pieces were taken to the adjacent warehouse for dispatch to customers. It will be noted that in their design the partners left space for a third kiln. It is highly unlikely that this was ever built but this foresight does show the optimism they must have felt after this change of site.

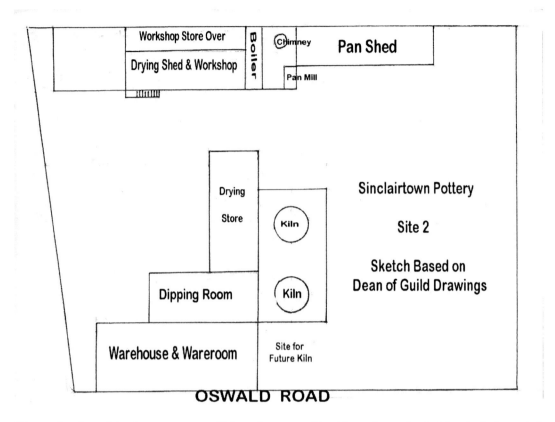

The total value of the investment would have been considerable and was funded by the balance left from the sale of the old Pottery, from personal and business funds and by a loan of £600 from Robert Blyth secured against the Pottery [16/11/1900 962-29]. It can be assumed that as this loan was taken after the Pottery was substantially complete that the funds were, at least in part, for starting the operations.

At this time the partnership remained the same being Lawrence [sen] and his three sons whilst other members of the family also worked in the Pottery without being partners. There is no doubt the business was successful and as early as May 1903 they were able to pay off half of the debt to Blyth [Lib. 863-198]. In the same year Lawrence [jun] purchased his own house in Oswald Road by borrowing £200 from the Dysart Provident Society [12/9/1903 10-11]. The business continued to flourish and the next year, 1904, they paid off the remainder of the loan from Blyth [13/2/1904 898-72]. It is shown in the various legal documents that sometime between 1900 and 1903 James left the partnership and was replaced by his younger brother, John William [born 1872].

Thus in 1904 the Buists must have been very content that after only some fourteen years of trading on this site they had cleared all of their major business debts and owned a modern and productive Pottery. They continued to make good profits and having no need to invest heavily in the business the lent various sums of money to private parties in the form of "secured loans" which totalled to some £200 in the period 1905/07. As would be expected the partners were also individually successful and Lawrence [sen] was able to clear his debt of £100 on his house in 1906 [1018-59]. Despite this obvious success the partners continued to live in their relatively small houses. John, the new partner, lived in a rented tenemented house in Sutherland Street.

Lawrence [sen] remained the senior partner until his death in 19ll when he was replaced by Lawrence [jun] who continued with his two brothers David and John. David the eldest brother was fifty years of age and although he had, in many ways, been the prime mover in the early days of the partnership must have felt it was better to leave his younger brother in the senior position. David remained in the company throughout the Great War until he retired at the end of 1919 [Company Records.14209]. On his retiral David also withdrew from the ownership of the Pottery and John who was a partner in the firm became a co-owner in the property with Lawrence [jun] [7/11/1914 Lib 1475-171]. This was a generous gesture by the two older brothers as the Pottery could have remained their property until their deaths under the conditions of the Title. Any financial arrangements are not recorded.

There are surprisingly few reports regarding the Pottery and even Lawrence [sen] death is not mentioned. It is safe to assume that the progress and on occasions the lack of progress during the first twenty years of the Century was roughly the same at the other Potteries in the area. It is reported that they settled the potters strike in 1919 quicker than the others by agreeing to the workers demand for an increase in wages but it is not reported if this was due to the employers' "fairness" or their inability to with stand a prolonged strike [F.A. 6/12/ 1919].

There were no further improvements or additions to the buildings and the increase of the R.V.s in 1912 to £90 and in 1924 to £II2 were due to general revaluations and not to improvements in the works as other commercial properties were subject to similar increases. During the period 1912 to 1916 they were also subjected to an additional tax in the form of an extra to the R.V. of £19.20 but no reason is apparent for this. Trading during the War must have been successful as the partners were able to make personal loans to house purchasers and to purchase property of their own.

The 1920s was a period of severe depression and several coal and railway strikes, which could only have had a very detrimental effect on the business. Indeed the situation was so bad that Lawrence [III] the grandson of Lawrence [sen] left the Pottery and immigrated to the USA in 1927 [F.A. 6/8/1927] followed by his cousin W. L. Buist the following year [F.A. 13/10/1928]..In the reports Lawrence[III] is credited with being "one of the members of the firm" which suggests he may have been a junior partner but if so this was not registered in the Company Records Office. W.L.'s trade is not mentioned

Through out the period Lawrence [jun.] was reported as being the driving force in the company. Unfortunately during this troubled time his health started to deteriorate in 1925 and he was seriously ill until his death in 1928 [F.A. 16/6/1928]. This death could not have come at a worse time as most businesses were struggling for survival and John, the surviving partner, closed the Pottery in October 1928 [F.A. 20/10/1928]. It is perhaps surprising that this closure should be recorded as the closure of the two other Potteries earlier that year had gone unmentioned.

Sinclairtown Pottery Closure Notice 20th Oct 1928

ANOTHER POTTERY CLOSES DOWN.—A third pottery in Kirkcaldy has been closed down this year. The latest is that at Sinclairtown occupied by Messrs Lawrence Buist & Sons Kirkcaldy. The business was founded in 1890 by Mr Lawrence Buist, who was a native of the town, and who died 17 years ago. Afterwards the business was conducted by his three sons, Messrs David, Lawrence, and John and under the chairmanship of the last mentioned, who later retired. Mr Lawrence then became senior partner, and carried on the business until he died a few months ago. The firm of Lawrence Buist & Sons enjoyed a world-wide reputation for their teapots, in the production of which they specialised. The closing of the pottery has arisen through the death of Mr Lawrence Buist.

John still had ambitions in "potting" and he registered the Title of the Pottery but not the adjoining pottery house, which was occupied by Lawrence [Jun]'s widow in August 1929 [Lib 1784-199] as agreed in the earlier Titles. John did not apply for a reduction in rates for the closed Pottery, which is listed in the Valuation Roll in 1929 and 1930 as having a R.V. of £II2 and apparently "open". In 1931 it is listed as "empty" and having a value of £56. No other proof has been found and it could be that John still hoped to restart production and did not challenge this valuation until 1931. On balance it appears unlikely that in those troubled times that a Pottery reopening would not have been noted in the local newspapers. Whilst there remains doubt regarding this "reopening" there is no doubt about that it was closed in 1931 and that it was sold to Lennie, a local scrap dealer, in 1934 for £650.

1928 was indeed a sad year in the history of potting in the Kirkcaldy area when the two largest and one of the smaller Potteries all closed within months of each other leaving only the remnants of a once proud and successful industry.

Chapter10   ROSSLYN POTTERY   1879 to 1932

This the last of the Potteries in Kirkcaldy has, in many ways, a similar history as its nearby competitors. It was, however, to out live them all perhaps due to the fact that it was so small.

As in the case of Sinclairtown Pottery the story begins in 1868 when on the 20th March William Crawford, "potter of Linktown", fued a section of land in Oswald Road from the Rosslyn Estate [274-43] subject to feu duty of £5. There is no doubt of his intention as the feu conditions clearly state that he had to build a Pottery to the value of £200 within two years and also fence off the land within one year. Crawford does not appear in either the 1851 or 1861 Census Returns but it is suggested that he was employed at the Links Pottery as a kilnman [K.M. files]. He must obviously have been a skilled and ambitious workman to undertake such an enterprise and since he did not apparently borrow any capital he must have been financially secure.

Despite his best intentions 1868 was not a sensible time to start a new Pottery as shown by the troubles at Sinclairtown Pottery and Crawford made little or no attempt to start building. Fortunately for him the Feu Superior accepted this and continued the feu although the conditions had not been met.

The construction of the Pottery did not start until 1879 [F.A.22/3/1879] and later that year the buildings were given a R.V. of £15 indicating a fairly small works. It is likely that the Pottery would have been only basically equipped and would only have had one kiln.

About this time Crawford entered into a business partnership with Adam Morrison who also had been employed at the Links Pottery. Morrison who was born in Kinglassie in 1850 [C.R. 1881] worked in the Links Pottery office at first and later was promoted becoming a salesman and business representative in London were he took the opportunity to study accounting and business practices [K.M. files Col. Hunter]. In many ways his early career mirrored that of A R Young who would have been involved in his early training. The precise date and details of the partnership are conjectural but, judging by his age, it is unlikely that Morrison would have had any influence in the original idea of starting the Pottery. Whilst Morrison's nephew and successor, Hunter, incorrectly claimed that his uncle started the Pottery in 1879 there can be very little doubt that Morrison had a major role in the foundation of the Pottery. The Title to the land clearly shows that Crawford was the sole owner. The Valuation Roll also records that in 1879 the Pottery was owned and occupied by Crawford and it was not until 1880 that the Pottery was owned and occupied by Morrison and Crawford. This would suggest that by that time the business partnership had been formed and that there was some arrangement with regard to the property although the Titles do not show this. On balance it seems likely that Morrison was a partner when the Pottery was being planned and built and certainly he was a partner by early 1880. Morrison would have invested capital in the project and obtained some rights to the property although the Title Deeds were not altered at this time. This combination of technical expertise and business skills was potentially a sound basis for a successful enterprise.

This partnership did not last long as in August 1880 Crawford died leaving Morrison in full charge although there was a family dispute about the ownership of the Pottery. This dispute although a distraction would not have troubled Morrison as he apparently had some agreement by which he would eventually obtain the Title. The problem with the Title was regarding who should inherit it. Crawford although married to Mary Ann Thomson of Glasgow had lived with Julia Paul who claimed to be his "wife". There were also three married sisters who felt they also had a claim. This dispute was settled by the Sheriff in favour of the wife and the sisters and he ruled that Julia had no claim on the Estate [F.A. 2/4/1881]. It is interesting to note that in the legal papers associated with the action that two of Crawford's sisters had married potters one of whom, Scouler, lived in Glasgow while the other, Cathgart, lived locally although he had lived in Angus at one time. The third sister was married to John Morrison of Glasgow. From this it is seen that Crawford had a strong connection with Glasgow and probably he worked there for some time. It will also be noted that one of the sisters was a Morrison but there is no apparent connection with the partner of the same name. Having obtained this ruling the Crawfords were in a position to dispose of the Pottery but for some reason, perhaps financial, the transfer to Morrison did not take place until 1884 [12/8/1884 274-45].

With the death of Crawford Morrison was left without the necessary technical support and it must be assumed that he either promoted one of his own work force or appointed one from outwith the works.

Unfortunately the Census Returns for 1881 do not record this person and it is only in 1885 that there is evidence of the foreman, William Cathgart, who had been listed as a potter in 1881. It may be that William was Crawford's nephew and that he and his father John had worked at the Pottery since it opened. Although the 1881 Census Returns do not allocate any worker to a specific Pottery it is recorded that Morrison employed 10 men, 2 girls and 2 boys. This work force corresponds to a small Pottery as indicated by a R.V. of £15. It seems likely that as well as being fairly small the Pottery would have been only simply equipped being manually powered with, perhaps, only the clay preparation being steam driven. This certainly not how how Fleming described it "...most primitive, only hand powered at that date..." [Scottish Pottery p. 200].

Despite the problems of the Title for the Pottery Morrison was obviously certain he would eventually acquire it as he entered into a lease with the Rosslyn Estate for land adjoining the Pottery in 1883 [8.12/1883 258-167] and agreed to erect buildings to the value of £200 "in so far as not already done". These buildings were completed early in 1884 [VR]. Assuming that Crawford and Morrison had fulfilled their feu conditions then the Pottery buildings alone should have cost at least £400. After this expansion the R.V. was raised from £15 to £50 which must represent a very substantial improvement.

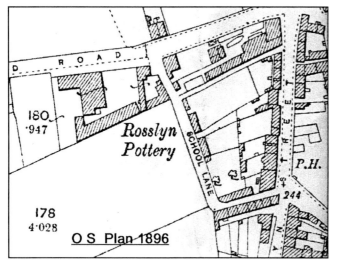

O S Plan 1896

Needless to say such an expansion must have required capital, which Morrison appears to have been able to find from the business profits and his personal funds. Surprisingly after completing the building of the new Pottery in 1884 Morrison used the property as security to raise a loan of £600 from Jackson, a local lawyer,[7/10/1884 276-51]. From this it can be assumed that the Pottery was now valued at a sum much greater than this. No reason was given for the loan but it can be taken that it was for the business either to complete the equipping of the works or for working capital to handle the expanded production. There certainly was some form of further improvement at the Pottery as the Assessor tried unsuccessfully to increase the R.V. to £75 in 1887. Morrison's financial situation during this period must still have been sound as although he inherited family property in Kinglassie in 1884 he did not sell it until 1889 [9/9/1889 387-107].

At the same time as establishing a potentially prosperous business Morrison married Elizabeth Hunter of Links in 1885. As a mark of their esteem the employees presented the couple with a clock at a celebration meal. In reply to this gesture as well as thanking his workers Morrison took the opportunity to urge them to work harder in a short speech reflecting a good "Victorian" working arrangement. One of the oldest employees referred "to the cares and anxieties and sorrows of existence as a Pottery" but Morrison "looked forward with hope and trusted they [the employees] would do their duty honestly not so much as servants but as friends their interests being the same. If they turned out good workmanship it would be easy to find a market for it and they were all thereby mutually benefited" [F.A. 21/11/1885]. This hope for the future of the Pottery was not misplaced.

Since coming to Gallatown to live Morrison had lodged in Rosslyn Street and he continued in rented accommodation with his new wife. This situation continued for two years until he bought his own home in 1883 [7/6/1887 333-73] by purchasing a house and byre adjoining the Pottery thus completing the block on the corner of Oswald Road and School Lane. This might have been as much an investment towards future expansion of the Pottery as the desire for his own home. However two years later he started to build a new house in Bandon Avenue. This building was finished in late 1891 after which he sold the house and byre in 1893 [502-75] presumably as he saw no need for further expansion of the buildings.

Throughout this period although fluctuating Trade was on the whole good. During periods of recession Morrison, in common with most employers, reduced his workers' wages and cut their working hours. He seems to have made an individual move of this type in 1890 when he alone of the local master potters reduced wages by 5% and would not increase them later when trade had improved. This, not surprisingly, was not accepted by the potters who came out on strike under the direction of the Potters Union. This strike was short lived but the outcome was not reported [F.A.5/9/1890].

There is very little reported about Morrison in the local newspapers and he appears to have taken very little active interest in local affairs except the occasional bowling match and works outings. Despite the lack of details there can be little doubt that the Pottery was successful as in 1895 he was able to pay off the loan of £600 to Jackson [30/3/1895 382]. It also reasonable to assume that as he had sold the house and byre adjoining the Pottery and therefore given up the room to expand he was content with the physical size of the Pottery. Perhaps he realised that his operation was the correct size for the market or more simply he had no further ambition to expand.

The 1891 Census Returns do not help much to establish the details of the Pottery as it does not give the number of employees in any work place nor is it possible to attribute any specific worker to one Pottery unless further information is available. It is known that Robert Halket, "pottery branch thrower" from Rutherglen, started worked in the mid 1880's and remained for many years to become one of the principal workers. A John Cathgart from Glasgow is listed as a Pottery Manager and as he cannot be associated with any other Pottery in the area he probably was the manager at the Rosslyn Pottery. John had been in the area for about eight years but it has been not known if he was related to William Cathgart, the foreman, or to Crawford.

By the end of the century Morrison at the age of fifty was a successful businessman with a prosperous, if small, Pottery. As suggested earlier he may have lacked ambition to expand further. If this description is correct then it can perhaps be partially attributed to his lack of a heir as he had no children. His nearest suitable relation was his nephew, Andrew Hunter, who had been brought up by his grandmother who was also Morrison's mother-in-law. Morrison would have been well acquainted with Hunter as they lived in adjoining houses in Bandon Avenue. Hunter joined his uncle in the Pottery when he left school and worked for him until he left to join the army during the Great War.

Again there is very little information in the local newspapers except for a minor fire in 1910. There can be no doubt that he Pottery would have been affected by the various strikes in the other Potteries especially the one in 1914 which exclusively involved the "Rockingham and Brownware potters" as those were the main types of ware at that time. It must also be assumed that Rosslyn Pottery suffered the same hardships experienced by its local rivals due to the importation of cheap foreign goods and the outbreak of the Great War.

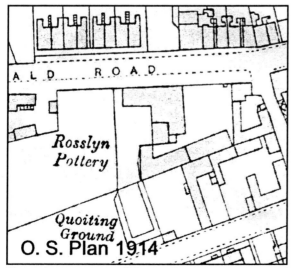

O. S. Plan 1914

The period during the war was fairly bleak due to lack of orders and of skilled workers many of whom had either been conscripted or had volunteered to join the armed forces. This lack of skilled workers was so acute that in June 1918 the Pottery was closed for three weeks due to the illness of one of the principal workers [F.A.22/6/1918]. This stoppage was even more serious at that time as the demand for earthenware of all types was exceptionally brisk and a stoppage at such a time would lead to a further delay in the output of orders.

The return to peace on 11th November 1918 should have brought great joy to everyone but this joy was short lived as by the 23rd. November so many of the workers were overcome by the influenza epidemic that the Pottery was closed for three weeks due to the lack of skilled workers [FA 23/11/1918]. During the next year Hunter returned from army service with the Black Watch where he had risen to the rank of Captain and had been awarded the Military Cross and Bar. He soon took over the running of the Pottery from his uncle who at the age of 69 years was no doubt glad to take a back seat. Things did not start well for Hunter as no sooner than he had come back the he was faced by the strike that affected the Potteries in the Kirkcaldy area. This strike had been brewing since June and as would be expected was for better wages. The negotiations had become protracted and communications with the workmen were so poor that the Rockingham Workers finally came out on strike early in December and remained out, with the support of their colleagues in the Whiteware Potteries. The strike was not settled for several weeks [see Kirkcaldy Pottery].

With this problem behind him Hunter introduced much needed improvements. These improvements were in the working methods no doubt with some new machinery but no new buildings were erected [K.M. files Hunter letter]. These improvements must have been fairly extensive as the R.V. was increased by approximately 25% to £68.50 in 1921. This increase was also in part due to a general revaluation of property in the area, which could have accounted for about half the increase. The Pottery continued to operate with two kilns and a two storied warehouse along with associated workshops.

At this time also Morrison formally handed over full control to Hunter by transferring the Pottery to him on an annual payment of £200 [5/5/1921 Lib 1540.91]. This appears to have been an arrangement whereby Hunter paid the £200 per annum as a rent and would inherit the property on the death of Morrison and his wife.

The period in the early 1920s was one of fluctuating trade and Rosslyn Pottery would have had the same problem as the other Potteries of the lack of skilled workers due to the wartime losses and the poor wages paid in the Potteries when compared to other local industries. This lack of skilled workers was so severe that when one of their principal workers was ill for three weeks in 1922 the Pottery was closed although the order book was full [F.A.22/6/1922]. Writing many years later Hunter stated that he had employed about fifty workers including 8 women, which is a low proportion when compared to the highly industrialised Kirkcaldy Pottery. Even after that time Hunter could recall many of the individual workers, whom he listed as Thrower [Robert Halket], Turner [David Adie], Kilnmen [Andrew and Robert Blair], Spout Maker [Miss Mathews], Pirlie Bank Maker [John Elie] and Handlers [William Green and George Bell]. These skilled workers were supported by the Warehouseman [A Cairns], Clerk [David Dingham] and Sales [Mr Cairns]. It is perhaps significant of his position that the traveller was "Mr" while the rest were remembered by their first name. As well as those listed there were others with less crucial tasks such as The "three Megs" who undertook the splatter colouring and the Clerkess, Mrs Walker, who reported that she started in 1922 as a girl on the salary of £15 per annum [KM files]. Hunter also reported that wages were in the region of £1.00 to £1.50 for women and £2.50 to £3.00 for men. These appear to be excessive and if correct they would represent very exceptional weeks and include overtime and production bonuses.

As already mentioned in Chapter 8 Carl Nekola joined Hunter in 1922 from the Fife Pottery to improve the decoration of the wares. He was at first employed to decorate the black, blue and green glazed wares such as teapots with overglaze silver and gold lustre and enamels, mainly in white. Carl's talents would also be required by Hunter as he introduced whiteware about that time. Production of this new ware was in full swing by following year [1923] when Mrs I Hutchison started her apprenticeship as a decorator of overglaze enamels and underglaze painting on the "new" whitewares. She was trained to paint roses, chrysanthemums, and cherries in a Wemyss like style which were sold under the trade name of Rosslyn Ware [KM Files].

It is an interesting insight into labour relation in the 1920's when Mrs Hutchison recalled how she started work at the Pottery. Hunter and Nekola recognising that skilled help was required saw the economic advantages of giving training to some young person although there would have no doubt been skilled decorators in the area who were unemployed. Instead of advertising the vacancy Hunter simply approached the Headmaster of the local Viewforth Secondary School to find out if there was a suitable child in the school. Mrs Huntchison was recommended and as she appeared to have the required artistic skill she was given a "note" for her parents informing them that the job was available and that their daughter could start the following Monday which she did.

Throughout most of its life Rosslyn Pottery had only two kilns both approximately the same size. With the exception of "Apple and Chicken Banks" all of the products required the normal two firings, biscuit and glost. Since, in general, biscuit firing takes up about 50% less kiln capacity than glost firing it is unlikely that one kiln was dedicated to one process and that kiln loads were mixed. The difference in temperatures could be handled by varying the position of the different wares in the kilns. It is unlikely that the temperatures required for each process were very different and the desired results could be achieved reasonably easily. However if a third much lower temperature firing was required for overglaze enamel or lustre then the problem was much greater but solvable with skill.

For many years prior to 1923 Rosslyn Pottery had been producing majolica wares that were decorated at the time of glazing. In this technique of decoration the biscuit ware was given a coat of glaze as normal. Once it had dried the colours were simply "flicked" by means of whin sprigs onto the dry glaze. This in turn was allowed to dry before being fired. There was no need to fix the colours in a kiln or oven thereby making a saving. By this method the coloured glaze could be fired in one glost firing to give the "runny" appearance that was typical of this type of ware at the Pottery. However this method could not be used with the new hand painted decoration on whiteware as the colours had to appear separate in the finished item. To achieve this each colours had to be set individually when merging of the colours was to be avoided. This could be achieved using the existing kiln methods although since the temperatures required were relatively low this would have been time consuming and uneconomic. By 1924 the output of whitewares was sufficiently large that Hunter no doubt wishing to expand the range and volume of whiteware products engaged a Mr Bickerstaff to build a muffle kiln, which was required for the decorated white ware production [K.M. Files].

The extra white clay required for this new ware was still obtained from Devon via Dysart Harbour while the brown clay was readily available nearby in Randolph Place and elsewhere. Coal at 35p per ton was readily available at the nearby coal mines [KM Hunter].

This new whiteware venture was of very limited success in the prevailing economic conditions and Hunter closed it down in 1926 as he had the opportunity to move to "Massachusetts to open a subsidiary company for on behalf of a Scots firm" [KM Files]. Hunter still had the problem of the annual payment to Morrison and to allow this move he leased the Pottery to Ken McKenzie, who was working at Fife Pottery, for a period of five years[K.M. Hunter]. As part of the deal McKenzie did not require all of the workers and especially the decorator, C. Nekola, who were discharged. The few decorators retained were all ladies and only undertook simple enamel work such as simplistic "forget-me-nots".

As all of the other Potteries were also struggling it is doubtful if any of the sacked workers would be able to find alternative work in their own trade. Nekola was perhaps a little luckier as he had a very specialised skill and was able to continue at least for a short time as a free lance decorator using his father's muffle kiln in Bandon Avenue and by giving lessons in art and pottery decoration at the local "Night Schools". Fortunately he was able to gain employment at Edinburgh Art College in late 1926 or very early 1927 in the newly formed Pottery Section where he was in charge of the technical side but not the design [WS 15/1/1927]. This reduction in the workforce seems to have been remembered by Hunter when he wrote many years later "We had a splendid crew of fine craftsmen who had been with us for years. Our people were both skilled and hard working. One of my greatest regrets in life was to be forced to leave behind those fine and loyal friends who had worked so long and so faithfully for my family"[KM files].

Hunter not only left Scotland but he also left the trade of potting and transferred his business skills to the flour industry when he opened a new mill in Springfield [USA] for "Youma Ltd" a subsidiary of a Kirkcaldy milling company [Springfield Museum]. With the advantage of hindsight he did not have much choice in the matter considering the troubles affecting the other Potteries at that time. Hunter and Morrison before him were generally considered to be reasonable employers although wages were on the whole low for unskilled workers. Skilled men, on the other hand were paid the "Union" wages and specialists much more. For example Andrew Blair, the chief firer and glazer, was paid £4.75 per week in 1922 with no doubt an extra bonus for each successful firing. This was a very handsome wage being at least twice that of a potter reflecting that he was the most important workman in the pottery. This wage would also reflect the extremely long working hours as the kilns required constant attention during firing. The employers also had an interest in the health of the workers and they paid the local doctor, Greig, 50p every six weeks to check the "girls" for lead poisoning [Greig family].

Hunter and Morrison before him also acted as wholesale and retail agents for both Bo'ness and

136

Portobello Potteries dealing in whiteware as they did not make this type of ware except for a very short time [circa 1923/26] and apparently never made flat ware. They also acted as agent for Fife Pottery and mixed loads containing their own goods and plates from Fife Pottery were regularly sent to Ireland.

Mckenzie cut the range of products severely and only produced teapots and concentrated on plain and cheap ones with only a very limited production of slightly "improved" but still cheap enamel decorated wares. Indeed when interviewed many years later when he was an elderly man he recalled sending teapots away in loads of over one ton and to the Woolworth Organisation. He managed to fulfil the terms of his five years lease until 1931 when he gave up being unable to compete with mass importation of cheap aluminium teapots from Japan.

Hunter was unable to find anyone else to operate the Pottery and he returned to Kirkcaldy from America to oversee the final closure making sure that he spoke directly to all of the workers. In their recollections of that time the former employees had fond memories of all of the employers and considered that they had been treated as well as could be expected in the conditions at the time. Certainly Hunter could have avoided the trauma of the final closure by staying in the USA to which he quickly returned and remained for the rest of his life.

With the Pottery now unoccupied it was unlikely if not impossible that a new tenant could be found to take it over as a "going concern" and Hunter who still had the problem of the annual payment was forced to find some other use for the property. Firstly the equipment of the Pottery was sold so that the buildings could be cleared for other uses.

F.F.P. Nov. 26 1932

AT ROSSLYN POTTERY, Oswald Road,
Gallatown, Kirkcaldy,
ON WEDNESDAY, 30th November
at II.30 a.m.
Auction Sale of
MODERN POTTERY MACHINERY AND PLANT
Comprising:-20 B.H.P. "Crossley" Gas Engine; "Edwards & Jones" 1 Ton All Metal Filtering Press, 56 Chambers. 24in.by 24 in: "Farmer Bros." 1 Ton All Metal Filtering Press, 30 Chambers. 24 in.by 60 in; "Edwards & Jones" Cast Iron Octagonal Blunger, 5ft 0in by 4ft 4in.; "Gosling & Gatensbury" Eccentric Driven Slip Pump; Pug Mill, Barrel 22in. by 20in. diam; "Sirroco"Fan and Piping; Thrower's Wheel: 2 Jiggers; Potters' Lathes; Shafting, Pulleys and Belting; 647 Iron Bound Carrying Boards; about 1500 Saggars; 40 cwt. "Anderson Bros." Dormant Platform Weighing Machine; Hand Winch; Wood Racks, Fittings and Partitioning; Glaze Dipping and other Tubs; New and Second Hand Filter Press Cloths; Roller Conveyor; about 95 Sq. Yds. Wood Flooring; Barrows and Boggies and General Pottery Loose Tools and Utensils. Etc. Brick and Ironwork of 2 Coal Fired Kilns 14ft 0in. diam: Brick Built Kiln House with Lavatory fittings and Tiled Roof; Sectional Corrugated Iron Hut or Garage 24ft. by 10ft 0in.
Thos Hill & Co. have received instructions from Alexander Hunter, Esq., to dispose of above.
Catalogues to be had from
THOS. HILL & CO.,
Machinery Auctioneers
67 Robertson Street, Glasgow.

The closure of any workplace must have a devastating effect on the owners and employees especially at a time when there was no alternative employment available in the area. This effect must also extend outside the work place as there would have been many people involved in support industries and suppliers. One supplier deeply involved was the tenant of a nearby smallholding, Birrell, who had augmented his income by digging clay on his land and delivering it to the Pottery. The loss of the income made his unit unviable and he left the district [Birrell family].

As Hunter was now not in the district to deal with the property it was transferred back to the "Morrison's Trustees" who acted on behalf of his aunt, Mrs Morrison, as Hunter was no longer able to pay the annual £200 as agreed earlier. To give her some income tenants were found for part of the Pottery buildings at low rents as the property was subdivided and used partly as stables and a piggery while remaining Pottery buildings remaining unoccupied until 1935 when they was converted into a "Tile Factory" by A Birrell who was related to the clay supplier mentioned earlier[V.R.1935]. Although this description of the works could suggest that the Pottery had been reopened as a Tile works this is incorrect. The roof tiles were made from concrete as a new experimental venture by a local builder who later established a successful business in this type of product [Birrell family].

It is perhaps a fitting epitaph to the use of clay in the Kirkcaldy area which owed so much to the manufacture of clay tiles that the final use of the last working Pottery should be for producing concrete tiles a situation which was repeated through out Britain.

CHAPTER 11
1855- 1860

Tyrie Brick, Tile & Fireclay Works

This ninth possible Pottery in the area has been left to the end as it was extremely short lived and there are still those in the Scottish Pottery field who still consider that such works are not true Potteries. However for the purpose of this publication Works which have only produced bricks & tiles have not been considered but in the case of Tyrie there is suggestion that the products were more sophisticated. The story is clouded in mystery.

On May 12th 1855 the Fifeshire Advertiser reported

Tyrie Brick & Tile & Lime Works
The buildings and appendages connected with the brick & tile work now occupy a site of ground nearly four acres in extent; and from plans shown to us when completed, it will bear comparison with any brick or tile work in the kingdom.. There are about 80 hands employed already, and bricks etc. manufactured are of a very superior quality arising, from the peculiar adamination [??] of the clay while the machinery employed is of the best description. A machine on an improved principle is in course of erection for the manufacture of drain tiles, pipes etc, which is calculated to throw of immense quantities of these useful articles. The fireclay in the locality is abundant and good and kilns are in course of erection for the burning operations.

Later on July 28th 1855 it was further reported

Tyrie Brick & Tile Works
Passing onto the brick & tile-work, we observe every indication of progress. Large commodious sheds for the drying of raw tile, drain pipes & other products, in course of erection, enclosure walls, skeleton roads and infant kilns for firing operations, all pointing to the rapid advancement with which this new field of industry is moving on now. The making of fireclay gas retorts is fairly commenced, and a machine remarkable for simplicity in construction and perfection in adaptability for the making of drain-tile pipes is a curiosity well worth attention and inspection of those who are interested in such matters. The bed of clay in the immediate vicinity of the premises is of great thickness, and will supply the raw material for ages to come...

....It is proposed to build a pier in the neighbourhood of the Seafield Tower a little beyond the brickworks with a railway connecting to the Lime Works.

This article is contained in a description of a walk north to south along Kirkcaldy beach

A third article appeared in the Fifeshire Advertiser of August 11th 1855

We regret to say that, on Tuesday last, a young woman, the second daughter of a gentleman connected with the brick and tile works, while engaged in attending to the machine for making drain pipes, very incautiously allowed her hands to come into contact with the rollers, whereby she was severely bruised...

It is no surprise that a new Brick & Tile Works was being considered at that time as the demand for the products was extremely high and new Works were being opened throughout Fife. However these descriptions of the Works certainly suggest a major operation which was intended to be much more than the usual Brick & Tile Works.

The Ordnance Survey Plan of the area published in 1856 shows the Tyrie Bleachfield with several buildings and a possible clay pit but there is no reference to a Brick & Tile Works. The presence of a clay pit would suggest that production of some sort had started. Unfortunately it is not stated which type of clay was excavated and it must be remembered that this plan was based on a survey undertaken at least one year before publication. It is perhaps best to assume the pit had some other use than clay excavation.

The other evidence is equally sketchy. As the July newspaper article makes it clear that the Bleachfield, Brick & Tile & Lime Works are all part of the same operation it is reasonable assume that the buildings shown as the Bleachfield also include the Brick & Tile Works. In the Valuation Roll [VR] for 1856-57 only the Tyrie Bleachfield is listed suggesting that when the details were collected [probably late 1855] it was not possible or practical to separate the two works. This would not matter for local tax purposes. The owners of the various Works were the "Swan Brothers" who were local linen manufacturers and dealers hence the need for a Bleachfield. These brothers were descendants of the "Swan" who had been an agent for bricks in 1822 [Page16]. The land was owned by Ferguson of Raith. In the VR 1859-60 the Bleachfield is listed along with "Limestone, Common & Fireclay & House" but no other buildings. By 1862 all references to the clays had disappeared.

While newspaper reports such as these must be treated with caution there is little doubt that the owners of the Brick & Tile Works had great ambitions for the project which included the Lime Works and if they were successful it might be viable to build a new pier for export. This pier was never built although later an abortive attempt was tried nearby to export coal. They are credited with making "gas retorts" and as these must have been made from fireclay at least it is known for sure that fireclay products were made. The type of the other fireclay products is not known but although not specially mentioned they could have included drain pipes. Drain-tile pipes would have been made of "common", local red clay, as they had to be porous. Other fireclay products would be speculative but as the Works appear to have lasted for a few years it is likely that other products such as chimney cans were made as along with gas retorts they only required fairly simple moulds and not expensive machinery.

There can be very little doubt that no matter how ambitious the dreams were for this new industrial enterprise it was not a success and only lasted for about five years. It was, however, within the criteria adopted for this publication a Pottery. On the same basis Works which only produced bricks such as at Gallatown or Denburn are not considered.

It is left to the reader to decide where this line should be drawn.

CHAPTER 12   The Wares

Unfortunately for the researcher or collector there are very few catalogues or lists of the many products from the Potteries in the Kirkcaldy area. The price list from Fife and Links Potteries in 1855 [pages 98 & 142] have already been discussed and although they are very interesting they only give an indication of the range of products. The only exceptions are catalogues for Abbotsford Ware from Kirkcaldy Pottery and Wemyss Ware from Fife pottery. Thus the only evidence available is from examples discovered over the years by many avid collectors and very limited shards.

Mathie Pottery, Links Tile Works Pottery & John Methvens Links Pottery

To date there is no evidence regarding the products of these Potteries and it can be only assumed that they would be typical for the period.

Combined Links Potteries under George Methven

As explained in the text although details of the individual Wares are not known from the details of the Court Case [page 46] it is seen that they made black teapots, gold lustre teapots and brownware along with garden pots and chimney cans. All of these were made from the local red clay and it is reasonable to assume that they also made teapots from this clay as well. Brownware probably included bowls in various sizes from the small table variety up to reasonably large sizes for use in farm dairies. It is also suggested that caneware might have been made and if this correct this is likely to have been bakers [pie dishes] or teapots.

No marked pieces have been seen to date.

Links/Kirkcaldy Pottery 1847 to 1928 [circa] - David Methven & Sons [DM&S]

It is only during this period that the different wares can be fully considered

Brownware

There can be very little doubt that the change of ownership can have had very little immediate effect on the products of the Pottery which were to continue for as long as the   brownware pottery was in production. There would have been changes to the designs and methods of production as improved machinery and techniques became available.

Unfortunately the owners continued the practice of generally not marking the brownware wares and it has not been possible to identify any of the bowls or containers made for the commercial market. The limited shard evidence does show that much of this output had an inner lining of white clay slip and frequently only the interior was glazed. Also it appears that these wares were usually fired to a stoneware state thus making them impervious to water perhaps suggesting the white lining was for hygienic reasons. Some of these are listed under "Pans" & "Basins" in the following Price List

Teapots were always the main product and a vast number were made over the years but, again, they are rarely if ever marked to identify the maker. The most important type of teapots was the extensive rockingham range. In common with many of the other Scottish Potteries this type of teapots were a principal product made for the Scottish and foreign markets. Indeed is amazing that these markets could accept such huge numbers.

**Extract from Links Pottery 1855 Price List showing Brownware
[NB the fuzziness in these copies is due to the quality of the original]**

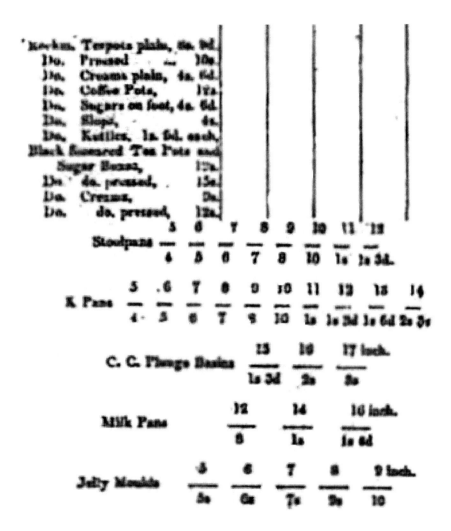

Although it is not possible to identify the teapots and associated wares from this list at least the range can be established. As would be expected "plain teapots" were thrown and turned while more elaborate finishes were achieved by press moulding probably in two pieces. In both types it is likely the handles and spouts would have been made separately by either extraction or moulding. Lids could have been made by either process. Teapots were supplied with matching cream jugs, bowls, kettles [normally used as hot water jugs] and coffee pots.

This range was available as "Rockingham" or "Black Smeared" which are types of glaze used to achieve either a brown or a black jet finish. It will be noticed that the black wares were much more expensive due to the extra kiln firing required and perhaps additional decorating although this is not specifically mentioned. The prices quoted are probably per dozen. There is no mention of lustre ware and it may be they had dropped these wares but if this is correct they certainly produced those at a later date.

When undertaking research such as this there is an ongoing problem of being shown pieces which the owner is certain came from a specific Pottery. In the research for this work such claims have not been quoted unless the provenance was very strong. Following this rule two teapots with lustre [gold & silver] are illustrated [Fig 1]. From the same source there are a black jet jug with over glaze enamel decoration and a black jet cow creamer with gilt over glaze decoration [Fig 2]. These four pieces were acquired from the Pottery during the Great War [1914 — 18].

Whiteware   Transfer Printed

While it has to be accepted that there is limited knowledge of the brown ware produced the situation with white ware is very much better. As explained earlier white ware production started about 1850 and was well established by 1855 when there was a very extensive range of products as shown in the **1855 Price List**

As would be expected the range covered all types of table, tea and bedroom wares along with kitchen ware such as bakers. Perhaps surprisingly cane bakers were slightly more expensive than cream coloured.

As well as offering this large range they also offered most of the white ware as "cream coloured" i.e. undecorated, "Blue Edged and Sponged", "Willow", "Printed" and "Flowing Coloured" i.e. Hand painted. These types of decoration were similar to those offered at other Whiteware Potteries. Blue Edge decoration appears to be the application of a blue line round the edge of the item as the name suggests. Sponge Decoration was the application of a simple repetitive pattern round the item by means of a sponge root suitably cut with the design. It is interesting to note that "Willow" pattern was quoted separately from the other transfer printed designs and it was cheaper especially for larger sizes. This is no doubt partly explained by the national popularity of the willow pattern but is still difficult to follow the price difference as it would appear that the labour and oncosts would be similar for any pattern.

PRICE LIST

DAVID METHVEN & SONS, LINKS POTTERY, KIRKCALDY

MARCH, 1855.

143

Page 2

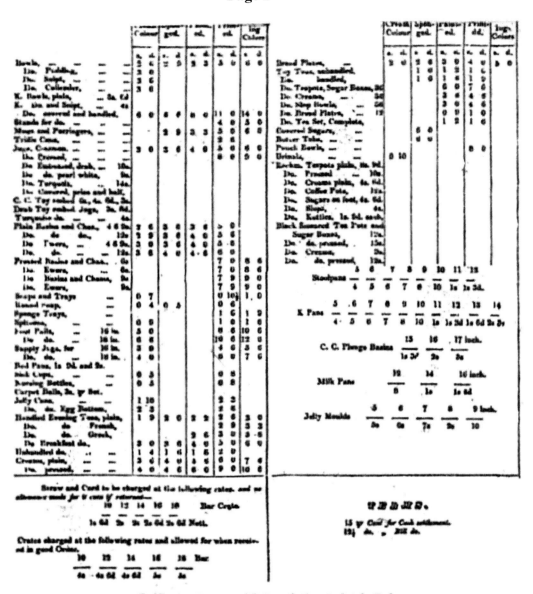

At the bottom of the left hand list on page 1 they offered "Best Printed Plates" which were substantially more expensive no doubt due to the extra care in both the potting and the application of and the quality of the print. Judging by examples such as Fig 3 special copper plates were acquired for this type of ware. This shows that they were capable of producing wares to high standard but they choose to work to a lower standard at a lower cost to maintain their target market.

Also listed are jugs with a "turquoise" finish which presumably was a coloured glaze or an under glaze colour and toy tea sets which probably did not have a large market at this early date. A Methven Child's tea set is shown in [Fig 4] which probably dates from a later period. The name "Farm" has been given to this transfer print by collectors of tea sets although the scene depicted is a water mill but no explanation is given for this.

Having produced an extensive range of products all manufacturers have the problem of continually finding new markets. Whilst there will usually be ongoing markets for such products as Willow patterns it is necessary to find new "fashionable" products which the customer will want although there is perhaps no need. The producer of Table & Tea Wares has an ongoing problem that it is difficult to change the basic shape of the individual pieces. This is especially true of flat ware such as plates although variations in hollow ware such as tureens & cups are easier but still limited.

To overcome this problem DM&S apparently accepted that their wares could not compete in quality with the multitude of English Potteries as many of these were producing china ware to a good standard. To overcome this problem it was necessary to find a niche market and much of the output was aimed at the emerging lower middle and working classes which although far from affluent still had a small disposable income and sought a little relative luxury and status in their lives. Having decided to remain with earthenware production which they could make to a good standard they appear to have accepted their market would accept that the quality of the potting and to a lesser degree the decoration could deteriorate slightly. To ensure that there was always new varieties of wares available it was apparently decided to use a large selection of different transfer patterns to vary the products.

To be able to offer a new design required a considerable financial outlay as different transfers were required for each shape and size of item to be decorated. Thus a separate copper plate was required for each individual transfer. The number of copper plates could be in excess of twenty for a dinner set but very much lower in the case of tea sets.

No official list from the Pottery appears to exist which is not surprising as it is likely that at any one time only a few of the patterns would be regularly in use. There would have been no problem in producing patterns which were not held in stock as long as the copper plates were still available. Presumably there was also an opportunity to supply items to replace breakages to wares previously supplied.

There can be little doubt that various owners of DM&S knew how to market their products and they used a large numbers of names to identify the items. In most cases this was the name of the pattern but other marketing ploys were used. A list of these names is shown on the following lists and is based on items and shards seen. There is no doubt that there would have been many more types of products which may never be known. It must be remembered that the use of identification marks on individual pieces must have added to the cost and was not done to help the collector but was simply to assist marketing. No doubt the chosen name was considered to be attractive to the eventual purchaser and when the pattern names are studied certain themes emerge.

One of the popular themes was to use names associated with the extended family of Queen Victoria. Indeed it appears that DM&S marked most of the Royal marriages/engagements although the patterns chosen have no obvious connection to the event. It is reasonable to assume that these patterns were first used at the appropriate date and remained popular for a period after the event. Equally it can be accepted that a pattern such as "Kaiser" or "German Stag Hunt" were not used after 1914.

Equally other popular interests at the time were the study of Classical and Chinese art along with nature and these are mirrored with appropriate patterns. As always care must be taken not to read too much into the choice of a pattern since probably many of them were stock patterns sold by agents on behalf of copper plate engravers as presumably it was more expensive to have set of special plates made to an original and exclusive design.

To add to the researcher's problems there is evidence that DM&S also used multi coloured transfer prints which were purchased ready for use. These appear to have been mainly used on children' ware and had appropriate themes frequently showing rosy cheeked children at play. Transfers of this type became available in the second half of the nineteenth century but would have been rarely used as they were gelatine based and only remained usable for a short time. About 1900 these transfers were much improved to give them a much longer life and make them available to Potteries such as Kirkcaldy. Transfers of this type [Fig34] do not appear to have been given the potters' mark and can only be identified if the item has a separate impressed mark.

Coloured Wares

As seen from the Price List DM&S produced wares which were decorated with under glaze colours specified as blue edge, sponged & flowing colours. Unfortunately these types of decoration were used until the Pottery eventually closed in 1928 and it is not possible to identify wares from this early period or indeed for most of the active life of the Pottery. As before to gain an impression of the output consideration must be given to the pieces available which fall into several categories.

White Ware   Sponge Ware & Hand Painting

This method of cheap but colourful decoration was very popular at many Scottish Potteries and DM&S was no exception. Like the other Potteries they only added an identifying mark on rare occasions and it is difficult to be absolutely certain of the origin of much of this ware. One method is by comparison of the individual parts of the design based on shard evidence or marked piece. This can be reasonably successful in a number of cases but must be treated with caution as the sponge roots if cut in the pottery could easily be copies of others seen from other Potteries. In addition sponges were also centrally made in Staffordshire and available to all Potteries.

Identification was much easier if hand painting was used in conjunction with sponge decoration. This is well illustrated by the design known locally in the Links area as "Maggie Roonie Roses" [Fig 5]. None of the former pottery decorators who were interviewed some forty years after the Pottery closed were able identify this Maggie although she was apparently well known for her style and speed of painting.

Always willing to supply any market DM&S were prepared to mark pieces with other than their own name if the order was large enough and wares with a mixture of sponge and hand painted decoration were supplied as **Nisbet Ware** [Fig 7] to a dealer in Edinburgh and as **Airlie Ware** [Fig 6] to a dealer near Glamis. Most of these wares appear to have been bedroom ware with associated ornaments. Also without giving the ware a specific name they supplied other dealers and marked them with the dealer's name.

By far the best quality decoration seen on this type of ware is seen on **Auld Heather Ware** which was apparently produced for the American market. This was made in the 1920's when DM&S employed an artist, Brown, who could be diverted to this work if he was not required else where. There is also a very similar ware marked **Dundee** but the market for this is not certain.

Self Coloured and Hand Painted

There can be little doubt that DM&S must have produced a large quantity unmarked ornamental wares from jardinières to small banks and egg cups. Similarly there can be no doubt that the best decorating was reserved for **Abbotsford Ware** [Figs 8 &33]. This ware was started in the early 1880s as self coloured ornaments on a classical theme and eventually expanded to hand painted fruits and flowers very similar to Wemyss Ware from Fife Pottery. It is far from certain which of these Potteries started first with self coloured wares but there is very little doubt that the fruit and flowers was a copy of Wemyss Ware. Indeed most of this work undertaken at DM&S was by decorators who had trained at Fife Pottery.

In the 1920's Brown who was the chief [if not sole] decorator produced a range of items with an unusual blue & green design [Fig 9] which was frequently given the back stamp showing the Kirkcaldy town crest. This style was continued by Brown either just before or after the closure of Kirkcaldy Pottery when he was employed to decorate **Lomond Ware** [Fig 9]. This gave rise to some confusion for collectors especially as the blanks used at first were old stock from Kirkcaldy Pottery.

Export Wares

These fall into the previous categories but help to show the enterprise shown by DM&S. While pottery had been exported for many years it was mainly to European based countries and customers. Later towards the end of the 1800's a new market was identified in the Far East and specially Burma. Wares were specifically made and marketed in that area. Water Vessels [Fig 36&37] had a specific use to the native population and were frequently marked with the Elephant mark presumably as this would be of significance to the customer. It is difficult to understand why the transfer printed patterns used [Wild Rose & Canovian] would appeal to this market but it must have as a new back stamp partially in the script of the country was featured [Fig 10].

Personalised Wares

DM&S were always willing to add personal messages to their wares and marriage jugs seem to have been a popular line along with small banks. They also added suitable messages to imported decorated china pieces [Fig 12]. Indeed A. R. Young used this method to acquire a christening mug for his son William which perhaps confirms he was well aware of the quality of the wares.

Blanks
Fired but unglazed wares were sold to pottery decorators to finish with Bough, Strathyre [Fig 12] where the plate has the impressed thistle and crown mark], Makmerry and Jessie M King being among the more notable customers. J. M. King also returned the decorated wares to the Pottery to be glazed and fired. DM&S also supplied blanks to other unnamed decorators and recognisable wares do turn up with unknown decorators' mark. Toby Jugs seem to have been popular for this use as seen in [Fig 13]. Similarly blanks were supplied for use at the ceramic painting classes which were popular for many years.

Impressed marks
DM&S used two impressed marks on an irregular basis. The first was a small rectangular containing *"Imperial David Methven & Sons"* Imperial being the name given to the undecorated wares. The second was a stylised thistle and crown either as a fairly crude image or occasionally very clearly marked.

Pattern Names Associated with DM&S
The following list gives some of the various patterns used by DM&S both with name given and others which have an attributed name based on the design. Other names used by DM&S are included with the brief details. It is not practical to attempt to describe the patterns and the few illustrated are also listed. Dating of many of the pieces is very difficult and dates are given where the pattern appears to commemorate a specific event. These dates are only offered as a suggestion and the reader must decide if they are reasonable or not.

DM&S PATERNS AND OTHER NAMES

NAME	COLOUR & DETAIL	TYPE, SUGGESTED DATE ETC.
Abbotsford Fig 8	Green	Table ware & plaques
Abbotsford Ware	Range of ornaments	See separate note 1880(c)
Airlie Ware Fig 6	Hand Painted see separate note	A Dealer Miss Burse Kirriemuir
Akabam	Two coloured transfer print	For Far East market
Alphabet Fig 10	Blue or green	Assumed name children's plate
Antique Fig 22	Purple	Dinner ware
Asiatic Pheasant Fig 24	Light Blue	Dinner ware
Aster	Green	Jug
Auld Heather Ware	Hand Painted see separate note	A Dealer 1920's
Bamboo	White	Moulded Jug
Barming HE..	partial shard	unknown
Beatrice	Blue	Bedroom ware b 1857 m 1885
Berries	Blue or red	Jugs
Berry Fig 29	Blue	Bedroom ware
Bird & Lily	Grey	Jug identified by shape
Bird in Arch Window	Black	Plate Impressed Assumed name
Bird on Fruit	Blue	Assumed name from design
Birds	Blue	Bowl
Blossom	Red	Jug Thane mark
Bough	Blanks only supplied	Decorated & fired by the studio
Boy on swing	Grey	Plate Dinner/ tea ware Assumed nam
Brig O' Doon	Blue	Plate
British Rivers	Grey	Jug
Bullfinch	Blue	Jug Assumed name from design
Bulloch Fig 11	Mainly flow blue sponge ware	Far East Dealer
Burgundy	Red	Plate
Burns	White	Moulded Jug impressed Burns ?
Butterflies	Blue	Bedroom ware
Caller Herrin'	Blue	Plate & Jug RHFP
Caller Ou	Blue	Plate & Jug RHFP
Camels	Blue	Assumed name from design
Canova	Dark blue	Dinner ware
Canove	Blue	Dinner ware
Canovian Fig 10	Dark Blue	Dinner ware for Far East Market
Ceylon	Blue	Dinner Ware
Chilli 1 Fig 30	Black & hand painting	Tea ware
Chilli 2	Black & hand painting	Large jug
China	Blue	Table ware
Ching	Blue	Table ware
Christmas	Several colours bought in transfer	Assumed name from design
Clarence	Grey	Table ware 1890
Classical Vases	Blue	Dinner ware
Colombo Crystal Palace	Sponge ware	A dealer in Sri Lanka also Shard
Convolvulus	Sepia with Bulloch mark	Design reg. DM&S 1911-16
Coronation Fig 27	Light Blue	Mugs & Plates 1902
Crystal Palace	Blue	Dinner ware 1854
Cumae	Blue	Table ware
Daisy	Sepia & pale blue	Jug
Damascus Fig 20	Blue or Sepia	Dinner ware
DCMH	Blue shard only	Unknown
Denmark	Purple	Jug
Derby	Green	Tea ware
Devon	Blue	Bedroom ware

DM&S PATERNS AND OTHER NAMES

NAME	COLOUR & DETAIL	TYPE, SUGGESTED DATE ETC.
Edina 1	Green	Dinner ware
Edina 2	Green	Dinner ware
Edinburgh Exhibition	Black or light blue	Cheese dish, creamer & vase 1881
Edinburgh Views	Black or Blue	Similar to "Edinburgh Exhibition"
Farm Fig 4	Black	Jug
Farm 2	Blue	Child's tea set attributed name
Fern	Grey	Tea Ware
Fibre Fig 31	Grey	Tea ware
Fife	Grey	Dinner ware
Flaxman	gold lustre	Bowl
Florence	Blue	Dinner ware
Fly	not known	Pottery gazette 1883
Forth	not known	Shard only mark seen
Fountain	not known	Shard only mark seen
Foxglove & Rose	Blue	Bedroom ware Assumed name
Fragara	red	Table ware
Garden	not known	
Garland	Blue or green	
Gathering Berries	Blue	Jug
Gazebo	Blue	Plate
German Stag Hunt Fig 23	Blue	Punch Bowl
God save the Queen	Blue	Bowl TP attributed name 1887
Gondola	Blue	Table ware
Grecian 1 Fig 24	Grey transfer printed	Table ware
Grecian 2	Grey or blue sponge printed	Table ware
Hawthorn	sepia, red. green & blue	Bedroom ware
Holly	Green	Jug
Humming Bird	Purple	Assumed name from design
Imperial 1	Dark or light blue	Table ware
Imperial 2	undecorated & decorated	Table ware Impressed mark
Inverness District Asylum	red shard only	Table ware supplied to that institution
Iona	Black	Plate/Plaque
Iona	Blue	Table ware
J Stewart	red shard only	Tea ware assume to be a tearoom
Japan	Blue	Tea ware
Jay	purple, red, green, blue & yellow	Jug
Jay	Black	Jug
Jessie M King	Hand painted	Biscuit ware supplied and fired
Jubilee	purple, light blue or black	Jug or plaque Queen Victoria 1897
Kaiser	red	Table ware
Kaiser	Black	Plaque
Kent Fig 25	brown with red, blue yellow & gold	Tea ware
Kilted Boy feeding dog	Blue	Child's plate assumed name
Labyrinth	Purple	Dinner ware
Labyrinth	Sepia	Assumed name from design
Lily	Grey	Assumed name from design
Lomand	Green	Bedroom ware
Lomond Ware Fig 9	Similar not part of DM&S	See separate note
Lorie	Grey	Plaque Assumed name from design
Lorne	Grey	Plate
Maltese	not known	
Marble	Grey appears to be a "block patter	Bedroom Ware attributed name
Milan	Blue	Table ware

DM&S PATERNS AND OTHER NAMES

NAME	COLOUR & DETAIL	TYPE, SUGGESTED DATE ETC.
Milkmaid	Blue	Plate
Mocha	Blue with brown staining	Jug Bulloch mark & impressed
Montrose	not known	
Mossgeil	not known	
Nankin	Black colour infill	Table ware
Ness Ware	hand painted shards only	Table ware assumed to be a dealer
Nightingale	Sepia	Bedroom ware
Nisbet Ware	Hand Painted see separate note	A Dealer
No 1000	Dark blue and gilding	Table ware
Oban	Blue	Table ware
Omagh Lunatic Asylum	blue shard only	Table ware Supplied to that institution
Osborne Fig 19	Green	Table ware
Palestine	Blue	Plate
Pansy	Light blue	Table ware
Pansy 2	Bought in coloured transfer	Tea ware Assumed name
Parrot	Transfer with multi coloured paint	Marriage Jug Mr & Mrs Brown 1876
Passion Flower	Brown TP with pink, green & gilding	Jug identified by shape
Pastoral	Dark blue	Table ware
Peace 1	Blue 1856	Jug Crimean War variation of No 2
Peace 2	Blue 1856	Jug Crimean War variation of No1
Peacock	Sepia	Jug Assumed name from design
Pelegorium	red	Dinner ware
Persia	Not known	
Persian 1	Not know	
Persian 2	Not know	
Peruvian Hunter	Not know	
Pheasant	Blue	Table ware
Phosphorus	Blue	Table ware
Pickwick	Black	Plate
Playmates	Blue	Jug Thane mark
Playmates	Black	Child's Plate
Pomegranate	Grey	Plate
Pompadour	Blue	Pottery Gazette 1883
Prince of Wales	Not know	Assumed name from design 1863
Queen Mary	Blue	Plate
Raith	Blue & coloured painting	Plate
Robin	Red	Jug
Rolland	Shards only Hand painted	Table ware A dealer in Folkestone
Roman	Blue	Table ware
Roman Temple	Blue	Table ware
Rose	Grey	Plate
Rose & Vine	Red	Bedroom ware
Roses	Moulded jug	Thane Mark
Scotia	Hand Painted	Bowl Assumed Name from Design
Scots Guards Badge	Red	Plate Assumed name from design
Seasons	Red or Blue	Jug
Seaweed	Blue	Block Pattern Assumed Name
Sebastapol	Blue	Jug 1854/55 (c)
Serapis	Green	Plate
Sicily	Blue	Plate
Songster	Blue	Jug
Souter Johnny Fig 39	Moulded Brown	Jug Design reg. in 1908 Thane mark
Spiral	Sepia	Bowl & plate

DM&S PATERNS AND OTHER NAMES

NAME	COLOUR & DETAIL	TYPE, SUGGESTED DATE ETC.
Sporting	Black	Jug marked DM&Ss
Springfield Hospital	Shard !	Table ware for use in that hospital
Squirrel	Sepia & gilt	Punch Bowl & tea ware
Stag	Sepia	Tea ware
Strathyre	Blanks only supplied	
Sulian	Not know	
Sultan	Not know	Jug
Swallow Fig 28	Blue	Bedroom ware
T F & Co	shard only impressed "Imperial"	Table ware assumed to be a retailer
Tam O' Shanter	Moulded Brown	Jug Design reg. in 1908 Thane mark
Teck	Sepia & colour	Tea ware 1893
The Crockery	Shards only Hand painted	Table ware for a dealer in Letchford
The Farm	Black	Jug
The Farmer	Black	jugs
The Turk	Blue	Jug
Tom Tit	Blue	Bedroom ware
Trellis	Sepia	Jug
Tudor Fig 29	Blue	Table ware
Tulip	Not know	
Turkey	Not know	
United We Stand	Coloured Flags bought in transfer	Jug Identified by shape 1914-18
Unity	hand painted	Jug with rose & thistle moulding
Vase	Blue	Jug
Verona	Mainly blue occasional sepia	Table ware SEPERATE NOTE
Victoria	Black	Plaque
Views	Blue	Jug
Views	Blue or red	Jug
Villa	Blue	Plate
Vintage	Blue	Plate 1883 (c)
Water Hemlock	Sepia	Bedroom ware
West Ham Union	red shard only	Table ware Supplied to that institution
Wild Rose	Dark blue	Table ware for Far East market
Willow Fig 11	Dark Blue recognised pattern	Marked as "stoneware"
Windsor	Blue	Dinner ware
Wolseley	Blue	Plate DM&Ss
Wolsley	Not know	
Woodbine	Blue	Jug
York	Blue	Tea Ware 1892

Verona Pattern

This pattern appears to have been the most popular of those used mainly or exclusively by DM&S. Many examples still exist bearing this name and numerically it rivals the Willow pattern. Presumably for marketing and cost reasons the design has many variations although they all have the same Classical theme and have similar back stamps. In addition the quality of the engraving and printing varies greatly and it would appear that the highest quality was used at first and deteriorated slowly to suit the market. It is not known how the producers identified the individual variations and in the following list an arbitrary numbering method has been adopted. Most of the examples are on flat ware and printed in blue with occasional sepia. Note these are major variations as there are other minor variations in the back and fore ground which are not listed. These could be within one set of copper plates for different items.

Verona 1   Standing lady with seated lady to left & reclining lady to right. Fig17
Verona 2   Seated lady with baby & child standing to right.
Verona 3   Seated lady & kneeling lady to left.   On punch bowls

Verona 4   Seated lady with child on lap

Verona 5   Standing lady with greyhound on hind legs to left. Also seen on the border of large plates and on small items such as sauce boats.   Fig 16R

Verona 6   Seated lady with child on lap & standing child to right

Verona 7   Standing lady & seated lady to left

Verona 8   Standing lady & standing child to left

Verona 9   Seated lady facing left towards a standing cherub   Fig 15

Verona 10   Standing lady with bird in hand & seated lady to left   Fig 14

Verona 11   Standing lady & seated lady to left   Fig 16 L

Verona 12   Seated lady with child on lap & kneeling lady to left   Fig 16 C

Verona 13   Seated lady with a child on each side

DAVID METHVEN & SONS TYPICAL MARKS

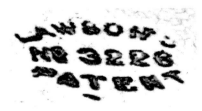

Gallatown Pottery   ? - 1822

As with the early potteries in the Links area very little is known about the products or the early days of this Pottery. The available evidence only indicates that white ware was produced from some date in the late 1700s until the closure in 1822 and the quality was such that it was suitable for export. There are apparently no marked pieces and few which have reasonable association with Gallatown Pottery. One is the Beveridge — Shoulbread mug [Fig 41] which is now in Kirkcaldy Museum and as explained earlier could date about 1777. Also in *Scottish Pottery* J A Fleming illustrates [Plate XII] an earthenware goat which he attributes to Gallatoun Pottery with a date of 1820-25 along with a Sauce Boat which is undated. It appears that Fleming based his book on information given to him at the various Potteries and his dates for Gallatown and Fife Potteries are not always accurate

Fife Pottery   Gray & Co. 1817 — 1829

The situation regarding authenticated pieces from this period is only slightly better than that from Gallatown Pottery as there are two similar marked white ware pieces held by Glasgow Museums. They are rectangular plaques with the relief of George 1V [Fig40] which are incised on the back *Fife Pottery 1827.* Other pieces which although unmarked has an excellent provenance and must be considered. As explained earlier [P26] Andrew Nicolson started his apprenticeship in 1817 as a plate maker. One of his descendants still has a small rectangular plate with red line decoration which is inscribed with his name [Fig 45A]. The family tradition is that this is his apprentice piece made before he became a journey man. This explanation appears to be very acceptable and this piece can be considered as typical of the wares at that time.

Although it is only conjecture at this time perhaps the impressed whelk mark that appears on Fife Pottery pieces only a few years later may have also been used at this period. Perhaps time will tell!

Fife Pottery   John Methven   1829 — 36

It has to be assumed that as he had little or no white ware experience John would have continued with the existing staff where available. Also that at first he probably continued making the same pots as the Grays until he was able to acquire more experience and equipment. Once he had settled in he soon started producing pieces to his own design using transfer prints and marking them as his products with an "*M*" [Fig 49] and on occasions with an impressed whelk. A list of the known patterns from this and later periods is given later although there can be little doubt there were others. From the pieces seen John was making table ware including jugs [Fig 43 & 44] which make up the largest percentage of the wares now seen. This high percentage is probably due to jugs being treated as special and shown greater care.

The descendents of Nicolson have a pair of mantle ornaments "Hope Decaying" and "Sailors Return" thought to be of this period [Fig 42]. Several of "Hope Decaying" still exist although the bases vary slightly and one is incised "Fife Pottery" while another is adapted to represent Robinson Crusoe.

In Kirkcaldy Museum there are a luggie [a bowl with handles at the rim] and mugs which are yellow coloured over a dark coloured body. These are reputed to be from Fife Pottery and made especially for fishermen. The provenance of these is not clear.

It must be stressed that although the use of an "*M*" or indeed an "*H*" in the next period to identify the manufacturer is a strong indicator towards Fife Pottery they did not have exclusive use of these marks. Also the later mark RH&S was also used by R Hammersley & Son, an English Potter. Generally the latter are recognisable by the inclusion of a crown but occasionally there are doubts. Where doubt exists it is shown in the lists.

FIFE POTTERY 1836-1930 Robert Heron, Robert M Heron & Williamson

This period covers the above owners although there were other partners both within and outwith the families. It can however be considered as a complete unit as there was a strong continuity in the succession. From 1850 [circa] it also very much mirrored the situation at the Links/Kirkcaldy Pottery which is hardly surprising considering the family connections.

In common with DM&S there is the problem of a lack of written evidence regarding the products as only in the case of Wemyss Ware no catalogues appear to exist. It is only by studying the items that still exist that an indication of the output can be found.

Whiteware   Transfer Printed Wares

Those seen so far are listed and it is very noticeable that the number recorded is substantially smaller than at DM&S. This can be partially explained by the comparative sizes of the two Potteries and the, so far unsubstantiated, suggestion that much of the output of Fife Pottery was sent abroad and especially to Australia.

While it must be remembered that that Fife Pottery throughout this period was never as well funded at it appears that during the two Robert Heron periods the marketing of transfer printed wares was not as aggressive as at DM&S. Certainly there was not so much attention to royal events. Perhaps a more profitable line was available with hand coloured decoration.

Whiteware   Sponge Printed

Although this type of ware was made from at least 1856 it appears that it was never marked to show the producer and to date there is little evidence that can attributed any pieces with any degree of certainty. A number of pieces found in the Kirkcaldy area which were supplied to a London Dealer, Norman Franks, are considered to have been made at Fife Pottery. These mainly have a mixture of sponge printing and hand painting and although very occasionally the shape of the item [specially the handles] is similar to products from Fife Pottery caution must be observed in attributing all or any of them.

Whiteware   Hand Painted

As explained in the text it seems reasonable to assume hand painting was used from the start of this period as shown by the two jugs [Figs 47 & 48] belonging to the descendants of Nicolson which have both been personalised with hand painting with the date of 1838. This skill was to continue throughout this period but, regretfully, most of the wares are unmarked and identification of pieces and the type of wares produced is often a matter of conjecture. Even when wares are identified it is difficult to place a date on many of them.

It appears that the decorators' skill gradually increased over the years no doubt encouraged by Robert Methven and his sister Jessie. The jardinière [Fig 53] and two white teapots [Fig 55] which are thought to date from the 1870's illustrate that the decorators had become artists. This artistry was to reach its peak shortly thereafter in the production of **Wemyss Ware** [Figs 57 & 58]. This very special ware started with single coloured finish on mainly newly designed pots but soon progressed into a multitude of subjects from nature There has been much written about and even more speculation regarding this ware but it can be said that it was and still is very popular and expensive. While it would be an attractive proposition to write about and illustrate this ware in great detail this work has already been completed and published. It is better therefore to refer readers to the book "*Wemyss Ware*" [details in Further Reading]. The same remarks apply to **Langtoun Ware** [Fig 58]. Although the decorator's skill was concentrated on Wemyss Ware it must be remembered that it was available for other wares. Two of the cheese dishes [Figs 54 & 59] show a reasonable amount of skill while the third, with local views shows a high degree of artistry.

Rosslyn Jet

This remarkable and attractive ware started some time before 1880 and it is tempting to suggest that it dates at least from 1861 when the Court went into mourning on the death of Prince Albert. It had the advantage of being made of local red clay and therefore cheaper than imported white clay.

Judging from the number of examples found this ware must have been very popular and held in high esteem by the purchasers as it is frequently still in good condition. The decoration is all over glaze in both transfer printing [usually gilt] and hand painted enamels [Figs 60-62]. This decoration is usually to a high standard as seen in [Fig 60] where the white enamelled bird is to the same high standard as used on hand painted white ware [Fig 55]. Indeed the birds are so similar in style that they appear to be by the same decorator. The same could be said of the flowers and lettering on the "Davie" jug [Fig 60] when compared to some monogrammed Wemyss Ware. The bulk of the output appears to have been teapots with matching water jugs including kettles, cream jugs, sugar bowls and stands. The same items were also decorated with transfer printing in gilt including a heron and Queen Victoria at her jubilee in 1887.

It will be noted that most of these wares have very distinctive handles which help identification of unmarked pieces including, perhaps the sponge ware mentioned earlier. These jugs also appear in white ware [Fig 63] decorated in gilt or in transfer printing.

Personalised Wares
In the same way as DM&S Fife Pottery would add a name or message to their wares. This was not a new idea as it will be remembered that this was done by John Methven and perhaps at the Gallatown Pottery.

Other items are known which have been decorated and personalised by one of the Wemyss Ware artists. These are on both earthenware and china and it is likely but not certain they were private work [Figs 73-76].

Blanks
In the same way as DM&S blanks were supplied for private decoration although few examples can be positively identified. Indeed Carl Nekola held classes for several years in the late 1920's. The few which have been positively identified all had the Wemyss Ware impressed marked and are, probably, on blanks sold after the closure of the Pottery. Indeed a number of such blanks were recently sold on an internet auction!

FIFE POTTERY PATERNS AND NAMES WITH OWNERS

Balmoral	RH	Blue	Plate
Bathers Surprise	RH	Grey	Plate Bathers being chased by a swan
Blythswood	?	Blue	Table ware made for "Bells" of Glasgow. The mar
Burns	RH	Black	Plate At least 2 designs of Robert Burn's characte
Canton	R.H.&S.	Blue	Dinner ware
Cygnet	JM ?	Blue	Jug "Identified by shape
Dancing Girls	JM ?	White	Jug By shape attributed name by design
Falconry	RH	Blue	Bedroom ware Impressed Whelk
Florence	R.H.&S.	Blue	Dinner ware
Florentine	JM ?	Blue	Jug Identified by shape
Forth Bridge	RH&S	Blue	Plate
Fragaria	RH	Blue	Jug
Garibaldi	H	Black	Plate Also impressed with Crown in oval garter
Garlbaldi	H&G	Blue	Plate
Glasgow	RHS	Blue	Plate Maybe Hammersley
Goat	H	Blue	Jug
Gondola	J M	Blue	Jug
Hawking	R.H.F.P.	Blue	Dinner Ware
Heron	R.H.	Grey	Dinner Ware
Heron	?	White	Moulded Jug with herons doubtful
Heron	RH	Black	Dinner Ware
Jara Masjid Dehli	RH	Blue	Jug
Jubilee	R.H.&S.	Gilt	Black Jug Recognised pattern Queen Vic. 1897
King George IV	Sequestration	White	Moulded plaque incised Fife Pottery
Lake	JM?	Blue	Identified by shape
Langtoun Ware	RH&S	Several	Tea ware and ornaments Hand painted in an art-d
Milan	H	Blue	Dinner ware
Monastery	JM	Blue	Jug Personalised for 1838
Montrose	H	Blue	Plate maybe Hammersley
Nankin	RH & Co	Black	Plate
Parrot	R.H.&S.	Blue	Jug
Pastoral	H	Blue	Plate
Peace	RH ?	Blue	Jug Crimea War
Peace	RH	Blue	Jug
Playmates	?		Plate
Polka Dancers	H	Brown	Moulded Jug Assumed name for design
Prince Albert	RH	Red	Jug
Prince Albert	H	Black	Jug Identified by shape
Regina Victoria	H	Red	Jug Coronation of Queen Vic personalised 1838
Roman	?	Blue	Dinner ware
Rose	?	Red	Jug Identified by shape
Rosslyn Jet	R.H.&S.	Black	Tea pots etc. often gilded and enamelled
Seaweed	JM	Blue	Mug & Jug Assumed name for a block pattern
Sicilian	JM?	Blue	Jug
Sportsman	RH & S ?	Black	Jug
Strawberry	H	Green	Bedroom ware
Sultana	R.H.& Co.	Blue	Dinner ware attributed to 1844 SPHR 15
Swan	RH FP	Grey	Plate Impressed Whelk
Swan 2	RH	White	Moulded jug with swan
Taymouth Castle	RH	Blue	Dinner Ware Also impressed Whelk mark
The Cottage	M	Blue	Jug also identified by shape
Wemyss Castle	RH&S	Various	Plate View of the Castle
Wemyss Hospital	RH&S	Various	Plate View of Hospital.
Wemyss Ware	R.H.&S.	Many	Bedroom & tea wares and ornaments
Willow	H.G.	Blue	Dinner ware recognised pattern
Willow	H & G	Blue	Dinner ware recognised pattern
Willow	R.H.F.P.	Blue	Dinner ware recognised pattern
Willow	R.H.&S.	Blue	Dinner ware recognised pattern

Fife Pottery Marks & One Rosslyn Mark

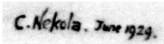

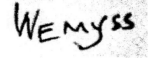

Wemyss
T Goode & Co

Rosslyn Pottery

'Bird' & 'Whelk'

Sinclairtown Pottery Number 1   G Mclaughlan & Kirk   1868 - 1890

As has become the normal the details of the wares during these two owners are not available. The generality of production under both owners has already been set out in the text and to date there are no known examples. However there is evidence from an archaeological excavation in 1990 when a large number of wasters [Fig 66] were found [see Further Reading]. In these were a number of teapots both plain and moulded perhaps amounting to 19 different types. Where finished they were all had a rockingham glaze. It appears that no effort has been made so far to find complete items which match the shards

Within the wasters there were a large number other domestic wares [bowls. mugs, bakers, chamber pots & salters]. These were made from both local and imported clays. A few shards of mugs and bowls with sponge ware decoration were found however these had been glazed and it is never certain if they had been made at the Pottery or imported baring in mind that both owners had acted as agents for other Potteries. However it should be remembered that when Kirk tried to sell the Pottery he advertised it as being equipped to make this type of ware. Indeed there is a mixture of periods within the shards although the only mark shard found was from a baker and impressed with *"L Buist & Sons"*.

Unfortunately there was no accurate dating evidence for the wasters and they may well belong in the next period.

Sinclairtown Pottery Numbers 1 & 2   L Buist & Sons   1890 -1928

At first Buist would have continued in the same way as Kirk and at least it is known they continued making bakers. There is no evidence the made white ware of any type. In the Kirkcaldy Museum there is a pair of "Wally Dogs" with a rockingham glaze which were gifted by the Buist family with the explanation that they were "apprentice pieces" made by one of the family and not part of the routine production [Fig 64] As explained in the text what ever the situation at first it was soon decided to concentrate on teapots and they only advertised such products. Again these were rarely or never marked with the name of the Pottery.

This practice was continued after the move to Site Number 2. Fortunately when a new road was being constructed near to this Pottery a few years ago the works passed through the former clay pit which had been used as a dump for wasters. Examples of these are held in Kirkcaldy Museum and it is seen that as well as plain teapots others were made with impressed and sprig decoration. The museum also has a teapot with a reasonable provenance with a green band decoration [Fig 55].

A number of shards were also acquired by members of the Edinburgh Branch of the Scottish Pottery Society who managed to match the handles and spouts to complete examples [Fig 68A]. These must be treated with caution as it is likely that the masters for the moulds were made commercially elsewhere and would have also been available to other Potteries in Scotland and elsewhere.

Rosslyn Pottery   Morrison & Crawford   1879 - 1932

Morrison and Crawford rarely marked their brown ware or cane ware except teapots which were occasionally impressed "M & C FIREPROOF". They did however mark the white ware which was produced for a short period 1924/26 [circa]. The most common mark was an oval cartouche usually by rubber stamp.

By far their principal item of manufacture was teapots which they had a ready market for throughout Scotland and Ireland although they did also make many other types of products. Most these teapots were made in the same methods as adopted by the Sinclairtown Pottery from the local brown clay and glazed in the rockingham manner. As a special line they also used blue, black jet and green glaze to give a more attractive finish which at least in the 1920's they decorated over glaze with silver and gold lustre. Over glaze enamel was also used as blue, pink and white "forget me nots" these being flowers with five petals often with a yellow centre and joined by simple swags in the same or alternative colours. Although the quantities are not known they used sufficiently large amounts of the lustre used to justify collecting all of the rags and glass palettes used by the decorators and sending them away to recover the gold and platinum.

They also carried a large utility line of baking dishes, bowls, sugar and creams etc. mostly made in cane ware being a mixture of the local brown clay, flint and imported white clay covered with a clear glaze. Bowls were also made in brownware usually with a white clay slip on the inside and frequently inscribed with couthy sayings [eg "Save yer breath to cool yer porridge"]. For some reason these were popular in Canada where loads were sent to the Eaton Tea and Trading Company [KM files].

By far the most distinctive and popular with collectors is the Majolica Ware in the form of bread safes, cheese dishes and storage jars marked rice, meal, flour, tobacco sugar etc. sets of which were a "must" in many Scottish kitchens [[Fig 70 & 71]. These jars were wheel thrown using predetermined weights of clay and profile markers to achieve a uniformity of size. When dry the green ware was given the final shape on a lathe. The name of the contents was usually applied as sprigs in either white or cane ware or occasionally by impressing the name into the wet clay. Items could also be personalised by the same method. The finish was both decorative and useful and also applied to jugs, jardinières, bowls, candle sticks [Fig 67 & 69] and pirlie banks [Fig 68]

The bodies of these products were usually made of caneware which gave a yellow coloured base for the other colours. Some of the smaller items were press moulded using an incomplete mixture of cane and brown clays to use up "scrap" brown and cane clays. As this type of ware was made for most of the life of Morrison and Crawford it is impossible to date them unless they were personalised with a date. Storage jars were, for a short time in the 1920's also made in white ware with the name of the contents painted, under glaze, in black. The maker's mark was, usually, added in black on the base by means of a rubber stamp.

A further popular line was in penny or pirlie banks modelled in the form of apples, pigs, cats, dogs, cottages, etc. which were all moulded usually in cane ware or brown ware and occasionally in agate ware which was exposed with a clear glaze to give the striped effect. The apple banks were a special cheap range being sold for 1p in 1922. These were made in biscuit ware which was sealed by size and coloured with green or red household paint thus saving on the second firing. They also made many globular banks frequently with finials which were invariably finished with majolica glaze.

As well as storage jars some of the products already mentioned [teapots, bowls, jugs and very occasionally banks] were also made in white ware during the Hunter period. These were frequently also given a back stamp mark by means of a rubber stamp. Some of these items were decorated under glaze. As explained earlier the "best" hand painted wares were given the trade name of **Rosslyn Ware** [Fig 72]. The pallet colours used were much more subdued than those used at the Fife Pottery but the quality of the pieces and the decoration was in no way inferior to those of their illustrious neighbour. Carl Nekola is also credited with painting small butterflies which were fixed to curtains by wire but no examples of these appear to exist. An ex-employee also reported the production of lamp bases for a Mr J D McCormack but did not explain the type of ware used [KM].

It will now be very obvious that although the products of these Potteries are greatly sought after there is still a great deal to be discovered and perhaps this work will encourage others to try to fill the many gaps.

Index

FURTHER READING

Fife Pottery Society has an archive of books and other material regarding the Kirkcaldy Potteries as well as Scottish Potteries in general. This is available to members and non- members will be helped as far as possible.

The following publications are recommended

Scottish Pottery   J A Fleming published 1923 in Glasgow reprinted by EP Publishing Ltd. 1973

Scottish Pottery   G Cruickshank   Shire Album 191

Scottish East Coast Potteries. P McVeigh   Published by John Donald Publishers Ltd ISBN 0 85976 0383

Wemyss Ware   Davis & Rankine   Scottish Academic Press 1986 ISBN 0 7073 0354 0

Scottish Spongeware   G Cruickshank   Scottish Pottery Studies 1   ISSN 0260-7972

Scottish Printed Pottery   Harry Kelly   Lomondside Press   ISBN 0 9521035 8

Kirkcaldy Potteries   C McNeill   Fife Publicity   ISBN 0 9534686 07

Scottish Pottery Historical Review   Scottish Pottery Society. An annual publication

The Excavations at Sinclairtown Pottery   Fife Regional Council [now Fife Council]

Archaeological Investigations at Linktown Pottery   SUART Perth

Photographs

These photographs were mainly taken by Don Swanson of Kirkcaldy. Others were provided by Fife Council Museums Central (Kirkcaldy Museum & Art Gallery Service) and are indicted by [FCM] and a few from private collections and so marked. The remainder were provided by the author. DM&S = Links/Kirkcaldy Pottery, FP = Fife Pottery & possible Gallatown Pottery, SP=Sinclairtown Pottery [both sites] & RP = Rosslyn Pottery. The use of ? is restricted to "private" work where the Pottery used for the glost firing is unknown

Fig 1   DM&S   3 lustre teapots. Unmarked   good province & shards.

Fig 2   DM&S   Cow creamer & jug black glaze over painted Unmarked good provenance.

Fig3   DM&S   4 Plates   Bread plate **Teck**, unknown impressed mark, **Imperial** & **Damascus**

Fig 4   DM&S   Child's tea set   **Farm** pattern impressed mark.

Fig 5   DM&S   3 porrage creamers Left & Right **"Maggie Roonie Rose"** decoration Centre stencil & sponge ware.

Fig 6   DM&S   Candlesticks **Airlie Ware**   Bowl Town Mark.

Fig 7   DM&S   2 Mugs   hand painted crude plums. Bowl & jar **Nisbet Ware**. Egg Cups unmarked.

Fig 8   DM&S   4 pieces of **Abbotsford.**

Fig 9   DM&S   2 pieces of **"Blue & Green"** & small lidded pot with cherries. Jug has Town Mark & small pots are **Lomond Ware** showing continuity of decoration.

Fig 10   DM&S   Export ware **Canovian, Akabam, "Convolvulus"** [registered design] & flow blue with **Bulloch** mark.

Fig 11   DM&S   Flow Blue Bowls **Bulloch** mark & shards.

Fig 12   DM&S   2 personalised china plates recognised by style of hand writing. Plate with impressed **Thistle & Crown** mark decorated at Stratheyre.

Fig 13   DM&S   2 **Toby Jugs** Right in traditional colours marked WC a Pottery worker's wedding gift. Left perhaps decorated out with the Pottery.

Fig 14   DM&S   Rectangular ashet Sepia **Verona 10.**

Fig 15   DM&S   Rectangular ashet   Blue **Verona 9.**

Fig 16   DM&S   4 Plates   **Verona**

Fig 17   DM&S   2 Ashets   2 types of **Verona 7** & plate **Verona 2**

Fig 18   DM&S   3 Covered dishes blue & sepia **Verona 4** and soup blue **Verona 2**

Fig 19   DM&S   2 Covered serving dishes   green **Osborne** pattern.

Fig 20   DM&S   Covered serving dish   sepia **Damascus** pattern.

Fig 21   DM&S   3 Dishes **Willow** pattern.

Fig 22   DM&S   Covered serving dish   dark sepia **Antique** pattern.

Fig 23   DM&S   Punch Bowl   blue **German Stag Hunt** pattern.

Fig 24   DM&S   5 Plates blue **Verona, Willow, Verona, Damascus, Asiatic Pheasant & Grecian**

Fig 25   DM&S   Part Tea Set   sepia & coloured **Kent** pattern.

Fig 26   DM&S   Cup, saucer & Plate   green   **Mill** pattern

Fig 27   DM&S   Mug   blue **Coronation** pattern

Fig 28   DM&S   3 Jugs   2 moulded [no shape names] & **Swallow** pattern.

Fig 29   DM&S   3 Jugs   **Tudor & Berry** [red & blue] patterns.

Fig 30   DM&S   3 Jugs   2 **Chilli** pattern & 1 moulded & gilt decoration.

Fig 31   DM&S   2 Bowls unmarked identified by shape & shards. 1 saucer grey **Fibre** pattern.

Fig 32   DM&S   2 Chamber Pots sepia   **Squirrel & Daffodil** patterns.

Fig 33   DM&S   **Abbotsford Catalogue**   front cover & 3 pages.

Fig 34   DM&S   **Coloured Transfers**. Acquired at Pottery.

Fig 35   DM&S   Ewer Sepia **Rose** pattern   part of bedroom set.

Fig 36   DM&S   **Water Bottle** made for Burmese market. This example is gilt decorated probably at the Pottery

Fig 37   DM&S   **Water Jar** made for Burmese market Elephant Mark. Unnamed pattern.

Fig 38   DM&S   Jug **Playmates** pattern sepia with colour infill.

Fig 39   DM&S   Jug moulded **Souter Johnny** registered design.

Fig 40   FP   Rectangular Plaque   George IV.

Fig 41   FP   Mug Beveridge & Shoulbread   [FCM]

Fig 42   FP   2 Chimney Ornaments [Private Collection].

Fig 43   FP   Jug marriage piece   [FCM].

Fig 44   FP   Jug marriage piece 1830 marked "Fife Semi China"   [FCM].

Fig 45   FP   Lidded Container **Hawking** Pattern.   [FCM].

Fig 1

Fig 2

Fig 3

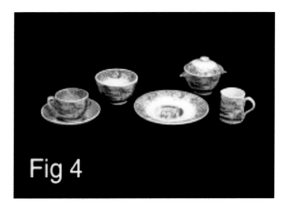

Fig 4

Fig 5

Fig 6

Fig 7

Fig 8

Fig 9

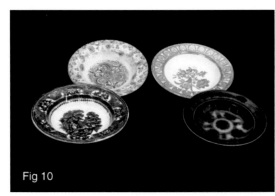

Fig 10

Fig 11

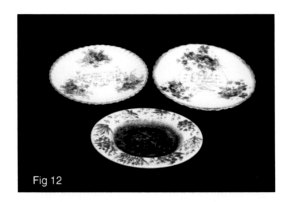

Fig 12

Fig 13

Fig 14

Fig 15

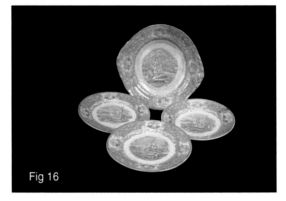

Fig 16

Fig 17

Fig 18

Fig 19

Fig 20

Fig 22

Fig 21

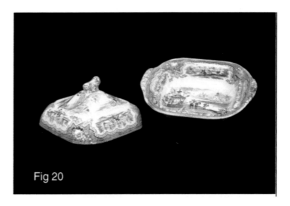

Fig 22

Fig 24

Fig 25

Fig 26

Fig 27

Fig 28

Fig 29

Fig 30

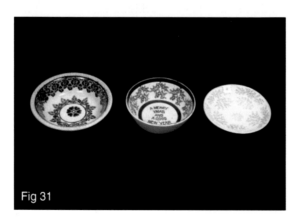

Fig 31

Fig 32

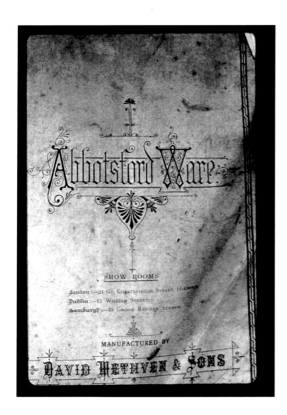

Fig 33   Cover & 3 pages from an Abbotsford Ware Catalogue [undated] supplied by the late Prof. P. Davis

Fig 34

Fig 35

Fig 36

Fig 37

Fig 38

Fig 39

Fig 40

Fig 41

Fig 42

Fig 43

Fig 44

Fig 45

Fig 46

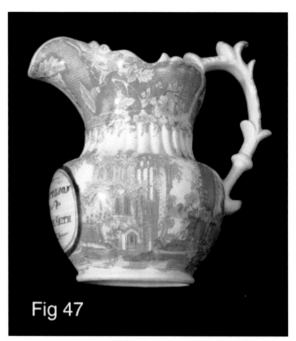

Fig 47

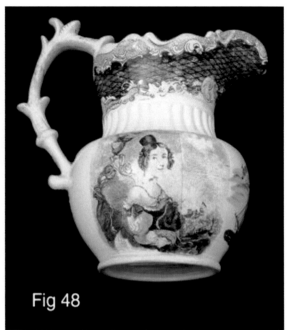

Fig 48

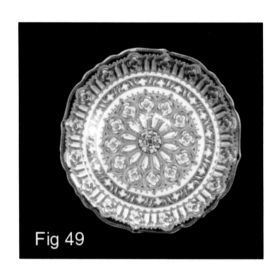

Fig 49

Fig 50

Fig 51

Fig 52

Fig 53

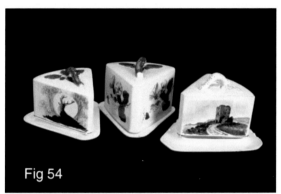

Fig 54

Fig 55

Fig 56

Fig 57

Fig 58

Fig 59

Fig 60

Fig 61

Fig 62

Fig 63

Fig 64

Fig 65

Fig 67

Fig 68

Fig 66

Fig 69

Fig 70

Fig 71

Fig 72

Fig 73

Fig 74

Fig 75

Fig 76